I Did As I Was Told

Prologue

My name is Addie and this is my story.There are many parts that I am amazed I lived through. Many that still give me nightmares. I carry with me the fear, scares ,lack of self esteem and anxiety to this day.

No child should ever have to go through such pain ,such striping of self worth . My childhood was stolen by my mother Esther. The one person who should have shown me compassion and love made it her personal mission to make me fear her and everything around me.

She controlled my every move with fear. The abuse both physical and emotional that I suffered at her hands has carried over to my adult life. I live my life always second guessing myself,staying in relationships that weren't healthy,but thinking that was all I deserved.Being so insecure that I felt uncomfortable in my own skin.Although the physical beatings were very painful I sometimes wonder if the mental abuse was more crippling.

When your told something often enough it becomes as real to you as the color of your eyes !

Dedication

This book is dedicated to children everywhere that suffered the unthinkable at the hands of those who should have loved and nurtured them in their lives . You are worthy of love. You have had a rough start but never stay quiet ! Speak your truth , love yourself , let the pain go . Your time is now , get out there and take back your life !

Chapter 1

I was a small frail child who lived with my mother Esther and my Father Joe. From the outside looking in we seemed like a normal family. Nothing could be further from the truth. Esther was 5 foot 8 inches of pure evil. She had long dark hair and eyes so dark, so piercing they could make a grown man cry. Joe was a lighthearted kind man with blond hair and blue eyes. He stood 5 foot 7 inches tall. How these two ever wound up together was a mystery. They say you can only be fake for so long and sooner or later your true self comes out well this is what happened to my family.

Esther and Joe were introduced by friends.Within a year they were married. They were a wrong fit from the start. From my first memory there was always fighting in my house. I would hear Esther and Joe screaming at each other and Esther saying the most hateful things. Joe was no match for her sharp tongue. It would always end the same way he would walk out and be gone longer and longer every time.

Joe really did try and I feel he had the patients of a Saint ! We didn't have a lot of money. Let's be real we were dirt poor ! He would say hey let's go over to my parents apartment my mom will cook us supper. Nothing could please Esther . Joe's Mom was the sweetest person, Joe's father on the other hand was an abusive drunk! He treated Joe's mom horribly which made me care about her even more! She would flinch when he came near her. She jumped when he told her to do something ,all the signs of abuse were there ! It was odd to me that the roles were reversed for Esther and Joe. She was the abuser and he was the victim . You would think growing up in that environment he wouldn't want anything to do with that way of life. Then even as a child I thought about it. He and his mom were controlled there whole life maybe he just stuck with what he knew. Maybe he sought out someone who would control him because that was his norm and he didn't know how to function without it . Joe's parents didn't have a pot to pee in they were just as poor as us but his mom always helped out when she could . She would stretch her meals so we had something to eat . If our power got turned off she would let us stay in her tiny apartment.

The fighting between Joe and Esther escalated. Soon he was away from home more than he was there. During this time is when Esther seemed to look at me in a different way. One night when the fighting had gotten really bad and Joe left Esther was in her room I went down the hall to the bathroom. Esther ripped the bathroom door open and glared at me as I sat on the toilet. The way she was looking at me sent chills down my spine. Then she spoke and my life would never be the same. You ruined my life. I should have drowned you when I had the chance turned and walked out of the bathroom! I sat in the bathroom terrified to come out! Finally I cracked the bathroom door and looked out to see if Esther was in the kitchen. The coast was clear , I ran to my room and shut the door. I couldn't shake the fear that night as I laid in bed. The way Esther hissed those words to me played back in my head over and over again. I grabbed my blanket and hugged it tight . I would be extra good from now on so Joe didn't leave .The last thinking I wanted was to be left alone with Esther.

The fighting was constant at this point. Esther and Joe couldn't even be in the same room without hurling insults at each other. This is when my stomach started to hurt. I would be bent over in pain . I did everything I could to hide it. There was enough tension already I didn't need to add to it. I stayed in my room a lot. I would sit on my bed hugging my knees ,rocking back and forth trying to drown out the fighting.

Chapter 2

About a month later Joe moved out. He sat down and talked to me explaining he would still come see me on weekends but it was better for everyone if he didn't live there anymore. I grabbed him around his neck and hugged him tight . I'm sorry I'll be good ,please don't leave I begged ! He knelt down and hugged me Addie you are a good girl this has nothing to do with you. It's not your fault. He picked me up giving me one last hug and walked out the door ! I had no idea that when he walked out that door my door to hell was opened and I would suffer unimaginable abuse for years to come.

I became very introverted. I would stare down at the ground afraid to look up . I lived in constant fear I kept playing back Esther's words"I should have drowned you when I had the chance ! My God what kind of person says that to their child? Now that Joe was gone I had no one to protect me. Why did Esther hate me as much ?. She would glance over at me and a darkness feel over her. Those eyes that made my blood go cold. Yet another reason I never liked to look up. I was haunted by those eyes in my sleep. They were truly what nightmares were made of.

Joe came around as he had promised every weekend in the beginning. Esther made his life unbearable. She would start fights the second he came to the door. He just wanted to take me for the day. Many times Esther would claim I wasn't feeling well and didn't want to go for visitation. He would return the next weekend and she would have another excuse as to why I couldn't go. The whole time I would be in my room crying . All I wanted was to go with Joe and never come back but I knew better than to go against Esther.

Finally Joe said listen I have a right to see her if this is going to continue we'll go through the courts and then you will have no choice in the matter! Esther wouldn't be told what to do ! She invited him in and with me sitting right there she started screaming stop don't hit me what are you doing and slamming her fist against her face and chest. Both Joe and I stood in shock ! What the hell are you doing Esther,Joe asked ? She didn't stop She yelled leave or I'll call the police ! Joe said your crazy ! She got right up in his face and said yep and don't you forget it ! I'll make it so you'll never see this little bitch again. He ran over to hug me and told me it would be ok .Even at my young age I could tell he didn't believe the words coming out of his mouth ! He tried to talk to Esther ,all I want is to see her I could take her for the day it would give you a break. Yeah that's not gonna happen Esther snared! He looked at her and said now listen I have a right to see her and you know it. They yelled back and for then there was a knock at the door. We all froze, Mam it's the police is everything ok in there ?

Esther turned and glared at both of us and said let the games begin as she opened the door ! She went from raving maniac to pretend beaten victum with tears and everything in the time it took her to open the door ! Oh thank God you're here he just started beating on me. Joe tried to defend himself but.. The cops took one look at Esther who was covered with red marks all over her face and handcuffed him. I stepped forward and was going to tell them that he didn't do anything when Esther scooped me up and put my head on her shoulder and said it will be ok honey and whispered in my ear say one fucking word and when they leave I will beat the shit out of you. I was terrified I started crying and said nothing. I watched with a broken heart as the police took Joe away.

When the police left with Joe she closed the door and glared down at me , your all mine now you little bitch your prince charming won't be here to protect you anymore! With that she grabbed me by the hair and drug me to my room. She threw me on the bed and said I don't want to see your face anymore tonight and closed and locked the bedroom door behind her ! When did she put a lock on my bedroom door? What was happening ? That night as I lay in my bed all I could think about were Esther's words! I had no idea just how horrifying it was about to get. Sleep didnt come easy that night but finally exhaustion won over and I drifted off. My bedroom door was ripped open sometime in the middle of the night and I could see Esther's silhouette in my doorway!. She stood in my room glaring down at me. I cringed because I could feel the rage in her presents.. I clenched my blanket closer and with that she lunged at me. She grabbed me by the hair and started shaking me back and forth saying you ruined my life you little bitch now I'm gonna ruin yours! I screamed what did I do and she slapped me across the face ! Shut the fuck up .! From now on you don't speak unless I tell you to got it she snarled? I was to afraid to respond! She shook me again and said bitch you better answer me when I ask you a question ! Yes I understand I replied. She pushed me on the floor and walked out of the rom. I crawled to the corner and sat on the floor knees to chest, rocking back and forth terrified ,trying to make sense of what just happened ! Little did I know this would become my new normal !

Chapter 3

Joe continued to come around but now it was more like every other weekend or once a month. He refused to ever step foot in the apartment again. He waited for me outside. he would never put himself in that situation again. He tried to convince me to talk to the police and that I could come live with him but by this time I had suffered many beatings from Esther and I was so convinced that her hold on me would never allow it. My fear of Esther ran to deep ! Joe contacted children and youth and explained what was going on. They said they would send someone out but if they couldn't prove there was abuse then their hands were tied. A case worker came to the apartment and questioned Esther . She then knelt down to talk to me with Esther standing in the same room! Does anyone hit you she asked? I thought for a minute, could this women help me? Even though I couldn't see Esther I could feel her eyes piercing the back of my head. Terror set in and I knew what I had to say. No no one hits me. Do you feel safe here ? Everything in my body was telling me to scream no I'm not safe here she beats me but instead I said Yes I feel safe,with that the case worker got up looked at Esther and said sorry to have wasted your time! In my head I was screaming wait please don't go take me ! I said nothing! Esther watched the caseworker drive away and glared down at me and said well who knew you're not as dumb as I thought you were ! Smart move on your part for keeping your mouth shut! Now get the fuck out of my sight and go to your room ! I did as I was told.

This is when Esther started to ration my meals . Some of it was because we were so poor and food was scarce but there were times she seemed to get joy out of not feeding me and eating right in front of me. She would make me sit at the table while she ate and watch her. All the time she would smack her lips and rave about how good the food was ! The first time she did this I said I'm hungry can I have some and she slapped me so hard across the face she knocked me out of my chair onto the floor! From that time on I never asked again.

Soon after the beatings started I started to wet the bed. The first time it happened I was frantic. I ripped the sheets off her bed and threw them in the closet. Quickly I pulled up the blanket so Esther didn't see the bare mattress. The next night it happened again. Why was this happening? I got one of my shirts and tried to clean up the mattress. At that moment Esther came into the room. She took one look at the wet stain on the mattress and lunged at me. You filthy little bitch are you that lazy you couldn't go to the bathroom to take a piss? It was an accident I'm sorry was all I had a chance to say when she grabbed me by the hair and pushed my face into the mattress. She held my face down and kept screaming you filthy bitch ! I was crying please I'm sorry but Esther pushed my face deeper into the mattress. It was getting harder to breath. I can't breathe I can't breath I was crying! Esther yanked my head up and threw me on the floor and walked out of the room. I ran to the corner of the room sat on the floor knees to my chest , rocking back and forth heart racing . All of a sudden I felt like I was going to get sick. God please no I looked around for something I could throw up in . I grabbed the shirt I had tried to clean the mattress with and held in under my mouth and got sick . I tied the sleeves of the shirt making a little sack out of it to contain the vomit and put it in the closet with the soiled sheets.

In the days that followed Esther instead of charging onto the room would pace back and forth in front of my bedroom door holding the belt in a circle making a snapping noise . Every time she passed the door she would pear in at me smile and snap the belt. My heart would pound so hard I honestly thought it would jump out of my chest. She would then run in the room ,arm raised and start beating me . With every strike of the belt my skin would mark and later form welts.. I would curl my little body into a ball and try to protect myself. After what seemed like an eternity Esther would glare at me, not speak a word and walk out of the room slamming the door behind her .

I continued to wet the bed every night . I would force myself to stay up as long as I could because I was afraid to sleep. No matter how many times I went to the bathroom before bed, or stopped liquids early it still happend. Esther would come down the hall every morning rip the door open and look at the mattress if it was wet I would get beat. Her new torture was after the beating she made me wear my soiled underwear on my head. She added insult to injury by making me pull them down over my face . There I would sit for hours ,I knew better than to even attempted to take them off!

Chapter 4

My life was a living hell ! The only joy in my life was the seldom times Joe visited and when I got to visit my Grandparents house.. These were Esther's parents and for the life of me I couldn't believe that she was related to them. My Grandparents were proper, respected people who had the life I dreamed of. They lived in a clean well kept house. They were kind and loving. Esther had told me more than once that my Grandparents hated me . I had no idea why a mother would say something so awful but I knew in my heart it wasn't true. ! Before every visit Esther would lay down the same rules. 1. You go in say hi and sit your ass down. 2. you know they can't stand you and they only tolerate you because I'm their daughter so don't you dare act up. 3 For no reason do I want you to be around them unless I'm right there. 4. If you know what's good for you you won't mention anything that goes on in this house. Do you understand ? Yes I would reply with my head down .

Esther's whole demeanor changed when she walked into her parents house. She almost seemed human. I could tell even as a small child there was a strain between her and my grandparents. They all still talked but the conversation seemed difficult at times. As soon as I stepped into their home I felt a peace come over me. Even though I had seen it all before I marveled at the furniture, the pictures on the wall and how clean it was. The familiar rocking chair, my Grandfather's recliner,the dinning room table where many holiday dinners were served but we only attended a few. As I looked around the house I always wondered how had Esther grown up in such a loving home and become such a monster !

My Grandparents always dressed so nice. My grandmother wore button front blouses with slacks and my Grandfather wore men's button front shirts with dress pants. Esther was what I would classify as a rebellious hippie. She always wore jeans and over sized tunic tops.

 My favorite room in the whole house was the kitchen. My Grandmother was an amazing cook. When I walked into the kitchen I would immediately look to the back counter that was lined with different size glass jars with screw on lids. Those jars were filled with cookies of many varieties. My favorites where the chocolate chip cookies. I would cherish every second at my Grandparents house even though Esther didn't let me leave her side. She was always afraid I would slip and say something about how horrible it was at home. There were times that I thought what would happen if I ran up to my Grandparents and said please help me she beats me ! Can I stay here ? I'll be good I promise. Then I would snap back to reality . My Aunt Linda ,Esther's sister was the total opposite of Esther . She was married and had two kids . She was well off , the sisters hated each other ! They would actually snarl when they spoke to one another. I couldn't blame Linda for disliking Esther she was a lot to handle and they didn't even know about the abuse. In her younger years Esther brought a lot of shame to my Grandparents. My time at my Grandparents always went by to fast. Every time I walked out that door I wondered if it was my last. Sooner or later I knew in my heart that Esther would do something and it would sever ties with my Grandparents. I got used to not getting attached to people that came into my life because they never stayed. Esther was toxic and people could only take that for so long before they had enough. I prayed everyday this never happened with my Grandparents.

Chapter 5

The beatings continued. There were times my cries were heard by neighbors and most did nothing but there would always be one that would confront Esther. The neighbors that did speak up were no match for her evil ! She would calmly walk up to them and say, go ahead report me I'll burn your house to the ground with you inside ! She would grab me by the arm and drag me home and I knew what was going to happen next ! I would get beat for crying to loud and alerting the neighbors. The whole time she was beating me she would say over and over again didn't I tell you to shut up you fucking bitch. With every hit of the belt it felt like she was beating the skin from my body.

Once confronted by a neighbor we would move . A lot of the moves were done at night. I would always be told to be quiet . I found out as I got older that we would move at night because Esther wanted to skip out on the rent. I had moved so many times as a child it just became second nature to never unpack. It was easier to live out of a box and garbage bags then have to pack everything up for the next move. With every move we would leave more and more behind. I had learned to keep the few items I held dear to me packed away .I didn't want to risk leaving or loosing them.

Beating me with a belt wasn't satisfying Esther anymore !
She graduated to metal spatulas , wire hangers and
extension cords. One day Esther called me into the
kitchen and turned the front burner on on the stove.She
said there's change missing from my purse and I know you
stole it ! I had never and would never steal from anyone
especially Esther ! She said tell me the truth did you do it
? No I would never steal from anyone I replied ! Your a liar
I know it was you she screamed ! I'll give you one more
chance to tell the truth you little bitch or your hand's
going on the burner! I swear I didn't do it . Get over here
and she grabbed me holding me under one arm. I'll show
you what happens to fucking liars ! She took my hand and
held it above the burner close enough for me to feel the
heat. I begged please no don't ! Then tell me you did it . I
didn't I swear ! Ok then because you won't tell the truth
your hands going on the burner! She put it closer and I
started screaming no no please don't ! As she yanked at
my arm to put it on the burner I said ok I took the money
I'm sorry ! We both knew that I didn't steal any money but
I was convinced that she would put my hand on that
burner if I didn't say exactly what she wanted to hear !

Well you little thieving bitch I'll teach you to steal from
me ! I wiggled free from her grip and ran into my room
and cowered in the corner ! I'm sorry I'll never do it again I
pleaded ! You bet your ass you wont I'll make sure of that
! She grabbed the extension cord and started to whip me

on my butt ! I tried to get away and that made her enraged ! She began to swing widely striking me on my back and thighs ! When she was done I crawled to the corner , knees to chest rocking back and forth! The welts were already forming on my legs.

Chapter 6

By this time there wasn't a day that I wasn't beat ! I developed a escape for my mind ! I trained my mind to think , in a few minutes it will be over ! You'll be cowering in the corner of your room knees to chest but the beating will be over ! From that day on I would go to that place in my mind to get through the beatings ! It was the only way I could tolerate the pain!

When I was almost six years old the summer before I was going to start kindergarten Esther started to watch kids in our apartment. I was thrilled to have kids around but couldn't believe anyone would leave their child with such a monster! How did she fool everyone into believing she was this wonderful person ?Couldn't they take one look at me and see the obvious ? See how neglected I was , how I never made eye contact and sense I was abused ? Or did the people who left their children with Esther follow the same practices as she or just not care about their kids at all ?

I became like a big sister to these kids. Esther had shown me how to give the little ones a bottle and how to change diapers. Many days she would lay on the couch watching tv and I was the one caring for the kids which was fine with me. If the kids got to loud she would take me to my room and grab me by the hair hissing you better shut them the fuck up if you know what's good for you. If I hear them cry I'll make you cry got it ! I would make up stories and act them out for the kids and build a blanket fort in my room . I would sit there and look at the kids when they would take their naps and wonder if their home life was like mine. Did they fear their parents ? Did they have food to eat and a warm bed to sleep ? I would always be extra kind to the them just in case it was the only kindness they were shown.

Chapter 7

We took a very rare trip to my Aunt Linda's house. Esther and Linda were sisters but they had no bond. Linda lived in a beautiful home in the country and it was a long car ride. Esther looked out her side window and saw the Goodyear blimp off in the distance traveling toward us. She sped up and got to a open field and told me to get out of the car. I was terrified of just about everything ! One of those things was huge objects. I don't know if you've ever seen the Goodyear blimp but it is gigantic. I got out of the car reluctantly because I knew better to protest. I stood pressed against the car in terror. She drug me by the hand to a open spot in the field and the blimp was approaching. My heart started to race and my ears were ringing. I tried to pull away but she was holding my wrist so tightly. As it approached the sound became very loud and I began to cry harder terrified. She looked down at me as said grow the fuck up already ! As it passed over us it made a huge shadow that I will never forget. My fear escalated so severe that I peed my pants. I stood there in the field with Esther who was still gripping my wrist and she looked up at the blimp like it was the mother ship ! I knew I I was going to get a beating for peeing my pants . When the blimp was a distance away Esther said get your ass back in the car and in the future don't be such a little fucking baby ! I was walking to the car and she screamed you fucking filthy bitch you pissed your pants ! She grabbed me by the back of the hair and started shaking me ! She pushed me in the car , punched the crap out of me right there ! The whole time she kept looking around making sure no on was watching ! We were almost to my Aunt Linda's house and Esther looked at me and said how the fuck am I gonna explain you pissing in your pants ? I'm going to tell them you saw a Dr and your having bladder issues ! We got to my Aunt's house, Linda her husband, two kids and my Grandparents were there. Linda came over to hug me and with everyone around Esther said I wouldn't hug her she pissed her pants! I hung my head in shame. Aunt Linda said accidents happen and put her hand out for me to take . I'll get you some clean clothes until I wash your's . I could feel my face burning from embarrassment. Thank you was all I said as I walked into the house.

A couple of weeks later Esther told me I was going to stay with Aunt Linda for a couple of days . I was so shocked I didn't reply. Hello did you fucking hear me she asked ? Yes I replied still shocked , this was huge . I never got to be anywhere without Esther . How long will I get to stay I asked ? Until I fucking pick you up now get the fuck out of my face. I just about floated down the hall. I was going to be Esther free for a couple of days ! No beatings and I would get fed ! I would have hot water to take a bath . I could hardly contain myself ! Esther ripped the door open to my room and I ran to the corner and crouched down shaking . Get the fuck over here she commanded! I slowly walked over and when I got within arms length she grabbed me by the back of my neck and said here's the rules ! You don't say anything about what goes on in this house ! If they ask you anything about anything you say I don't know ! You better be on your best behavior ! Don't embarrass me and if you know what's good for you I would't mention anything about your beatings unless you want one when you get home ! Got it she asked as she squeezed the back of my neck ? Yes I replied ! She looked at me and said well I guess I have to buy your stupid ass some clothes so my bitch of a sister can't run her mouth and say you were wearing rags ! No way I was going to be Esther free and I got new clothes ! This day was getting better and better!

We stopped at a little strip mall on the way to my Aunts house. I got a new pair of pajamas, a housecoat, two shirts, a pair of pants and a pack of underwear. I was thrilled, this was more clothes than I had ever gotten at one time and they were new ! Esther put the bags in the car and pulled out the housecoat and looked me dead in the eye and said I want this on you every second if you have pajamas on do you hear me ? Yes I replied and she grabbed my face and repeated herself , every second your in your pajamas ! I nodded my head in reply. When we arrived I was met with a warm hug from my Aunt. Esther and Linda looked at each other , few words were spoken and just like that Esther was gone !

I was like a fish out of water at my Aunts house. I loved being there but I had no idea how to act without Esther planning out every second of my day ! It was like my life was a play and I followed the script . When Esther wasn't around I was clueless! I constantly apologized for the smallest things . If I was playing and she said time to get washed up for bed I apologized. If it was time to eat and she called for us to come in I apologized because I thought I was holding up dinner. My Aunt looked at me and said honey you did nothing wrong no reason to apologize. She looked down at me with such pity in her eyes I had to look away! All I could think was don't draw attention to yourself she'll say something to Esther and I'll get beat ! I know my Aunt would never try to get me in trouble on purpose . How could Esther and she be sisters ? It just didn't make any sense to me. They were so different. My Aunt's house was just like my Grandparents. It was bigger but just as clean. Decorated with beautiful furniture. They had sit down dinners every night , no one got beat and they had warm beds to sleep in. We would go out and play everyday which was so foreign to me. The freedom her kids had was something I only dreamed about and it was their everyday! They were so lucky to have the childhood they did. My Grandparents were closer Aunt Linda's Children than they were to me. It wasn't my Grandparents fault they never really got a chance to bond with me. I didn't resent them for it I loved them with all my heart. I vowed that when I was an adult and free from Esther that I'd have a relationship with them and allow them to get to know me. For right now I had no say but when I got older hopefully they would love me as much as my Aunt's children. I stayed there for just a few short days and then Esther returned! I didn't want to go and I remember thinking for one split second maybe my Aunt and Uncle could help me . Then Esther rang the doorbell and I snapped back to reality ! I knew my fate. No one could save me from her ! My Aunt hugged me and said her good byes .She tried to tell Esther about my stay and Esther could care less ! She said is this all her stuff pointing at the bag on the floor next to me ? Yes my Aunt replied and we got her a few things. A couple of outfits to take with her. Esther glared at my Aunt and said we don't need your charity I can take care of my own God damn kid ! She grabbed my arm and just like that I was headed back to hell !

Chapter 8

Esther was in a exceptionally bad mood when we woke up . She said were going to my parents house today. I have to leave for a few hours ! You know the drill say anything and I'll beat your ass got it she snarled? You're going to drop me off at Grandma and Grandpas house and your going to leave I asked confused ? Yes you dumb fucking shit that's what I said ! They hate you so don't you dare miss behave ? I was going to be able to be with my Grandparents without fear ! Get your ass in your room and get dressed Esther ordered ! I was going to be able to talk to my Grandparents and just be around them like a normal child. I burst into tears at the shear thought of it ! Esther ripped open my bedroom door and I quickly wiped my tears away. I didn't want to do anything to jeopardize my trip ! One more thing she said when you get there you have to ask your Grandparents to buy you a pair of sneakers for school ! My heart sank ! The only reason I was aloud to go was because Esther wanted something ! I should have known ! Instead of going and asking them herself she was going to make me do her dirty work ! Can you ask them before you go , about the sneakers I mean ? No you fucking little baby you ask and wait until I leave to do it ! I no longer wanted to go ! What was going to be a nice time with my Grandparents had turned into me begging for sneakers. Well get your ass in gear she said as we headed for the door. On the drive over I became sick to my stomach. How was I going to ask for these stupid sneakers? As we were walking up to my Grandparents porch Esther said now remember wait until I leave before you ask ! Don't screw this up you hear ! Come home without those sneakers and I will beat the shit out of you ! As I went into their house I knew what I had to do. Esther left giving me a fake hug and my stomach churned ! My grandmother said are you hungry ? Yes I replied in such a soft voice I wondered if I said it out loud. Come on in the kitchen and I'll get you something to eat.

I followed her into the kitchen and even though I knew Esther wasn't there I still felt her presence. I sat at the table and thought well I better get this over with. Grandma did my Mother ask you about the sneakers I asked ? No she didn't , what sneakers ? Oh I'm sorry she said she was going to ask you if I could get me a pair of sneakers for school . She must have forgotten or changed her mind I said. Do you need sneakers for school she asked ? Yes was all I said feeling horrible for the sneaky way I was asking. Ok when your done we'll go and get you some. I sat there looking at my snack hungry but to ashamed to eat. I had just been so dishonest to my Grandmother ! We went to the local store and there was a tall bin of sneakers each pair was attached with a plastic ring though the loop on the back . what size sneaker do you need ? I'm not sure . She looked at the shoes I was wearing and grabbed a navy blue pair out of the bin . Here try these on she instructed . I did and they were so comfortable I didn't want to take them off . Can I wear them now I asked ? Well we have to pay for them first but then you can put them back on . I strutted around with pride. Then my Grandmother tossed my old shoes in the garbage can outside the store. I gasped! I think I am supposed to bring my old shoes home . Nonsense they're so worn out no sense in keeping them . All of my joy left knowing I would surely get beat because my old shoes were thrown away . Esther came to pick me up and I couldn't wait to show her my new sneakers. She took one look at my feet and said Mother they're boys sneakers ! They're what she wanted ! Jesus Christ Mother she's a kid she doesn't know ! With that she grabbed me by the arm and was walking so fast to the car she was just about dragging me ! As soon as we get in the car you take those fucking boys sneakers off and put your old shoes on you hear me ? I froze , my heart pounding I don't have my old shoes Grandma threw them away . Are you fucking kidding me she said as she stopped in her tracks ! Where did she trow them away ? Outside the store in the garbage can . Well guess what you're getting your ass kicked when we get home for stupidity ! The whole way home Esther screamed about the old shoes and the new sneakers . When we got home I indeed get a beating for the tossed shoes and for not knowing the new ones were boys sneakers !

Chapter 9

The big day was finally here! I was going to start kindergarten! I got up early and quietly went into the bathroom to get washed. I had a brand new uniform with a crisp white short sleeve button shirt . I had brown hair that rested at the middle of my back . I brushed my hair and put it in a ponytail. I was so excited to be going to school. Esther came into the bathroom and said look at your hair can't you do anything right? She grabbed the brush from the sink and ripped the rubber band out of my hair . Smacking me in the head with the hard plastic brush so hard my head hurt immediately . She wet my entire head and put it in a ponytail. When she was done she stood behind me . We both looked at our reflections in the mirror. I thought surely she would have to say I looked nice now. Instead of praise she looked at me and said you still look like a pile of shit . I'm not a miracle worker , laughed and walked out of the room !

She walked me to school and said The rules are simple. 1. Listen to the teacher. 2. Don't draw attention to yourself. 3. This is the most important one if you know what's good for you you'll keep your mouth shut about our home life. You know by now I can make your life a living hell ! We came to the fenced playground of the school and all I wanted to do was run. Run straight into the school and scream someone please help me. I knew better! The fear of Esther outweighed the fear of the beatings. I truly believed that she could and would kill me if given a reason. Esther grabbed my hand and squeezed it hard , remember what I said ! A teacher came over and said hi my name is Mrs. Jenkins what's your name? Addie I said softly with my head down. Well welcome to your new school I hope you'll like it here. She put out her hand out and I took it . Mrs. Jenkins looked up at Esther and said she'll be fine. Esther with her fake outside voice said have a great day honey!

Mrs Jenkins spoke softly and had a happy tone to her voice. Come on I'll show you to your classroom. I was so excited I felt I would burst. As I entered the room I saw round tables with colorful chairs. Each table had a basket full of crayons and a pile of white paper. The walls were covered with pictures of letters and numbers. Mrs Jenkins walked over to the teacher in the room and said this is Addie. The teacher bent down and shook my hand hi my name is Miss Howard nice to meet you . Nice to meet you I said with my head down. Let's go find your seat . There were stickers on each table with everyones name. They found my chair and I sat and waited for the rest of the kids to arrive.

The first kid I met was Becky I could tell right away that she wasn't a nice person. She stared me up and down then wrinkled her nose and said you smell ! I could feel my face burn with embarrassment. I just bowed my head and didn't say anything . The next kid to come into class was roaming around looking for her name on the tables. She walked up to my table and said hi my names Harriet and it looks like I'm at this table. Becky took one look at her and said great another smelly kid ! Harriet looked Becky right in the eye and said ha is that all you got and brushed off Becky's insult . It worked because Becky just sat there with her mouth open not knowing how to respond ! I was in awe of the way Harriet handled the insult. I turned and said hi I'm Addie . We could tell immediately we would be friends. There was something so familiar about her but I knew I had never met her before . Then I realized that it wasn't that I knew Harriet it was that we had the same mannerisms. I saw a lot of myself in her. I loved school. not only because it was time away from Esther but because I had made a friend in Harriet. We sat together at lunch and played together at recess. We often talked about going to one another house after school but both knew it would never happen. I feared Harriet's home life was very similar to my own. Some how Harriet instead of internalizing everything like I did had tough skin and stood up to bullies ! I wish I had that trait !

Harriet and I became best friends. It was only during school hours but it was everything to us. We talked about what we wanted to be when we grew up and simple things that little girls talk about. Those talks kept me going when I was at home after school and weekends. We never talked about our home life. It was like we didn't want to tarnish what we had with the evil we lived everyday. I held this tiny piece of normalcy very close to my heart. No matter how bad it was at home knowing I would see Harriet in school made it all tolerable.

Chapter 10

 When I was about seven years old we moved into a second floor apartment . My first full day there I could hear someone playing on the inside steps. I laid on the floor at the apartment door and tried to see who it was but I could only hear them. It was a girl, I could tell by the voice . The girl said oh Barbie your dress is so pretty. I had no idea what a Barbie doll was I thought it meant there were two girls playing one who was named Barbie. As I laid there on the cold wood floor I imagined I was playing too. I got lost in the moment and didn't hear Esther sneaking up behind me. She yanked me up by my hair and screamed you sneaky little bitch who are you eavesdropping on? She ripped open the door and the little girl who was playing on the steps jumped up looking terrified. She ran down the stairs and into her apartment. When her door slammed shut Esther spun around and looked down at me. With that same dead stare that I knew all to well and said so your a sneaky little bitch who likes to spy on people ! Well I'll beat that out of you! She drug me by the hair to my room , turned on music to cover the cries and beat me with the belt .This time she used the buckle of the belt marking my back and legs. When she was done she said if I ever catch you doing that shit again you'll get a lot worse !

I laid on the floor of what was my new room covered in welts from the beating and took my mind to a happier place. I thought of Harriet. I replayed our days together as I laid there in pain. It helped me get through the night. When I got to school the next day it was like Harriet knew I had a bad night . I can't explain it exactly other than it was a feeling. We shared our lunches that day and for that moment everything was ok.

It was at this time I was going to make my First Holy Communion. Joe's Mom bought me the most beautiful white dress with sheer white floral gloves This dress meant everything to me not only because it was beautiful but mostly because Joe's Mom had so little and somehow she scraped the money together to buy it for me ! I got in line with the other kids making their communion and as I looked around a few thoughts went through my head. First how could Esther walk into a church kneel to pray and then the second she left beat the crap out of me ? Next I thought today I look just like all the other kids! I was wearing a dress that was just as fancy as the other girls and no one could tell I was the poor smelly girl ! I walked up the isle and received my First holy communion and as I went back to the pew and knelt to pray I prayed please God make Esther a better person ,please make her stop beating me ! I prayed so hard thinking if ever there was a day God would answer my prays it had to be today! There was a small party for all the kids who received communion and then it was time to go home. As soon as I got home Esther said get your ass in your room and take that dress off before you ruin it ! I did as I was told. I carefully took the dress off and laid it on my bed. I put the pretty white gloves, rosary and tiny bible along side the dress. I would remember this day for a long time.

Chapter 11

There were times when Esther would stay out all night .
Before she would leave for the night she would open my
bedroom door to let me go to the bathroom. Then she
instructed me stay quiet and not draw attention that I was
home alone ! There were other nights that she would
bring men home. On those nights I would hear her say I'll
be right back . She would walk down the hallway to my
bedroom look in and say I better not hear a fucking sound
from this room do you hear me! I would nod my head and
she would slam and lock the door with a key . I would
hear her go back down the hallway to the living room. I
could hear them talking and then they would go to
Esther's bedroom and I could hear strange noises . At the
time I had no idea they were having sex but over the years
I had figured it out. Most of the men left in the middle of
the night but a rare few stayed until morning They would
walk right passed my door , Esther not so much as
cracking the door to see if I was ok. What kind of man
would know there was a child locked in a bedroom and be
ok with that? I knew the answer to that question . A vile
low life drunk. It seemed every adult I knew with the
exception of my Grandparents , Joe and Maria's Parents
were horrible people .

Esther would go into the kitchen cook breakfast for the man and herself. I would lay on the bed having to pee so bad and listening to my stomach growl because usually I hadn't eaten since lunch at school the day before . Soon after eating the men would always leave. I would hear the front door close and pray that Esther went with him but she never did. She'd walk down the hall unlock my door and say I'm going to bed , go clean the kitchen and I don't want to hear any noise .I would wait until I heard her bedroom door close and quietly run to the bathroom. It was all I could do to hold it in until I sat down. I washed my hands and looked at myself in the mirror. I was always dirty with greasy hair and wore old clothes unless we were going out of the house. As I stared back at myself the one thing that caught me right in the throat was how old my eyes looked for my age. I shook myself back to reality and went to the kitchen. I scrounged whatever leftover food I could find on the plates which was never much.I washed the dishes and went back into my room. As told I stayed very quiet, Esther would sleep most of the day which was fine by me. I would go out one more time to use the bathroom because I didn't know if I would be locked in my room all night again. I would also go into the kitchen and make sure everything was clean and put away. If I did everything right maybe Esther would be proud of me and I wouldn't get beat. I looked around for something anything I could sneak back to my room to keep for later so I wouldn't be so hungry. I would usually take a piece of bread and wrap in in a piece of newspaper and hide it under her bed.

When she would finally wake up I would hold my breath to see what kind of mood she would be in. I would always know as soon as I saw her eyes I learned to read the signs If she walked passed my room and totally ignored me I would be spared but if she walked passed the room and stopped and glared at me sadly I knew what came next.

Chapter 12

It was around this time in my childhood that Esther would take me on a bus to the city about once every month. After we got off the bus we would walk ,what seemed like miles to my little legs. It was more like I was being drug for how fast she was walking ! She was a woman on a mission ! We would reach the same destination every time. It was a huge red brick building with big bay doors. Esther would stand me against the building and tell me not to move ! Don't draw attention to yourself and then she'd disappear into the building! I would be terrified! I had no idea where I was, people were busily moving around me . After what seemed like forever she would reappear with a happy expression on her face. That's something that stuck in my head because she rarely smiled ! So even as a kid I knew she must have been up to no good ! Every time she came out she had money and we would go get something to eat . She would always say eat now this is supper. Well she didn't have to tell me twice I inhaled the food. For a little kid I could sure eat! After eating we would make our way back to our apartment on the bus and then it was back to life as I knew it! Once back in our apartment evil Esther made her appearance. She would tell me to "go take a piss and get in my room for the night" . I loved these days because for whatever reason I never got beat ! It was one of the rare times I could fall asleep without fear of being ripped from my bed . I never knew if it was because she was tired from all the walking we did on those days or she was still on a high from whatever she did in that building! Either way I was thankful I would lay in my bed in total peace with a full stomach and sleep.

I'd been invited to a birthday party for one of the kids in my class. From the second I got the invitation I was trying to figure out a way to bring it up to Esther. I already knew I wouldn't be allowed to go . One day after school I opened the front door I saw her on the phone so I went to my room. I heard thank you for the invite and yes Addie would love to come! Did I hear correctly ? Was I going to be allowed to go to the party ? She hung up the phone and yelled for me . I ran to the living room as fast as I could. She glared at me and said well isn't this just fucking wonderful ! Some little brat from your class is having a birthday party and that was her mom calling to confirm that you're coming. With a shaking hand I held up the invitation and said we just got these in school today. I was going to tell you about it but you were on the phone when I came in. Well she caught me off guard so I guess your going to the stupid thing ! I could hardly contain myself ! Thank you so much for letting me go . Get out of my site I want to take a nap. I didn't want to give her a reason to change her mind so I went back to my room quietly closed the door and cried. These were happy tears. Maybe just maybe things were going to get better.

The birthday party was everything I imagined it to be and more. There was pink as far as the eye could see. It was held in my classmates back yard. You had to walk through her house to get to the backyard I couldn't believe this was the way some people lived ! The interior of the house was amazing. So clean and you could tell a happy family lived here. Esther dropped me off at the front door . I had no idea how to act around my peers without every move planned out for me. I had no social skills so I hung back and watched the kids interact with each other. It seemed to come so natural to them. I watched their mannerism, I didn't realize I was mimicking them from afar and caught myself just in time before one of the parents came over to me . Go on over and join the fun. I wanted to walk over to the group and fit in but as I took a few steps toward them I felt nauseous . I was going to get sick, I asked one of the parents where the bathroom was and as quickly as I could shut the door and vomited . Had anyone heard me ? Would I be in trouble because I vomited? I stood in the bathroom until there was a knock on the door. Anyone in there ,a voice said from the other side of the door. I'll be right out I replied. I splashed water on my face, opened the door and tried to look calm.

When I had returned to the party I looked across the yard and saw Harriet! My heart leapt ! When Harriett saw me a huge smile of relief came over her face. We met up in the middle of the yard and both said at the same time I'm so happy you're here ! Harriet said come on we'll go over to the group together. We joined the group and together we gave each other the strength we needed to interact. The group was snooty but I didn't care Harriet was there with me. There was cake and presents and then it was time to go. Harriet and I hugged and said we'd see each other in school. I went outside and stood on the curb to wait for Esther . When she pulled up she said what the hell are you smiling about? Nothing I replied head down. The whole way back to the apartment I relived the day I just had to be careful not to show any emotion so Esther wouldn't be suspicious. When we got inside I heard the oh so familiar go take a piss and get in your room ! I hope

you ate at the party cause there's nothing here to eat .
Yes I ate . Well get the fuck going . I did as I was told.

Chapter 13

My birthday was in a few weeks. Birthdays were just
another day in my house but I would always take a few
minutes every year on my birthday and smile. Even if
there wasn't any celebration or cake it was my day. I
would sit in my room and pretend I had a fancy dress, lots
of presents and a huge cake. Then I would hear Esther's
shrill voice and snap back to reality. She could take a lot
from me but she couldn't take my imagination ! She called
me to the living room. I guess now that your in school
people will expect me to throw you a birthday party. Wait
,what ? I just stood there frozen in time ! Well you dumb
shit do you want a party or not? Yes , oh yes I want a
party ! When you go into school tell those brats that
you're having a party here on the 29th at one o'clock. Can
you remember that or do I have to write it down? I can
remember I replied with such joy I thought I would
explode. Well here's the way it's going to go she said. You
clean the apartment and I mean clean it good then we'll
discuss your party. It's going to be here , don't expect and
fancy bullshit like the party you went to a couple of weeks
ago ! Thank you oh thank you I replied !

I stood there just in case there was anything else. She glared over at me and said well what the hell are you waiting for an invitation ? Get your ass moving and start cleaning this shit hole of a place ! I spun around so quickly I slammed into the wall. She looked at me and said Jesus you're dumb as rocks ! Her insult slid right off me ! I was going to have a birthday party ! I would make this place shine. A party, me I was having a party! This was huge ! I tackled the kitchen first. I scrubbed the kitchen floor,making sure to get into the corners, I had to change the water three times it was so dirty. Esther wasn't much of a cleaner! Next I wiped the wood work down. She walked by and instead of praise said don't forget to change the water before you wipe it down again so you get all the soap scrum off! Yes mam. I was so hungry but didn't dare touch anything !I've been hungry before and lived through it ! I wasn't going to do anything to jeopardize this party !

Next I would clean the bathroom. I scrubbed everything until it shined. We didn't have a vacuum so I grabbed the broom to sweep the carpets. I got as far as the hallway when Esther screamed can you stop making so much fucking noise I'm trying to watch tv. So I decided to clean my room instead . My room would be easy there was only a bed and a dresser . I had one doll which I had no idea where it came from but I adored it . It was hard plastic and stood about 3 feet tall . It had on a bright yellow dress with lace that had begun to show wear. It gave the doll character. I swept the floor in my room and I was sitting on my bed when she came down the hallway . Must be fucking nice to be able to sit around! Don't you have anything you could be doing? Can I clean the living room now ? Yeah I'm going for a nap , make any noise and I'll come out and kick your ass !I cleaned the living room and as I took a look around was very proud of myself for a job well done ! The only thing I didn't clean was Esther's room but I wasn't allowed in there so I was done. I walked through the apartment again just to make sure I didn't miss anything. This was the cleanest it's been in a long time. As I turned the light off in the kitchen I saw a banana on the counter but heard Esther's words consider that piece of bread your lunch and supper so I went to my room.

When I got to school the next day I timidly walked up to the teacher's desk before class . Excuse me my mom said I can have a birthday party at my house on the 29th at 1:00 . That's wonderful the teacher replied . You can hand out your invitations after class. I froze ,I didn't have invitations ! I was embarrassed I knew Esther would never buy them I was lucky to be having the party. Um I left them at home. Ok no problem bring them in tomorrow and you can hand them out. I walked back to my desk and all the joy I had left me. What was I going to do now ? I would make invitations on school paper and hand them out tomorrow.

As soon as I got home I went right to my room and got to work. My printing wasn't great but I did it. Twenty hand written invitations all done.

When I got to school the next day I was so excited. I couldn't wait to hand them out. I walked up to Miss Howard's desk and said I have my invitations . Can I hand them out now.? You sure can she replied happily. I walked around the room and put one on the table in front of everyone's chair . Becky took one look at them and started to laugh ! Are you kidding me, you couldn't even afford invitations you made them on school paper ! I felt my face burn. I walked back to my desk feeling defeated. The teacher became aware of what was going on and just as I was going to say something Harriet walked over to the table and said wow cool invitations ! That's all it took I had a huge smile on my face . Thanks , Harriet turned and looked in Becky's direction and said these are so much better than those store bought invitations that everyone hands out. Becky glared and said whatever ! I got a list from the teacher with everyone's home phone number on it. Miss Howard said take this list home to your parents . They can check off the names of the children when they call to RSVP . This way your parents will have an idea of how many kids will be coming. Thank you I replied. This was really happening ! I was going to have a real party with cake and classmates !

The night before the party Esther said check everything and make sure it's clean I don't want these rich snooty bitches talking about me having a dirty home. I gave the apartment a final check and everything looked great. She said you better be very thankful that I'm letting you have this party you hear? Yes I replied. Now get your ass to bed so you can get up early and set everything up. I was to excited to sleep. I still couldn't believe I was going to have a birthday party ! When I woke up the day of my party I immediately knew something was wrong.

Chapter 14

Esther stormed into my bedroom and said well your parties off ! What did I do wrong ? I told you to clean and this apartment looks like a shit house she replied ! Even though I knew I cleaned everything from top to bottom I wouldn't dare argue. I'll clean again I'll do it right ! No I told you to do it right and if you didn't there wasn't going to be a party. You fucked it up so no party. Please was all I said before a hand struck me in the face and I hit the floor! Don't argue with me get me that fucking paper so I can call the parents and cancel ! The paper Oh no where did I put the paper? I froze right where I stood ! Well what the fuck are you waiting for get me the God Damn paper ! I ran to my room, I started to panic Oh my God where did

I put it ? I looked all over my room,then in my back pack,
on my bed but it wasn't there ! Esther screamed from the
living room you have 10 seconds to get your ass out here
with that paper do you hear me! I stared to pray please
let me find the paper please !

I heard her footsteps thumped down the hallway ,where's
the fucking paper? I just stood there shaking in fear. I'll
ask you one more time where's the paper? Shaking I said
I can't find it ! Esther grabbed me by the hair and started
to shake me like a rag doll ! I'm sorry please don't , I'm
sorry was all I was able to say before I got the worse
beating of my life ! She drug me from one end of the
room to the other by my hair. She started kicking me so
hard that she actually lifting me off the floor I landed with
a loud thud ! She then drew her leg back looked me right
in the eye and kicked me in my private parts! The pain
was unbearable and I screamed it burned like fire ! This
sent her into even more of a rage ! Oh you want to
scream ? She grabbed me by the head slammed it on the
floor and sat on me ! She covered my mouth, she got so
close to my face that spit was flying out of her mouth
when she hissed ! I told you to never scream! I couldn't
breath my nose was full of snot from crying, she still had
her hand over my mouth! I tried to wiggle loose from
under her but there was no use I was to small ! I started
to flail my arms and pleading with her with my eyes then
everything started fade. It was like a light was being

turned off with a dim switch! The next thing I
remembered she was shaking me by the shoulders saying
wake up you little bitch wake up ! Everything came back
into focus and the first thing I saw was the hate in Esther's
eyes as she glared down at me ! You're not worth it she
said as she slammed and locked the door behind her!

Sometime had passed , I not sure how much but I heard
her at my bedroom door. As the door swung open I ran to
the corner of the room and crouched down shaking ! She
looked at me and laughed you better fear me ! She threw
clothes on the bed and said I have to go out and pick up
your stupid fucking cake ! Get dressed and be ready when
I come back ! All the little brats should be here in a couple
of hours ! I just stared at her . Did you hear me ? I just
shook my head yes . Well get moving ! As I heard her
leave I tried to stand up.the pain was unbearable ! Every
inch of my body ached. I had a lump on the back of my
head where it had hit the floor . I felt like I was going to
get sick. I limped to the bathroom , spun around and
threw up in the toilet. The whole room was spinning ! I
knew I had to do what I was told so I got dressed. All I
wanted to do was go lay down .

I wet my head and tried to brush my hair but the pain
was to much ! I touched my head and when I looked at
my fingers they had tiny blood spots on them . I knew I
had no choice so I held my hair at the top of my head and

brushed the ends. The pain made me get sick again. I took a wash rag and wet it in the sink and began to wash my body. Welts were starting to form . I soaked the rag in cold water and placed it on the welts. I stood there and looked at my reflection in the mirror . The eyes that stared back at me were so filled with pain , so fragile. How could no one see this? I had no time to feel sorry for myself now. She would be home soon so I got dressed. I put my hair in a ponytail and began to brush my teeth. We used baking soda instead of toothpaste and I was worried that it wouldn't mask the vomit smell so I brushed and rinsed twice . Every time I moved the nausea intensified. I only had a few minuted to get it together. I had to act like everything was ok because I knew there was no way I could tolerate another beating today !

She came home took one look at me and said you better straighten up ! This is your party and you better act like you're having a good time! Just a couple of days ago this birthday party meant so much to me now I just wished it was over.My body was starting to stiffen . I didn't think it was possible but it hurt more now than it did before.

The kids started to arrive and I was instructed put a smile on my ugly face and pretended to be having a wonderful time. Esther always seemed to have one or two normal friends. They would be around for a couple of months maybe a year and then just as they came into our lives they disappeared. At this point in our life her normal friends were Agnes and Eddie . They were married and had kids of their own. They thought the world of Esther and had no idea that she was evil ! They even let her watch their own children. They were both very kind to me. They came to the party and had gotten me a doll. Dolls usually creeped me out other than the one I had in my room. I thanked them and said I'd be right back . A wave of nausea had come over me and I barley made it to the bathroom before getting sick. I was in so much pain. I didn't know if I would be able to keep this "happy little girl" routine up.

With every knock on the door I had hoped it was Harriet but she never came. The last to arrive were Becky and her friend Pam. My stomach did flips when I saw them in my apartment. They walked around giggling and whispering to each other. I watched them walk right up to Esther with their fake smiles and say You have such a nice home . She looked down at them with that cold glare and their smiles disappeared from their faces. With a snide voice Esther said why thank you girls. Both Becky and Pam turned to walk away and kept looking back over their shoulder at Esther . Becky whispered wow that is one creepy lady ! I thought to myself you have no idea!

The party was finally over. Esther shut the door as the last person left and said so glad all those brats are gone. Get this shit cleaned up. She walked over to the table were the presents were and said I'm taking the cards with the money in them , consider it payment for the cake and party shit. With that she walked out of the room and I sat down on the couch so relieved that everyone was gone . I looked around the room , at the mess I had to clean up and cried. By this time I felt so weak but I did as I was told and gathered all party trash , I swept the rug ,took the bag to the garbage and brought the party snacks into the kitchen. I gathered the birthday cards that had money in them and placed them on the kitchen table . I had no use for money she could have it! After wiping the table down and drying the dishes I went to the bathroom and stared at myself in the mirror. If I had a normal life I would see a little girl who just had a birthday party instead a little girl with hollow eyes stared back at me. Esther walked by the bathroom saw me staring into the mirror and said no matter how long you stare you'll still be the same ugly little shit ! Now get done and get in your room. I finished up ,went to my room and cried myself to sleep.

Chapter 15

Monday when I got back to school I looked for Harriet but couldn't find her. When class started she wasn't in her seat. She must be sick that would explain why she didn't make it to my birthday party. Harriet wasn't there for the rest of the week. School just wasn't the same without her. Hopefully she would be back on Monday. When I waked into the classroom on Monday Harriett still wasn't there. I walked up to the teacher and asked if Harriett was still sick . She replied honey she moved she goes to a different school now ! I thought you knew she said, I'm sorry. That's ok I replied and walked back to my seat I started crying . As I sat down Becky said Whatcha gonna do now that your only friend is gone loser ? I looked at her and thought what would Harriett say but then realized I had no fight left in me and cried even harder. Awe little baby gonna cry ? Miss Howard came by the table leaned down and said Becky that's quite enough ! Becky spun in her seat not realizing the teacher was standing there. Addie take the pass on the desk and go to the restroom and take a few minutes. Becky see me after class said Miss Howard. When I got to the restroom I looked under all the stalls to make sure no one was in there and went into the last stall a cried a heartbroken cry for loss of my only friend.

When I got home from school that day I found Esther and a man I had never seen before sitting on the couch. Come here sweetie Esther motioned to me. I walked over and Esther said this is Billy . Billy barley looked away from the tv long enough to say hey. Nice to meet you I said . Billy had no reply! I could smell the booze on him from a few feet away. Come on now Esther said I'll get you a snack. They walked down the hall as soon as they got to the kitchen Esther grabbed me by the shoulders and said stand here for a few minutes then go to the bathroom because your going to your room for the night.I don't want you coming out for any reason do you hear me ? Yes I said as they stood there in the kitchen Ok Addie sweetie Esther said in her fake loud voice totally for Billy's benefit go clean up and go to your room. She shook her say ok loud enough so he can hear. I did as I was told . I went to the bathroom and they walked down the hall to my room Esther pushed me in as they passed and closed the door! Thats where I stayed until morning when I had to get ready for school I didn't get much sleep all I could think about was never seeing Harriett again. I got dressed , crept passed Esther's room and left for school.

No Esther again the apartment was empty . There was a note on the table , went out be back late wash up and go to your room . Thank God for free lunch at school or I'd never have anything to eat. How could a mother leave her child with no food and alone and just go out ? I was so hungry I knew I wasn't allowed but I looked around for something small to eat. I was so paranoid that I kept tip toeing back to the hallway to make sure Esther wasn't coming around the corner ! I looked through the cabinets and found a sleeve of open saltine crackers. I took four crackers and carefully put the sleeve back into the cabinet. I grabbed a glass and filled it with water from the faucet. I carefully ate the crackers so not to leave any trace of crumbs behind. I drank the water down fast to fill my belly. After going to the bathroom I went to my room sut the door a and laid on my bed . I cried myself to sleep thinking about Harriet . I missed her so much ! Yet another person I've lost !

Chapter 16

Esther started to be gone more and more which was fine with me ! She couldn't beat me if she wasn't around ! I got home from school and looked forward to the quiet ! I was walking up the inside stairs to the apartment and a girl came out from he first floor apartment ! We just stood there looking at each other! Finally she said my names Maria what's yours ? I looked up at my apartment door nervously ! Was Esther home ? Would she hear me talking to the neighbor ? As if Maria knew what I was looking for she said your mom went out ! I spun around and looked at her nervously ! So what's your name she asked again ? Addie I replied. So Addie you wanna play in the hallway ? I can bring my dolls out ! Sorry I can't play today maybe another day . Ok Marie said and she went into her apartment . I run into the apartment and closed the door my heart pounding ! I was terrified that Esther would find out I was talking to the neighbor and I would get beat ! It was a rule she had drilled into my head for as long as I could remember ! I went to the kitchen , no supper again ! I went to the cabinet to get a few crackers , I opened the cabinet and they were gone ! The only thing in the kitchen was a loaf of bread, some tea bags and a can of milk . Since the day I helped myself to a piece of bread without asking Esther started to count the slices ! She told me about it so I knew not to take any ! I'd rather be hungry and spare myself the beating ! So I grabbed a tea bag and made myself a cup of tea ! It would have to do !

The next day when I got home from school Maria was waiting for me on the stairs ! Can you play today ? No not today maybe another day I replied. How old are you Maria asked ? I'm eight I said how old are you ? I'm seven I think we go to the same school she said with a smile . I was getting nervous I had to get upstairs . Maybe I'll see you in school sometime Maria said. Yeah maybe I gotta get upstairs now bye. I ran up the stairs to the apartment . Thankfully Esther wasn't home ! I went into the kitchen to see of there was anything to eat and there sitting on the table was a single piece of bread with a note that read supper ! It was only a piece of bread but I was grateful for it ! I made myself a cup of tea and sat at the table and ate my supper !

The next day I looked for Maria in school but didn't see her . As soon as I got to class Becky was ready with her arsenal of snotty remarks ! How's your creepy mom doing smelly ? It's like Becky's day wasn't complete without making fun of me ! Oh how I missed Harriet , I stared at her empty chair and my heart ached ! When I got home there was Maria waiting at the bottom of the stairs for me . Can you play today ? No sorry not today maybe tomorrow I replied . As I was walking up the stairs Maria said your mom isn't home again I saw her go out ! I froze in my tracks , this was getting to dangerous ! Now Maria was keeping tabs on when Esther left ! If Esther caught on I would get a horrific beating ! I lied and said oh she'll be back in a few minutes ! I hated to lie to Maria she was so sweet . Maria's mom opened their apartment door and called for Maria. The sound of her voice made me jump , I gripped the banister . Time for dinner Maria she said and then she saw me . Oh you must be Addie , Maria never stops talking about you . Why what is she saying I asked with fear in my voice ? Oh just that you go to the same school and you live upstairs that's all honey . Maria's mom could sense that I was nervous, I'm sorry I didn't mean anything by it she said . Oh no play it cool I thought , don't arouse suspicion or we'll have to move again ! Oh ok I said faking a smile. Well I have to go upstairs now. It was nice meeting you . Nice meeting you to honey . Can Addie come in for supper Maria asked her mom ? Sure come on in . Oh how I wanted to I was so hungry but I knew better ! Oh thank you but I have to get upstairs ! Oh it's no problem we have plenty of food and I saw your mom go out . I always make to much . With this I started to freak out ! Now Maria's mom was keeping tabs on Esther when she left ! I have to go upstairs I said as I ran into my apartment and locked the door !

Once inside I started pacing back and forth in the living room. Oh please don't let Esther know that I was talking to the neighbors I'll get such a beating and we'll have to move again. I went into the kitchen and there was another piece of bread on the table with a note that read supper and nothing else. As I sat at the table eating my piece of bread and drinking my tea I imagined what they were eating downstairs. It smelled heavenly. I imagined them all sitting at the table together talking about their day. How wonderful Maria's life must be! There was a knock on her door that made me jump. No one ever came to our apartment except for Joe and whatever drunk Esther brought home. Joe's visits were always scheduled and I hadn't seen him in weeks. I tiptoed toward the door . I was halfway down the hallway when they knocked again. Who could it be? What if Maria's mom called children and youth or worse the cops telling them I was home alone!

There was another knock this time it was followed by Maria saying Addie it's Maria open the door I have a surprise for you! Was this a trick ,was she just trying to get her to open the door so the cops could take me ? What do you want? I'm not supposed to open the door? Just open it for a minute I'll be quick I promise. I put my ear to the door I didn't hear anyone talking. Keeping the chain on I open the door a crack. Hey silly it's only me. Open the door I have something for you. I opened the door and Maria handed her a plate covered with foil . What's this I asked. My mom sent some supper up , she always makes so much and we have tons of leftovers. Oh I cant but tell her thank you anyway. Don't be silly just take it. You can give me the plate back tomorrow after school. Ok well I have to go back down now. See you tomorrow ! With that she ran down the steps and into her apartment.

I lifted the foil and couldn't believe what I saw. The plate was overflowing with food. There was meat ,veggies , mashed potatoes with gravy. This was more food then I had seen on one plate in a long time. I knew if Esther caught me with this I would surely get beat. I was so hungry and I wasn't allowed to leave the apartment so I couldn't bring it back downstairs to give it back and there was no way I was going to throw this out so I made a decision. I was going to eat it.. I put the plate on the table and got myself a glass of water. I sat down ready to eat then all of a sudden thought oh no the kitchen was enveloped in the wonderful smells of the food and they would permeate the kitchen . I ran out to the back porch left the door open to air out any lingering smells and enjoyed one of the best meals I had ever eaten! I had no idea what kind of meat it was all I knew is was a huge step up from her stale piece of bread that would have been my supper! When every scrap of food was gone I brought the plate in, washed and dried it and put it in my book bag . I put the plate in front of Maria's door and attached a note which read thank you for the food it was very good. I didn't want to sign my name although I knew Esther wouldn't see the note I didn't want any proof left behind .

Everyday from that day on Maria would be waiting for me when I got home from school. Can you play today she would ask ? No sorry not today maybe tomorrow and I would head up to her apartment and wish I could sit in the hallway and play dolls with Maria. I knew better than to take that chance.

Chapter 17

Mrs Giorgio was a older woman who lived across the street. One day when I got home from school there was a note on the kitchen table it said as soon as you get home from school go across the street to Mrs Giorgio's house. The address was on the note. I was so confused then scared. Why was she going over to this women's house? Was she evil like Esther? Would she hurt me? Fear came easy to me but trust was different. I had huge trust issue. I did as I was told and went to Mrs Giorgio's house. When she opened the door she looked harmless . She wore her white hair up in a bun. She had a house dress on with an apron. Hi honey I don't think we were ever formally introduced my name is Mrs Giorgio . Hi I'm Addie. Come on in we can get to know each other. Are you hungry? I nodded my head yes . Well you come right in wash your hands and sit down. I made homemade sauce with calamari. Have you ever had it she asked? No I haven't but it smells amazing. She smiled, you're such a little sweetie. Go on now the bathrooms right through there . Go wash up and I'll fix you a plate. I did as I was told .

When I got back to the kitchen there was a huge plate of pasta on the table. Here you sit here she said. I hopped up on the chair still very nervous as to why I was there. She must have sensed it because she said how would you like to come over here a couple of days a week after school? Um I would have to check with my mother to see of it's ok. Your mom's the one that suggested it sweetie she said with a smile. I was still trying to read her. She didn't seem mean but I wasn't going to let my guard down. Ok if it's ok with my mom I'll come over. Great she replied, let me get you a fork so you can eat.

I finished every drop on my plate . She was amazed ! Wow for a little girl you can surely eat. I'm sorry did I eat to much I asked ? Oh no honey you have a great appetite that makes me happy. Did you enjoy it? Oh yes it was very good Thank you. I continued to go over to Mrs Giorgio's house for a couple of weeks . Then just like that I never went over again ! I got home from school and I was going to change out of my school clothes and go over and there was a note on the table ! When you get home stay there ! No more going over to Mrs Giorgio's house ! What happened I wondered ? I knew better than to go against what I was told so I stayed put ! For the next week when I walked home from school I would look over at Mrs Giorgio's house and wonder if I did something wrong ! Didn't she want me to come over anymore or was it Esther's decision ? My money was on the latter ! Esther had the uncanny ability of introducing people into my life and then ripping them away !

Chapter 18

Esther had been gone everyday after school for about 3 weeks which was wonderful . Then one day I got home from school and saw Maria peeking out from her apartment door but she wouldn't come out. I waved and she shut the door. I went upstairs and immediately saw her sitting on the couch. She must have broken up with Billy . I assumed that's were she had been staying. Get your ass in here she yelled. I went into the living room and she glared at me. The first thing that came to mind is oh no she found out about the plate of food ! I was so careful making sure every trace of it was gone. She jumped off the couch and grabbed me by the hair just so you know I'm back now so things will be changing around here ! I didn't say a word . I still didn't know if she knew about the meal or not. No more lounging around after school there will be a chore list on the table everyday when you get home. I want all the chores done before you go to bed understand. Yes I replied. How was this different I did all the chores anyway I thought but didn't dare say anything. Now get the fuck out of my sight. I hurried down the hall and went to the bathroom and straight to my room.

Esther came charging into my room, I jumped up and ran to the corner . So you think your going to just sit in here and do nothing the rest of the night ? I knew she wasn't looking for a reply I also knew what was coming next. She grabbed me and got real close to my ear and said I wish you were never born you ruined my life! Although I knew this was the way she felt hearing the words still cut like a knife ! For some sick reason I always tried my hardest and thought if I did everything right one day Esther might be proud of me and not hate me so much. I now knew that day would never come. She started slapping me but this beating was different . She was more filled with hate, it almost seemed like she was blaming me for being born and was willing to take my life ! She kept saying over and over again you ruined my life ! I tried to curl up in a ball to protect myself and then I there was a knock on the door!

We both froze! Then there was another knock. Don't move , don't make a sound she said to me . There was another knock and then another. Esther realized whoever it was wasn't going away. She looked down at me on the floor crying and said I'll be right back !

Who is it she yelled ? Hello it's Camila from downstairs. I froze , oh no please don't get involved. We'll have to move ! What do you want she asked without opening the door? Can I talk to you for a minute? About what still not opening the door ? It will just take a minute. Reluctantly Esther opened the door. Yes what is it ? I was wondering if your daughter could come down and play with my Maria? There aren't a lot of kids around here and I just thought they could play together. I was laying on the floor listening. I already knew what the answer would be. No Addie's busy she can't ! It would only be for a little while Camila said . They could play in the hallway so you can keep an eye on them or they can play in our apartment. Either one is fine with me. Again there was silence. It would give you some free time to yourself Camila said. I know moms don't get much of that. They both stood there in total silence for a minute and then if I wasn't already on the floor I would have fell over ! Esther said I'll send her down in a few minutes. I sat there in disbelief ! What just happened! Ok that's great Camila said Maria will be so excited. Do you want them to play in the hall or will the apartment be ok? Whatever doesn't matter to me

. Ok when you want her to come back up just yell for her I'll send her up. If you ever need someone to watch her after school I'm always home . The girls can play together . Ok I'll send her down in a few minutes. Esther shut the door and stormed down the hall to my room. I coward in the corner .

Esther looked at me and said fucking neighbors ! The noisy bitch neighbor from downstairs wants you to go play with her brat daughter! I didn't say a word. I'm letting you go down say one word about anything that goes on up here and you'll never go again understand Esther asked? Yes I replied. Get your ass in the bathroom and clean yourself up. I don't want that noisy bitch saying you were filthy when you went down there. I couldn't believe it Esther was letting me out of the apartment and I was going to be able to play with another kid! I got washed up and was ready to go but I stood in the hallway afraid to go into the living room because I might do something to set her off. Then she'd change her mind. Finally I heard her say what the hell is taking you so long ? Get your ass in gear and get in here! She went over the rules again and told me she would call me when she wanted me to come back up . You better get your ass back up here when I call . Don't make me have to come get you . I won't thank you for letting me go . Yeah whatever get out of my sight and don't slam the door! I was so excited I ran down the stairs straight to Maria's door but couldn't knock !

What was I doing ? Just knock on the door ! I waited for a day like this for so long. Now that the day had finally arrived I was afraid to knock ! What if I went in and Maria decided she didn't want to be friends with me? Finally I gathered all my courage and knocked. Maria ran to the door and hugged me and said you came you finally came ! I stiffened when hugged because hugs were so foreign to me then I leaned into it. I felt such joy in that moment . I had found a friend.

I'm not sure why but Esther started to let me go to Maria's a couple of times a week to play. I didn't care what the reason was for her change of heart I was just so glad I could go. Maria's family was so nice . Her mother was the kind of mother I always dreamed of having. She spoke softly and genuinely loved her family that was evident to anyone. Her father was a large quiet man. Her brother Jr. was five years old and a handful but a nice kid. Their apartment was so cozy. I could tell right away that Maria had a great life. She was free to be a kid with no fears of abuse.

It was never spoken but I think Maria's mom knew what my life was like. She was always very kind to me and would always hug me and tell me how special I was whenever I came to play. "If you ever need anything she

would say,you know we're alway right downstairs" No
matter what time of day. Maria's mom was always
cooking. She made the most amazing food. One day I said
I never had any of the foods that you make before but I
love them all. Camila said we're Spanish that may be why.
I said well I don't know what Spanish is but I love it. This
made everyone laugh.

Maria & I played in the back yard and the one day she said
I want to show you something. I followed her up to what
was a shared attic space for all the apartments. It was
filled with old furniture , decorations and toys. It was
magical ! She took me over to a small toy cola machine. It
had plastic cups and you could pretend you were at a
restaurant and getting a cola . There were all kinds of
random toys we would play with. Maria would tell me
stories that went with each toy. They were from her
childhood and were stored away because she had
outgrown them . They still held a very special place in her
heart so her parents put them in the attic so that one day
she could pass them along to her kids. We would sit up
there and play and for that short time my life was normal
! Her stories were told with such detail I felt like I was
there with her in her memory.They were some of the best
times of my life. Just us playing being kids ! Our friendship
continued to grow and we became more like sisters than
friends .

Joe's visitation was less and less. He only came around about once a month if that at this point. I missed him terribly but part of me was also upset with him for leaving me in this environment . If he couldn't handle it as an adult how was I supposed to handle it as a defenseless child ! Still I was happy to see him when he came and he did try and make the most of his time with me. We would go to the park and out to eat. The ride home was always the worst. I knew he would be leaving and I would have to go back upstairs to Esther! At least I had Maria. I was so very thankful to have her friendship .

Chapter 19

Right before my ninth birthday Esther came home and said we're moving tomorrow pack up your shit tonight ! Whatever you don't have packed will be staying here! What about Maria ? What about her Esther replied? Will I still be able to play at her house? I doubt it since were moving out of state! In the past when we moved we always stayed in the same city and certainly the same state. What about Joe ? How will I see him? You won't she laughed ! What about Grandma and Grandpa I asked? They hate you anyway so why would you care about them ? I only got to see my Grandparents a few times a year because Esther didn't want to go but at least I got to see them. I stood frozen , so I won't see them or Maria

anymore? Boy you're fucking quick aren't you she snarled
! I broke down in tears Please don't move please I cried !
Shut the fuck up and get in your room and pack! We only
have room for one box of your stuff so choose carefully!
Can I go down and say goodbye to Maria ? She'll figure
out you're moving when she sees the u haul truck Esther
laughed ! Please at least let me say goodbye. Listen you
little bitch I have a lot to do before tomorrow so get the
fuck out of my sight and go pack your shit ! One more
word out of you and I'll beat your ass now move! I walked
back to my room devastated! Why was she doing this ?
How could she leave and not let me say goodbye to my
Grandparents , Joe and Maria ? I sat on the floor and
sobbed. The only thing I put in the box was my doll , a
dress I wore when I was about five and some clothes and
that was an effort. I felt like part of me had died.

Esther came into her room and saw that I was sitting on
the floor crying and snatched me up by the throat. She
held me up against the wall and said listen you little bitch
if it was up to me I'd leave you here ! My life would be so
much easier without you but the law tends to frown upon
leaving strays when you move out of state ! So for the last
time pack your fucking shit! With that she threw me to
the floor! I crawled over to the corner and then realized I
had peed my pants. Esther took one look at the puddle on
the floor and said stupid little bitch ! You can clean that

up as soon as your done packing and she walked out of the room !

What was I going to do without my Grandparents , Joe and Maria ! Was she even going to tell Joe we were moving ? As far as Maria and her family went I considered them family.! How could she just take all of that away ? There had to be something I could do! I heard the downstairs doorbell ring. It was Joe ! He would know what to do! Esther said go the fuck away it's a done deal we're moving ! The hell you are he replied ! They started yelling back and forth through the intercom and finally Esther ripped the door to the apartment open and flew down the stairs to the downstairs door. It was a partial wood door with a glass top. She was yelling through the door for Joe to go or she was going to call the cops ! Go ahead and call them he said , you'll save me the phone call ! When they get here I'll tell them how your taking my kid out of the state without my permission ! I don't need your fucking permission to move she replied ! The hell you don't you can't just take my kid! At least let me say goodbye to her you fucking bitch Joe screamed through the door !

Esther screamed up the stairs Addie get your ass down here and say goodbye to your good for nothing father ! I ran down the stairs sobbing, and opened the door . Joe hugged me and said it will be ok don't cry. I hugged him and whispered in his ear please take me with you please !

He said I can't but I will find out where your moving and I'll come visit. The hell you will Esther snarled ! I'm leaving this fucking state and you behind ! Joe said what the fuck is wrong with you ? Why are you doing this ? Because I can, now leave . She pushed him towards the door and tried to shut it . He put his arm up as the door was closing and his arm went right through the glass making it shatter ! I looked down at Joe's arm and blood was squirting everywhere ! What the fuck did you do Joe kept saying over and over ! I was screaming hysterically and Esther looked right into Joe's eyes and said with any luck you'll bleed to death and die right here and I'll be done with you forever !

Call an ambulance Joe screamed Holding his arm ! Sorry can't our phone's disconnected Esther laughed ! Sucks for you huh ! I'll knock on Maria's door and ask them to call I screamed hysterically ! You fucking move and your dead Esther screamed! She knew Maria and her family had to hear the commotion but they didn't come out of their apartment. Joe looked right at Esther and said you better hope I die right in this spot tonight because if I don't I'll do whatever it takes to get your crazy ass thrown in jail ! She got right in Joe's face and snarled many have tried but I'm still waking free so go for it! Joe looked at me and pleaded Addie honey go knock on your friends door and ask them to call an ambulance ! I turned and Esther said go across the street to Ann's house and ask her to call. Ann was one of Esther's friends. It would be a miracle if she wasn't drunk and passed out. She said I'd rather one of my friends called instead of the fucking neighbors that hate me. Chances are she'll never answer the door but I can say I tried to get help Esther laughed ! I ran barefoot in the dark to Ann's house. When I got to the porch I saw all the lights were off but I banged on the door like Joe's life depended on it . No answer ! I started screaming Ann's name . Ann please it's an emergency Please open the door! Nothing, but my screaming woke up Ann's neighbor who called the ambulance.

I ran back across the street to the apartment and within a few minutes the police and ambulance pulled up..Esther said there's my daughter ask her she saw everything. He forced his way in and I was just protecting us . I thought he was going to kill me so I slammed the door ! The cop walked over to me honey , what did you see he asked ? This was my chance to break free from Esther and I was going to take it ! Just as I was going to answer Esther knelt down and hugged me and said you know what to say right in my ear. I looked at Joe on the front step being worked on and looked up at Esther and said I'm not sure it all happened so fast . Ok honey thank you the officer replied. He started writing in his notebook and said were taking him to the hospital now and we'll contact you if we need anything else. Ok thank you so much for coming out. It's our job ! Maybe it was just me but the officer seemed to feel there was more to the story than Esther had said by the way he looked at her. She grabbed my hand and squeezed it until my fingers overlapped. You think your so smart lets see how smart you are in a few minutes when I have you upstairs! I knew what would happen next. After the beating I laid on my bedroom for the last time and weeped. We were leaving in the morning . Leaving the people I loved . What would happen to me now.

Chapter 20

When I woke up Esther said I want you to go to the grocery store to pick up a few things! I stood there confused ! First of all I was nine years old and extremely backward for my age. We lived in a city, the grocery store was about 12 plus blocks from our apartment ! Never had she asked me to go to the store before .

Esther looked at me and said hello did you hear me? I felt sick to my stomach. I didn't want to go ! I was terrified! It's really far away can you go with me I asked ? Oh grow up already here's the list and here's ten dollars . You better not loose it and I want a receipt! I just stood there I couldn't move! What the fuck are you waiting for get going. As soon as you get back we're leaving . The truck will be packed so hurry it up. Still I didn't move. I was literally frozen with fear! She lost it and slapped me across the face ! I said get fucking going! With that she pushed me out of the apartment and slammed the door ! I stood in the hallway for what seemed like forever trying to convince myself that I could do this ! I walked down the steps and the first thing I saw was the door that Joe's hand went through. Someone had boarded up the top half of the door where the glass used to be. It looked like someone had made a sloppy attempt to clean up the blood leaving behind smears on both the floor and door. I opened the door and stepped onto the porch . I knew I had to do what I was told so I started on my way .

My head was darting left and right I was in a panic. I got to the first corner and timidly stepped off the curb my heart pounding ! I was so small I couldn't to see if there was traffic coming . I poked my head out and ran across the street ! When I got to the other side of the street my hand were so drenched with sweat the ten dollar bill felt damp. I shoved the money in my pants pocket and kept walking ! On the way I had to cross railroad tracks . I was stepping over the rails and looked down and there squashed to one of the rails was what looked like a crushed cat! I jumped back in fear and then my heart broke for that poor cat !

I was about two blocks from the store when I heard footsteps behind me. I turned around and saw two men. I don't know why but something about them made me feel very uneasy. Living with Esther and her endless array of drunk men I kind of got a sense early of evil ! I started to walk faster. When I walked faster so did they. Something was very wrong ! I turned around again and they were much closer to me now. My heart started to pound and I started to cry and walked so fast that I was almost running! I got in front of the store but there was a fence all the way around it so I had to go the length of the fence to the opening to get in. Out of no where a man driving really slow in a pickup truck who pulled over .He got out of the truck and told me to run into the store and not to stop ! Don't look back , just run ! I did as I was told and ran like my life depended on it! I got into the store and was shaking so bad that my legs felt like they were going to give out! I was terrified to look out the window in case those men were still there. What just happened ? Why were they following me ? Who was the man in the truck? I had no idea what was going on the only thing I knew is to me the man in the truck had just saved me!

I got the few things on her list and as I checked out I peeked out the huge widow of the store to see if the men were still there. They were no where in sight ! I clenched the bag tight and ran the whole way back to the apartment in tears ! If ever there was a time that Esther had compassion please let it be today ! I just needed someone to hug me, to be glad I was ok. Instead of compassion and love what I got chilled me to the bone !

When I returned I ran up the stair and into the apartment.I was drenched in sweat and tears. Esther was in the living room and when she saw me she just stood there staring . Like she'd seen a ghost ! We both stood in silence and finally she snapped out of it and said why are you such a sweaty mess ? I started to tell her everything that had happened and about the man in the truck who helped me .Sheasked what did he look like and I described the truck but for the life of her couldn't remember the man's face. Her eyes got huge and she said oh that was your Uncle Randy . I cringed a little because Esther referred to all her male friends as "Uncle" so and so when she talked about them to me . So this man that saved her was someone that Esther had dated ! That really saddened me. I would forever think of him as my hero but wished I had never found out that he was "Uncle" Randy !

Chapter 21

The truck was packed and Esther said she was going upstairs to do one more walk through to make sure she didn't forget anything and then they we're leaving. She told me to sit on the bottom step and not to move. I waited until she went into the apartment and ran to Maria's door. I knocked lightly so Esther didn't hear me and hoped Maria would. Almost immediately Maria answered the door. I don't have a lot of time I told her but

I wanted to say goodbye. We're moving I said sobbing so hard my chest hurt. Maria started to cry and said I know I'm going to miss you so much. We hugged and Maria's mom came to the door. She had a paper bag and said here honey here's some food for the road. She bent down and hugged me and when she stood up I saw she was crying. You always remember your a special little girl and we love you. I will I replied I love you all too. I hugged Maria and said I have to go . I'll miss you. Thank you for being my friend. I ran back to the step and sat down just as Esther closed our apartment door for the last time.

She came down the stairs and and asked what's in the bag? Maria's mom made us a snack for the road. Crazy bitch probably put poison in it. Leave it and lets go . I put the bag down on the bottom step and walked out onto the porch. I saw a man get out of the U Haul . This is Uncle Mike he's going to be driving. Looking down at my feet I said hi. My heart ached , I turned to get one last look at my apartment and saw Maria and her mom peeking out from behind the open door. I wanted to run up to them and beg them to keep me but I knew it was no use. Esther looked at me and said your riding in the back of the truck! For a minute I thought there was a back seat in the truck and then I realized she meant in the back with the furniture! She walked me to the back of the truck and said get in ! My heart raced , I had a terrible fear of the dark and tiny places. Who was I kidding I feared just about everything ! Get your ass in the back of the truck now Esther screamed. I stood there looking into the dark truck and felt like I was going to get sick. She looked at me and said don't make me tell you again. Get the fuck in the truck! I crawled up o the back bumper and stepped inside . Fear took over and I peed my pants. You stupid disgusting little bitch Esther screamed when she saw the ever so familiar puddle at my feet. Well you can sit in your own filth I'll see you in two hours she laughed as she pulled the door down and left me in total darkness!

The complete darkness and little air was really playing with my mind. There was a awful smell ,it was making me nauseous ! I felt like I was going to get sick ! I chocked it down. I knew what would happen if she opened the back of the truck and I was covered in vomit. I sat holding my knee close to my body and rocking back and forth. We drove for what seemed like forever and all of a sudden the truck came to a stop. I heard the door of the truck open and close then I heard movement at the back of the truck. I braced myself not knowing what would be on the other side ! Where would I be? Would my life be more violent ? Would I ever see my Grandparents , Joe or Maria again? The door opened and the sunlight was blinding. It took a few minutes for my eyes to adjust. Esther looked into the back of the truck and said It smells like a fucking stable in here piss the pants. Dig around in your box and find something clean to put on and then get your ass out here.

I changed and hoped down out of the truck. We were at a place with a couple of picnic tables and vending machines. The "Uncle" who was driving the truck had gone to the restroom. Esther looked at me and said when he gets out you better be polite. Don't speak unless you're spoken to and even then keep it short ! Do you understand? Yes I replied. We are going to live with a family for a little bit until I find us a place to live. You better be on your best behavior if you know whats good for you ! Don't think just because there's people around that I wont kick your ass! Get your ass in the restroom and wash up you smell like piss! I did what I was told. I grabbed a few disposable paper napkins and squirted them withe soap and took them in by the toilet .I washed my private parts trying to get the pee odor off. I threw the napkins in the toilet and the emotion of the day hit me like a ton of bricks. I stood there and sobbed.

After a few minute I went back out to Esther. "Uncle Mike" was sitting on the bench with Esther . He looked like one of her typical drunken bums that came to the apartment. What was different about this one though was she wasn't putting on her kind mom act and pretending she gave a crap about me which terrified me. She didn't even attempt to be nice in front of him leaving me to believe he was as evil as her. I over heard them talking about how far we had to go to get to our destination. About 15 more minutes and we'll be there he said. I guess the brat better ride in the cab with us. Can't roll up with her in the back of the truck . They both started to laugh. We could just leave her here Esther said with a snarl ! They both broke into more laughter! Let's go get your ass in the truck. At least I didn't have to ride in the back of the truck again. I sat in the truck looking out the window . With every mile I was going further and further from the people I loved . Would my Grandparents think I didn't care? As I sat there I could feel the tears well up in my eyes but I knew better than to cry in front of Esther. So I chocked them back and thought of something else.

Chapter 22

We arrived at our destination. Esther grabbed me by the arm before we got out of the truck and said listen you little bitch this is our home for now so don't fuck it up ! I got out of the truck and looked at the people standing on the porch waiting for us. They looked normal enough , at this point I was numb. Esther went into full fake mode as she hugged everyone ! All smiles and sweetness. She put her arm around me and said this is my Addie. I swear I could feel the evil from her touch through my shirt. I did what I was trained to do I smiled and said nice to meet you . There were four adults and a child. They all seemed very nice. Why the hell were they friends with Esther? They invited us in and from the second I walked through the door I could tell they were as poor as we were. The rugs were all worn, the furniture what there was of it was in very poor condition but the house was clean. Everyone in the house smoked and it immediately gave me a massive headache.

They said come on in the kitchen we made dinner. As we walked into the kitchen Esther tugged on my hair and I spun around she shot me an evil glare making sure I knew she was always an arms length away. We sat at the table and the adults talked about possible jobs for Esther. They apologized that they didn't have a spare bedroom for us that we would have to sleep on the couch and floor. Esther said we're thankful that you opened up your home . Like we discussed I will look for work first thing in the morning and we'll get an apartment as soon as I can. "Uncle Mike " said his good byes and he left. I never saw him again. In the days that followed it seemed like they really were a nice family. They were kind to me and there were no beatings because someone was always around. I missed Joe, my Grandparents and Maria so much. I cried myself to sleep every night for weeks. I was enrolled in a new school and had no friends but at least the abuse had stopped.

Chapter 23

Esther found a job as a waitress. She worked the mid morning to closing shift. I rarely saw her which was fine with me.I walked to and from school with the daughter of the one couple. She was nice enough but I could tell she wasn't to happy about us living in her house. They barley had enough room or food for themselves and now they had to share with us. I ate very little it was a small price to pay to have a safe place to live. I was always very polite and helped with chores around the house. One day Esther came home and said she was going to look at an apartment . She was thrilled I was terrified. I knew the second we got our own place the beatings would start again. I actually prayed that night that we didn't get the apartment. Please God keep me safe if only for a little bit longer.

My prayers we not answered. Esther got home from work and ran into the kitchen telling us she got the apartment! I excused myself and went to the bathroom and threw up . That weekend we took what few belongings we had and moved in. The family said we'll ask around for used furniture and kitchen items and get this place filled up in no time . Esther walked everyone out and thanked them for all they had done. I could feel my insides shake anticipating what was coming next. She came in shut the door and just looked at me. Like a switch her eyes went dark ,she lunged at me and I dropped to the floor and crawled backwards to a corner. She towered over me and slapped me so hard across the face I felt the burn instantly. Neither of us said a word. I didn't dare move. I just sat there cowering in the corner waiting just waiting to see what would happen next. All of a sudden she pounced on me like a wild animal unleashing all that pent up rage! She literally beat me until she was exhausted.. When she was done she walked out of the room without a word.

I laid on the floor sobbing and when I looked down I realized I was sitting in a puddle of urine. I quickly crawled over to the garbage bag that contained my clothes and pulled out a sweater and tried to wipe up the floor. Oh please let me get it cleaned up before she comes back please ! The floors were bare wood ,thankfully there was no carpet. I wrapped the sweater inside it's self and put it back in my bag of clothes. Hiding all evidence of my accident. She walked back into the room a couple of minutes later and said get your ass to bed and take your shit with you. I grabbed my bag of clothes and went into the room that would be my new prison. We had no furniture or blankets so I laid on the floor and cried myself to sleep.

The next morning I woke with the pain I knew to well. My body ached all over . As I laid there I wondered now that I was hours away from anyone I knew how would I survive! In the past I would try and detach myself when getting beat and think about my Grandparents house or playing with Maria. It didn't always work especially when the beatings were severe but there were times my thoughts would take me away, away from the pain if only for a little while. Now I had nothing, my heart was broken.

Chapter 24

My first day back at school since we moved was a major adjustment. I missed my loved ones so much but I had learned over the years to bury the heart ache and push on. I thought of them everyday but I knew better than to start crying. Esther drilled it into me at a young age that tears were weakness. They brought unwanted attention so I was told I better not ever get caught crying or I would pay for it. I was very much a loner in this new school. Everybody had their cliques as with every school and I was the new kid. Being the new kid was hard enough. Being the new kid that was dirty , stunk , wore old clothes and received free lunch was at times unbearable.

I got made fun of every day. I wouldn't let them see their words hurt me. I held it in until I would go to the bathroom and I would stand in the stall and sob . It became a daily thing, I would take the name calling for so long and then I knew if I didn't ask the teacher to go to the bathroom . I'd pulled myself together and went back to class.

We moved when I was entering fourth grade. Our move was in the middle of the school year. I was so far behind I never got caught up and I flunked that year. I stood there in front of the school holding my report card looking at the comment saying I was being held back and being to scared to take a step to start my walk home. My heart was pounding so hard my ears started to ring. I thought of running away for a moment then knew I had to go home. I had to face Esther . As soon as I walked through the door she looked at me and said what the fuck took you so long ? I thought of not giving her my report card then she looked and me and said well let's see your report card ! What the hell are you waiting for. I stood there staring at her. I didn't dare move a muscle. You dumb bitch did you hear me give me your fucking report card! With that I could feel the pee running down my leg ! As it hit the wood floor it got her attention ! What the fuck she said as she jumped up off the couch ! All I remember is saying over and over again I'm sorry I'll do better I'm sorry and I held out my report card.

She grabbed it from my shaking hand and as she read I could see the rage building in her ! She dropped the report card on the couch and lunged at me ! Why you fucking retard who the fuck flunks fourth grade she asked ? I'm sorry I said as I dropped to the floor I'm sorry ! Your fucking sorry? Oh you will be she said as darkness came over her eyes! She grabbed me by the hair and drug me down the hallway to my room. She started to slap me in the face and then her hand clenched in a fist and she hit me in the stomach. Before I knew what was happening I threw up You fucking gross pig she said as she grabbed me again by the hair and started shaking me violently back and forth . You have to be the most disgusting thing on the planet. I wish I would have drowned you when I had the chance! Sadly this wasn't the first time she had said this to me but it was filled with more rage than I had ever heard. She let go of my hair and I crawled to the corner . I curled up in a ball and tried to protect myself from the beating I was about to get. As I lay there head down and knees to chest there was silence. I was so scared to look up and then I did !

An evil smile came across her face as she said I want you to see this coming and she drew back her leg and kicked me in the leg so hard it actually lifted me off the ground. As I landed I remember the agonizing pain ! She came toward me and cleared the room in three steps and drew her leg back again this time I begged. Please don't I'm sorry and she kicked me in my private parts. The burning was instant. The pain was so bad it made me throw up again. I had no more fight left in me. I laid there on the floor hearing her say get up you stupid bitch ! I just laid there ! If she wanted to beat me some more she was going to have to drag me up from the floor to do it I was in such horrible pain I couldn't move. She hissed get the fuck up ! When I tell you to do something you better fucking do it ! I looked up at her hovering over me and said I can't move my leg .She looked down and said well if you can't move I'll move you and kicked me again ! With this I let out a scream that almost didn't sound human. I was convinced this is where I was going to die.

She looked down at me and said if you think your life was hell before wait and see whats coming your way ! She walked out of the room slamming my door behind her. I laid on the floor broken , sobbing because I was in so much pain and because I had given up. That night I laid on the floor afraid to sleep . All I could hear were her words "wait till you see what's coming your way" ! I could imagine her sitting in her room coming up with ideas of ways to torture me! My childhood was a terrifying cocktail of both physical and emotional abuse ! She would get such pleasure of terrorizing me mentally. Watching me cower in the corner or seeing me sitting with my knees to my chest just rocking in shear panic was her entertainment ! I would see her smile grow when I was in fear anticipating a beating. There were times she would build up the fear in me , leading me to believe a beating was imminent . I would be shaking and pee my pants in fear and she would laugh and walk away! I was both thankful and baffled by these times! So very grateful that I didn't have to endure another beating but baffled that a mother could inflict such emotional terror on her own child.

Chapter 25

The next morning I woke up and could feel the pain instantly. I ached from the top of my head to my toes. I tried to stand , it was incredibly painful to put weight on the injured leg.I prayed Esther was still sleeping . I didn't hear anything and went back and sat on the floor to look at my leg. There was a huge bruise forming on my upper thigh. It was raised and swollen. My private parts burned so bad where I had been kicked. My head ached and lumps had formed from where she had yanked me around by my hair. I had to pee so bad but didn't dare open my door. As I sat there fear took over! What did she have in store for me? Now that it was summer vacation there would be no break from her.

I heard movement in her room ! My heart started to race ! I heard her footsteps in the hall getting closer and closer to my door! She ripped the door open , took one look at me and laughed " wow somebody really fucked you up didn't they"? I sat there afraid to respond. Well get your ass up you stupid bitch. Don't think your going to sit around on your lazy ass all summer. Get in the bathroom and get washed I have a huge list of things for you to do today! I got up and limped to the bathroom. She looked at me and said "your leg hurting you"? Yes I replied. Good I hope when you feel that pain you think about doing better in school ! I continued walking to the bathroom and didn't reply. . It was at this moment some of my fear became hate ! I could feel it festering in me a small little twinge of hate taking up some space in my body. I wasn't proud of it but I welcomed it. To me it meant there was a little part of me that would no longer be consumed by fear. As small as it was I would take it !

When I got into the bathroom I shut the door and looked at myself in the mirror with horror. My God my face was so swollen I barely recognized myself! There was a patch on my head where she ripped the hair from my scalp! I sat to pee and as soon as I started the burning intensified ! I took my clothes off to examine my wounds in the mirror. I had a huge bruise on my arm that I wasn't sure how it got there. I stood on the tub so I could see my leg in the medicine cabinet mirror. The bruise seemed to have grown since I looked at it in my room. The colors were getting deeper, the swelling increasing. I painfully got down off the tub and stared at my reflection in the mirror. My eyes were not that of a young child! They were that of a person who saw to much pain for one lifetime ! I grabbed a wash rag and started to get washed. With every pass of the rag the pain intensified ! When I had gotten to my private parts I saw blood on the rag ! I was terrified ! It burned so much but I continued washing because this may be the only time today that I would have the chance. I soaked the rag in cold water and dabbed it on my private parts. It offered a tiny bit of relief from the pain. I heard Esther's yell from the other side of the door . Here some clean clothes. Really doesn't matter what you wear because nobody gonna see you this summer ! I got dressed and came out of the bathroom. Esther handed me a list of chores that was two pages long and so my summer began.

I finished one of the pages of chores while Esther sat on the couch watching TV. She came into the kitchen , grabbed a gallon of milk out of the fridge and drank right from the container! Mind you I hadn't eaten since lunch at school the day before. With every swallow of milk she took she glanced over at me with a smirk on her face! She put the milk back in the fridge turned to me and said "bet your hungry aren't you" ? I just stood there head down saying nothing. Well she said you'll eat when I say you eat! Get your ass moving and get that list done. I wasn't proud of it but I hated her with everything in my being ! I was raised catholic and if you could believe it Esther went to church every Sunday ! She made it a point of sitting right up front ,singing and praying and acting like the most loving mother then as soon as we got home she reverted back to satan! I one hundred percent believed in God and heaven but didn't understand why God was letting this happen ! One saying I have always hated was everything happens for a reason ! Really what was the reason for me getting the crap beat out of me and stripping me of every ounce of self dignity ?

That night I was almost done with my chore list and Esther called me into the kitchen. My leg ached so bad at this point that walking was almost impossible . I walked into the kitchen to see Esther with the gallon of milk to her mouth again guzzling it like it was her job ! She made a satisfying content sound as she wiped her mouth on the back of her arm. Boy that milk sure is good she said smirking ! You hungry yet she asked? Yes I said as my stomach growled. Well dumb little bitches don't get regular milk and she pulled a big box from the cabinet . You can have powdered milk. I watched as she drank more of the milk from the container then she added this powder and water to the milk gallon. She gave it a shake and said from now on this will be your milk . Say thank you and sit at the table. I did what I was told ! She poured the powdered milk mixture into a glass and huge clumps of of unmixed powder plopped into the glass.Looks yummy doesn't it she asked as she laughed ? Yes it looks good thank you I replied. She went to the counter and got a piece of bread threw it on the table and said enjoy your supper and walked out of the room! I was so hungry I ate the piece of bread and smelled the glass of "milk" which smelled horrible but it was food so I drank it. It made me gag but I got it down. At least I had something in my stomach and I was grateful not to be going to bed hungry.

Get your ass in the bathroom and piss so you don't piss the bed then go to your room ! I went into the bathroom peed and washed up and brushed my teeth. I listened to see if I could hear her it was quiet. I reached under the bathroom sink and pulled out a empty pickle jar I stashed there when I was cleaning . I tucked it under my shirt and went straight to my room. I put the jar under my bed. I would keep it under my bed just in case I had to pee in the middle of the night . I was exhausted but to scared to sleep . Esther was known for night beatings ! Out of no where she would come into the room in a fit a rage,beat the crap out of me and go back to her room. Sometimes it almost seemed like she was barely awake ! After the first couple of night beatings I became a very light sleeper. Only when pure exhaustion kicked in did I fall asleep.

There was a friend of Esther's who was as creepy as the day was long! He just wasn't right I could jut feel it ! Whenever he was around my gut told me to stay away ! One day when Easter was MIA he came over. I didn't open the door I told him she wasn't here and I wasn't allowed to open the door and to come back later ! I wasn't aware he had a key ! He let himself in and I backed into the kitchen !He was making small talk and my skin was crawling ! I said maybe you should come back later ! He walked toward me until I was backed against the wall. He looked down at me with a smirk and I started shaking ! I could tell he loved the fact that he was intimidating me ! I had no idea what was coming next ! He grabbed my arm and drug me upstairs I fought him every step of the way ! This made him smile more ! He pushed me on the bed and started ripping my clothes off ! I fought him, kicking ,punching and I started screaming ! His eyes got wild and he said scream again and I'll kill you ! He took his pants off and climbed on top of me ! I tried with everything I had to fight him off but I was no match for his size ! He pushed himself inside of me grunting like an animal ! I screamed in pain and he covered my mouth with his hand and finally collapsed on top of me ! I lost it I screamed get off of me ! He rolled off and laughed ! I grabbed my clothes and ran to the bathroom hysterical ! He pushed open the bathroom door and said you liked that didn't you ? I shook in fear ! Tell anyone and I'll kill you ! He stepped toward me and I pressed myself against the wall ! Now that I got you broken in I'll be back ! You can be my regular piece ! He left and I laid on the bathroom floor broken ! I felt so violated and dirty ! I should have fought harder I should have stopped him ! The shame was all consuming ! I felt anyone that looked at me could tell !

This happened two more times and then I never saw him again ! Even though he was gone I could still feel him on top of me ! I could he the filthy things he said to me ! He may have been physically gone but he lived in my head ! I never told anyone what happened ! I knew I couldn't tell Esther some how she would blame me so I buried in deep down inside with the rest of the horrors of my life !

Chapter 26

One day I came home from school and there was a dog chained to the radiator in the kitchen ! Esther came in from the living room and said this is Max He's you responsibility. Oh my God a dog ! My heart leapt with joy! I bent down to unchain him and Esther said what the fuck are you doing? I'm unchaining him so I can play with him. No he stays chained to that radiator ! The only time you let him off is to take him out to piss and shit ! I dropped down on the floor next to him in horror! Please don't keep him chained ! I'll take care of him. I'll clean up after him. Shut the fuck up and don't you dare ever talk back to me again . If I catch that dog off the leash other than to go out to take a piss he's gone ! . She went back into the living room and I sat down next to Max . Don't worry buddy I'll take care of you. we'll be best friends. Life became almost bearable with Max there. I knew he had a hellish life being chained to that radiator all the time but I would give him love and sit with him so he would have something to look forward to.

Everyday when I got home from school I would let him off the leash to go out in our small yard to pee and run free for a few minutes. I knew better to stay out there to long. I lived in fear everyday that she would get rid of him . I played by her rules so he could stay. He was so skinny . She had a big bag of dog food but only fed him the smallest amount everyday. It seemed like she fed him just enough to stay alive. When she would take off for a few days I would share what little food I had with him. The first time Esther was gone I took Max out and let him play in the yard. I had a chance to give him some freedom and I was taking it. Then I started to get freaked out thinking somehow , someway she would find out. I brought him back in and chained him to the radiator. The sadness in his eyes made me look away. My heart broke for him. Why would she get a dog only to make him a prisoner ? Because she was the devil that's why I thought !

That first night Esther was gone I slept on the kitchen floor with Max. He would jump when he heard the cabinets and doors slam shut. He would tilt his head looking in the direction of the sounds and growl. I would try and calm him, I know boy it's ok I'm here I would say trying not to let him know how terrified I was. This time

Esther was gone for three days so far. It was wonderful. I came home one day to find she had returned! My heart sank! I stuffed the scraps I saved from my lunch deep in my coat pocket. I'd give them to Max later. There was a box on the kitchen counter. I peeked inside it was filled with food. A bag of rice, peanut butter, a long cardboard box of cheese and more of that disgusting boxed powdered milk. Esther came into the kitchen and said keep your filthy hands off that food ! I got it from the soup kitchen . It has to last all week. That was more food than I had seen in this house ever. That night was a rare occasion Esther cooked ! It happened so infrequently that I thought maybe she was trying to poison me ! She took her plate in the living room to eat and I sat at the table which was fine with me. She made grilled cheese sandwiches. I saved a little piece to give to Max when I took him out.

The next day Esther said she was going to work late at the restaurant and her boss wanted to meet me ! Tomorrow on your way home from school stop in . Be polite or I'll kick your ass. Make sure your clean when you come in don't embarrass me ! I won't I replied. No talking about anything that happens in our house that's our business ! You got it. Yes I answered. Now go take that fucking dog out and pick up the shit in the yard before people complain ! I went over to Max who was more than eager to be set free from the radiator and opened the back door. He ran with delight jumping and was so happy to be free. It amazed me that he was such a mild tempered dog considering how he had to live his life.. I wonder where he came from. What awful event led up to his owner giving him to Esther ?

The next afternoon after school I stopped in at Esther's job. She came up to me with her fake loving mother voice ! Here she is this is Addie she said to the short dark haired woman behind the counter. Oh she's just as lovely as you said she was ! Hi sweetie my name is Connie nice to meet you. Nice to meet you I replied. Come on sit down we'll make you a little something. Oh that's ok I have to get home I have homework. Nonsense Connie said this is a restaurant ,we feed people that's what we do. You sit right up there on that stool and I'll fix you something. I looked over at Esther who had a fake smile on her face ,waiting for her to jump in and protest but she said nothing. I sat at the counter Connie asked me if I liked burgers and fries Yes I replied ! Well then that's what we'll fix you. Do you want a coke to go along with that ? I'll just take water I replied. Oh come on try a coke, in order to get the full restaurant experience you have to have a coke with your meal. Ok thank you I said. A few minutes later Connie placed a huge plate in front of me with a burger,fries and a pickle. She brought over a glass with ice and I had a coke for the first time in my life ! The bubbles tickled my nose ! I felt like a queen eating this wonderful meal. I slipped a piece of the burger into my napkin and put it in my coat pocket for Max . When I was all done I thanked Connie and told her it was nice to meet her and Esther walked me out. I hope you enjoyed the royal treatment because it will never happen again ! Now get the fuck over her and hug me they're watching us through the window she snapped. The mere touch of Esther made my insides go cold. Everything about her embrace screamed evil.

I got home and spent the rest of the night with my one and only friend Max. I gave him the piece of burger I'd saved for him and took him out. Every time I took him out he looked at me with gratitude ! It seemed he understood my life was as miserable as his but we were there for each other. The first time that Easter beat me when we had Max he went nuts . He instinctively wanted to protect me. Although I was being beat all I was thinking was no Max please don't if she senses she wasn't the alpha you'd be gone. When she was done I looked over at Max as if to say thank you boy for caring enough to try and help. Our bond was formed. When she left I went over to sit by Max to have a heart to heart. Max thank you so much for wanting to protect me but please don't . I don't know what I would do if I ever lost you. I can take the beatings but I wouldn't be able to take losing you. He looked into my eyes and it seemed he looked into my soul and got it. He licked my face and I hugged him so grateful I wasn't alone anymore.

Chapter 27

By this point I had seen Joe a total of two times. I was starting to really resent him. He knew the hell I was living and he basically wrote me off. He resurfaced a couple of months later. He came to the house and Esther refused to let him in. He said you know I have visitation , it's court ordered and I'm not going to let you keep me from seeing her any longer. I'll see you in court ! Wait what ,he did try and see me and she was keeping me from him ? I felt such guilt for the feelings I had toward him. I honestly thought he had abandoned me . I wanted to scream please don't go ! Break the door down if you have to but please don't leave me hear. Instead I said nothing. Fine I'll see you in court as he turned to leave ! Esther ripped the door open and said you'll never win , they always side with the mother ! Try me he replied. They stood there in a stand off for a minute and then I heard her say Addie get her ass over here. I ran as fast as my legs could carry me. You have to go with this piece of shit even if you don't want to ! Don't want to I was thinking are you kidding me ! For Christ sake you're filthy she said. Go get washed! Listen if this is another attempt at keeping me from seeing her Joe said, Esther cut him off calm the fuck down she's just getting washed . She'll be right out and she slammed the door in his face!

I ran upstairs and washed quickly . I put on clean clothes , brushed my hair and then remembered I better make it look like I don't want go Showing loyalty to someone other than Esther would earn me a beating later ! I walked down the rest of the stairs and she said get over here ! I went into the living room and she said say one words about what goes on in this house and that fucking dog is gone ,you hear me? My heart sank, yes I replied. My life was hell but I would never ever do anything to hurt Max. Get out she snarled. I walked through the kitchen , gave max a hug and opened the door. Joe looked at me with the saddest eyes. Where's your car I said calmly to him just in case Esther was watching. I parked around the corner. When we got around the corner , out of eye range I hugged him and sobbed I missed you so much. He hugged me back and seemed to realize why I had acted so cold when I opened the door . I missed you to Addie. Do you want to go get something to eat? Yes I replied not wanting to let go of him. We went and ate and talked. He told me he had gone to court to get legal visitation ,that it was a uphill battle because Esther had him arrested on false charges of battery a couple of times and claimed I was dangerous! I didn't realize I did it out loud but I laughed ! This made him smile. He said I know right ! If that isn't the pot calling the kettle black ! We both laughed for a second and then our eyes filled with tears. In that moment I realized yes I was physically and mentally abused but he was also abused by Esther.

How have you been he asked. All I could hear is Esther saying one word and that fucking dog is gone. I'm ok I got a dog I told him ! Did you that's wonderful he said. I love him so much his name is Max. I'm so happy for you Addie. How are you doing with everything else he asked? Again I could hear her in my head, good. everything is good. He tilted his head and looked at me as if to say I know your not being truthful but he said nothing. Now that our visitation is court ordered I'll get to see you more. would you like that? Yes that would be wonderful. You may be able to stay at my apartment once in awhile . Is that something you would like to do? The immediate picture of Max sitting in the kitchen all alone wondering where I had gone, if I left him popped in my head. I think visits would be great but I don't know about sleeping over I replied. That's fine I'm good with whatever you want. He took my hand I just want you to know I've missed you and I thought about you the whole time . I tried really hard not to cry but those are words I've never heard from anyone and they made me happy and sad both at the same time . So happy that I was loved , so sad that I couldn't tell him the truth ! We went to the local playground next and I went on the swings . Something I'm sure is taken for granted by other kids to me it was everything. Finally he said I guess I better be getting you home. Again I felt the tears well up but this time I held them in. He looked at me and said I know honey I feel the same way . He held my hand as we walked to the car.

On our way home I said can you park where you parked when you picked me up so I can say good bye? Sure honey no problem, He knew exactly why I was asking. When we got back to the house I couldn't take it anymore. I tried so hard not to cry but the tears just came. I was crying so hard I couldn't catch my breath. Addie I'll see you again . It'll be ok he said. I know I just missed you . I really wanted to say is you stay here I'll run in and grab Max and you can take me away from here ! I sat there for a minute and tried to calm down. If Esther knew I was crying I would surely get beat. Well I guess I better get in there . When will I see you again ? I get to see you every other Saturday. I'll be here at 1 o'clock is that ok he asked? Yes that's great I'll see you then. He grabbed me and hugged me so tight I felt the tears coming again so I said I better go. Ok honey he replied with that I got out of the car and headed towards the house I turned to see him drive away. Don't cry I kept telling myself don't cry. I got to the door and I just stared at it. What would happen if I took Max and some food the next time Esther left and I ran away? Could we make it on our own? It had to be better than the life I had now! Who was I kidding I was afraid of my own shadow I would never do it! All I could imagine is doing it

,getting caught and Esther getting rid of Max as punishment ! That was a risk I wasn't willing to take so I opened the door and went back into hell !

As soon as I got into the house I went straight to Max. He was looking so pitiful but when he saw me he perked up. Hi boy I missed you I said as I hugged him. He wagged his tail and licked my face. I heard Esther bellow from the living room. Get your ass in her. Coming I replied. Well I want details she said. I want to know exactly what you did , & what you talked about. We went to get something to eat and Joe just said he missed me and that he can see me every other Saturday. What else she hissed. Nothing that's all I replied. Did you open your mouth about this house? No I swear I replied. If I find out you did that fucking dog is gone got it ! Yes I said. Now go take that piece of shit dog out before he pisses on my floor. I happily took Max out so he could go to the bathroom and stretch his legs. It broke my heart that he had to live his life like a prisoner I wish he knew a life of freedom. I couldn't unchain him but I could let him know that I loved him and he was my friend.

Chapter 28

The only positive was I had Max . It amazed me that Esther just wrote off all the odd happenings of the house. Me on the other hand they terrified! We had lived here a little over a year and the house just seemed to get more angry by the day. The kids at school would comment as I walked by that I lived in the haunted house! Evidently the house had been empty for a couple of years and rumor was everyone that lived there had the same story. Doors ,cabinets and windows opening and shutting. Footsteps through the halls at night! Then one day it happened,Esther said were moving ! Oh thank God I said not realizing I said it out loud! What the fuck did you say she hissed? Nothing sorry I replied . When are we moving I asked? In two weeks so get your shit together ! Were moving up the street in the same block. For the first time in my life I was thrilled to be moving ! Good riddance to this place. Then she tore my world apart! This place doesn't allow pets so your flea bitten buddy has to go ! No please can't we find another place please I asked? No we can't you crazy bitch I was lucky to find this one ! It's just a dog get over it! I didn't think I could stand the pain my heart ached ! He wasn't just a dog he was my friend , my family ! Just like that Max was gone ! I'd lost so much in my short life ,losing max was so excruciating I didn't think I could go on !

We moved into the house up the street it was just as run down as all the others. All I could think about was Max ! Where did he go ? Was his new owner kind to him ? Did he finally know a life of freedom> Did he know I would always love him ? My heart felt like it was dying! It's been through so much ! My hope for him was that he lived a wonderful life never to be chained again . I will always love you Max I whispered in hopes that somehow where ever he was he could feel my love.

My bedroom was downstairs. It was the first room you came into when you entered the house. I robotically threw my garbage bag full of belongings on my bed and started to unpack. I didn't care about much at this point! This place had a hole in the floor in the living room with a round braided carpet over it ! Let's just say I found the hole just in time ! One more step and I would have fell through the floor to the basement ! The landlord came and put a piece of plywood down , we threw the rug back over it and that was that. Soon after moving in Esther said I'm gonna be gone for a few days. Don't answer the door do you hear me she asked? Yes I replied. She looked at me with that evil grin and said just so your not tempted to sit on your ass and watch tv the whole time I'm gone I'm taking the extension cord to the tv with me! She bent down pulled the cord plug from the wall and disconnected it from our tiny black and white tv and threw it in her purse ! This place better be clean when I get back she said as she pulled my hair and walked out the door ! I waited a few minutes to make sure she wasn't coming back for anything and I laid on my bed and cried a heartbroken cry for Max !

I started to walk around the house. I checked out each room one more depressing than the next. Well I didn't think it was possible but this place was more dilapidated than the previous but at least it didn't feel haunted ! I went into the kitchen to see what food we had if any . There was a box of crackers , teabags and a couple cans of veggies. That was it for the cabinets. I opened the old barrel fridge and there was one small pack of ground meat. So tea and crackers it was ! I wasn't aloud to use the stove so I ran the water until it was hot and filled a cup. I dropped in a tea bag, grabbed some crackers and sat on the kitchen floor to eat my supper. As I sat there my heart ached thinking about Max . When I was done I grabbed the broom and started to sweep the kitchen floor. Next I moved on to the living room. It was sparsely furnished with a couch and chair. I swept the floor around the braided area rug. I stood there staring at the TV . Why didn't it shock me that Esther took the cord ? At the very least she could have left the tv in working order when she left ! She barley left me any food,left me alone for God knows how long and took the cord to the only thing that could have given me company when she was gone ! She wasn't happy unless she was making me miserable. It became like her oxygen.

I went back downstairs and got the mop and bucket so I could wash the floors. Esther only bought lysol ,oh how I hated the smell of it! She would pour it directly from the bottle onto the floor and swish it around with the mop. My feet would stick to the floor because all the lysol residue was everywhere. She insisted it was the only way to clean ! I filled the bucket with the tiniest splash of lysol and hot water and moped the floor like a normal person. As the scent waifed up into my nose it made me nauseous. That smell was everything I hated ! It reminded me of the years I spent so far in this prison that was my life! I dumped the filthy water out in the sink and repeated the cycle in the living room and in what was now my room. The raw wood floor was a splintery mess ! I put my flip flops on after the first couple of splinter got caught in my feet. I laid back on the bed and dozed off I woke and it was dark outside . I was terrified of the dark . Just another thing to add to my endless list of fears ! Being this was a new house it was even more creepy. For some reason I felt a sadness from the house. Not within myself but from the actual house ! Ok I'm loosing it I thought ! It's a house it doesn't have feelings ! I went into the kitchen and made another cup of tea I was starving! I opened the fridge again even though I knew the only thing in there was that pack of ground meat. I knew better than to touch that , meat was like gold in our house. It was rationed and I was not allowed to ever touch it. I closed the door and went back to my room. I laid there on the bed listening to my stomach growl . Letting my mind take me away to anywhere other then my life! When I woke it was daylight! I had finally slept the whole night ! I was so excited. So this is what it felt like to actually sleep I thought!

Chapter 29

Two days later Esther returned. She wasn't in the door two seconds and all my anxiety returned. I had 2 more nights of uninterrupted sleep. That was about to change. She walked around the house and inspected it . Making sure I cleaned as I was taught ! She opened the cabinets and said Oh I see you were at the crackers Now I have to buy more ! In my head I thought you left me alone for days with nothing ! I scrounged a few crackers a day and I'm the wrong one here ! I bet she ate when she was gone ! I knew I better reply quickly if I didn't want a beating so I said I'm sorry with my head down . She just glared at me and walked out of the kitchen.

She went upstairs and called me get your ass up here. I ran up the steps, she was in the bathroom. I thought I told you to clean this bathroom? I did I replied, I scrubbed the tub ,toilet and floor. Well do it again it looks like shit! I'm tired I'm going to take a nap. Don't make any noise , you hear me? Yes I replied with my head down. She brushed past me and slammed the door to her room. I did as I was told and cleaned the bathroom again . No matter how much I scrubbed I couldn't erase the years of neglect and decay. I went back downstairs to scared to sit in case she came down. I paced back and forth and just as I was going to sit down I heard her bedroom door open . Get the fuck up here I heard her yelling from the bathroom ! I ran up the stairs and my face was met with a slap so hard I hit the floor ! You call this clean she asked as she looked around the bathroom? I scrubbed but the stains wont come out . You're going to do it over and over again till it's done right you hear me? Yes , and I turned to go out of the room. Where the fuck do you think your going ? I'm going downstairs to get the cleaning stuff . Don't talk to me like that you little bitch . She grabbed me by the hair , maybe the next time I leave I'll stay gone and you can be someone else's problem ! What do you think of that ? In my head I thought Bye see ya but I said I'll clean it better this time. She yanked my hair again and said you better and went downstairs. I sat on the bathroom floor and cried for a few minutes then did as I was told. I scrubbed until my fingers ached and to me it still looked dingy and in need of repairs. I heard her coming up the stairs and I backed to the far wall in the bathroom. She looked around and said finally looks clean and went down the hall to her room.

I gathered all the cleaning stuff and went downstairs. I looked at my bed all I wanted to do was lay down. I knew better , at any minute she could come down the stairs. If she found me sleeping she would take great joy in beating me . I leaned up against the wall and could feel myself drifting off so I moved into the living room. I wouldn't dare fall asleep now because she would see me immediately when she came down the stairs. I stood there for what seemed like forever and realized it was dark outside.I looked at the wall clock in the kitchen and it was 9:30 . I weighed my options. I could sit on the floor in the living room and take a little break from standing or I could go to bed. Sit on the floor it was! I didn't want to take the chance of falling asleep. I sat on the floor and sure enough I dozed off. Before I knew what was happening I was being kicked and slapped. Esther grabbed me up by my arm and said if you can't find anything to do I'll make you a list. With that she drug me into the kitchen by my hair and said write this down and gave me a long chore list. This was my last weekend before I started the sixth grade. I was probably the only kid I knew that couldn't wait for school to start!

The first day of school was here. I had nothing new to wear, I carried my beat up paper lunch bag with my stale white bread peanut butter and jelly sandwich to school that day and was so thankful to have time away from Esther ! Free lunch would start for me as soon as I filed out the paperwork and returned it to school. I would hear kids complain about the school lunches and thought you've never been hungry enough to be grateful for every meal. When I got to class The teacher was standing out side the classroom door .She was a small older woman who looked very stern. We all settled in our seats and I noticed a wooden paddle on the chalk board that had circles drilled into it. This was a time when teacher's were allowed to paddle students. Our teachers name was Mrs. Swartz She introduced herself and then said I do not put up with any nonsense in my classroom. She pointed to the paddle and said everybody take a good look at that paddle if you misbehave I can and will use it. Do I make myself clear she asked? We all squirmed in our seats and said yes . True to her words she used it the first day on one of the boy students who was acting out in class. She turned from the board and said you Timmy is it , come up to the board. He walked up trying to be cool and she instructed him to face the board and put his hands on the chalk tray. He did as he was told and she drew back the paddle and struck him on the butt. I turned my head because I couldn't bear to see someone being hit. A lot of kids in the class laughed and all I could think was you've never been beat or you wouldn't find this funny ! I just kept my mouth shut. I felt the tears well up in my eyes. I looked up when it was all over and she said now get back to your seat and let that be a lesson to all of you There will be consequences for bad behavior ! She was not a nice women!

I loved school although my grades were horrible. I tried I really did but when I was at school I would watch the clock and countdown to when I had to return home . I had a horrible time concentrating and retaining information. When I was home I was in constant fear of getting beat. There was no time for studying or homework at home. I had a daily list of chores that had to be done to Esther's liking or else. She would make me do them over and over again until they met her standards. Which was ironic since she was a slob and never cleaned ! I knew my grades were getting worse and worse . We would get our test back in class , the teacher would hand them out by rows and the first person would pass them back. I was in the third seat from the front which meant suffering the humiliation of other people seeing my bad grades . I would go into the bathroom at school

and cry. Maybe if I told someone what was going on they could help me. I already knew the answer! Esther owned me there was no help coming ! I passed sixth grade by the skin of my teeth. I walked home the last day of school sick to my stomach. When I walked in the door Esther said well let's see your report card Einstein and laughed ! I handed it to her and she laughed and said holy shit you passed. They must have lowered their standards at that school ! I felt the tears well up but I wouldn't give her the satisfaction of crying. Your chore list is on the table. Get your ass moving! I love summer your basically my slave she said mockingly! I thought to myself Summer isn't

special I'm your slave everyday of the year! I said nothing I
did as I was told .

Chapter 30

Two days after school let out for summer break Esther
said I'm going somewhere for a couple of days. You know
the rules , no going outside, don't answer the door or
phone and keep the curtains closed . You got it ? Yes was
all I replied! She grabbed her beat up bag and walked out
the door . The first thing I did was go to the kitchen to see
what food was in the cabinets . It had been two days since
school let out and I had had little more than bread
,crackers and some powdered milk. I was so hungry. I
looked in the cabinets and there were crackers, tea bags
nd a jar of B&M beans . I looked on the counter and there
was a half of loaf of bread and one banana. I opened the
fridge and there sat that horrible watery powdered milk ,
the rectangle cardboard box of government cheese and a
small package of ground meat. Now that I took inventory I
had to decide what I would be able to eat without getting
into trouble ! Tea was a given. I looked at the crackers and
saw that one of the sleeves were open I was thrilled ! I
could take about two crackers a day. Then I pulled out the
government cheese box. Please oh please let it be
opened. I lifted the lid and no such luck ! The cheese was
sealed all the way around in the original wrapping. No

cheese for me. I didn't dare touch the meat or the beans . Knowing she counted the slices of bread that would be my last resort . I would save the bread for when I was really hungry. If she was gone for more than two days I would have half a piece of bread for breakfast and half for supper. So tea and crackers it was for breakfast.

 I was going to sit at the table but then decided to go sit in the big red over stuffed chair in the living room. It was a ugly chair covered in scratchy floral material. I looked down and couldn't believe my eyes, the extension cord to the tv was still there ! I jumped out of the chair and stared at the tv! Did I dare turn it on ? It had to be a trick! I walked over to the tiny black and white tv and pulled the knob on . With a wooshing noise it started right up and the picture became clearer. I turned it off . I spun around half expecting Esther to grab me from behind . I'd get the beating of a lifetime if she ever caught me watching TV ! I went back and sat down on the chair. I ate my crackers and drank my tea. That night I went to bed thinking about the tv. It took everything I had not to run in there and turn it on.I just wanted something to break the deafening silence and loneliness. Instead I drifted off to sleep and in the morning I ran in the living room just to make sure the cord was still there and it wasn't a dream! There it was just hanging out of the outlet taunting me to be brave , to take a chance! I couldn't do it ! I went to the bathroom to wash up. Then I went into the kitchen to make some tea.

By this time I was so hungry ! I didn't want to take the bread yet because it was only day two . I had to save that just in case Esther was gone for four or five days. I stood in the kitchen sipping my tea and thought about the wonderful meals Maria's mom would make. I could almost taste them. I had to snap out of it all I was doing was torturing myself. I looked around the sad lonely house and thought I might as well clean something. I grabbed the bucket , a rag and filled it with hot water and that dreaded lysol and went to work scrubbing the baseboards. After I got done with the kitchen, living room and my room I sat on the big ugly red chair. I was so hot and I was so hungry. We shared a alleyway with the neighbors next door. I could hear them talking in their yard. At first it sounded like only a couple of people then it sounded like a larger group. I went over to the window in the kitchen and looked out. There were a bunch of people in the yard and more walking up the alley. They must have been having a party. There was a table set up with food and in the corner of the yard a man was lighting a grill.

I stood there spying on them trying to imagine what it was like living their carefree lives. In my day dreaming I didn't realize instead of peeking out of the window I had moved the curtain to far over and the older woman who was bringing all the food out of the house caught me looking. I jumped back from the window in a panic. I ran out of the kitchen and jumped on my bed. I sat there knee to chest rocking back and forth. Oh no if she tells Esther I was looking out the window I'm going to get beat. What was I thinking I knew the rules. No answering the phone or door,keep the curtains closed and no going outside! Maybe she didn't see me maybe I was just being paranoid. Yeah that was it I'm fine. I breathed a sigh of relief and got off the bed. I grabbed the bucket and went to the kitchen to dump the dirty water in the sink and there was a knock at the kitchen door. It scared me so much I dropped the bucket and water went everywhere. I ran back into my room ,jumped on my bed ,my heart was pounding so hard I thought it would leap out of my chest! Please make them go away I kept saying over and over. There was another knock followed by a womans voice . Honey are you ok she asked? Oh no what did I do ? She knew I was in here and now she'd call the cops. The cops will come and see I'm alone and they'll ask a bunch of questions ! I'm in so much trouble! Ok I just won't answer the door ,they'll go away right I said to myself ?

There was silence,oh thank God they just went away! It was a huge change living in a small town. When we lived in the city you become almost invisible because of the mass of people. Only your immediate neighbors sort of know you. In this small town everyone knew everyone and new people stuck out like a sore thumb. I learned my lesson I won't look out the window again ! All of a sudden there was a knock on my front door ! I jumped off my bed and ran to the corner of the room. What did they want? Why wouldn't they just go away? Another knock followed by the same female voice I'm just checking to see of your alright honey she said. I stood frozen afraid to move. Just let me know your ok and I'll go away she said. Do I trust her ? Do I open the door ? I tipped toed over to the door ,there was silence I looked out and saw an eye looking right back at me ! I jumped back and feel on the floor! Honey it's ok just let me know your ok she said again ! I stood up and decided to just crack the door let her see I was ok then she would go away. I cracked the door she took one look at me and said Oh my . That was it only Oh my. We both stood there for a second staring at each other. She peeked around me trying to look into the house and I panicked and said I'm fine thank you . I went to shut the door and she said we're having a cookout why don't you come on over and get something to eat? Oh no thank you I'm not hungry I replied. Which of course was the furthest thing from the truth. Oh come on we have so much food and I don't want it to go to waste. Only for a few minutes she said. You can make a plate and bring it right back to your house. She didn't seem like she was going to take no for an answer so I finally said ok I'll go out through the kitchen. Great she replied ,see you there !

I shut the door and freaked out ! I wasn't allowed outside ! What was I doing? If peeking out the window was going

to get me beat what would going outside get me ? I
decided to go . I told her I would go out the kitchen and if
I didn't she would just start knocking on the door again. I
cracked the kitchen door and tried to get enough courage
to go outside. I felt sick, You can do this I said to myself.
With that I opened the door I looked over and everyone
from the neighbors yard was looking directly at me! All at
once they all gave me a sympathetic head tilt with sad
eyes. The way people would look at me most of my
childhood ! I walked out , stood on our back porch and the
older woman that came to the door said come on over
honey and get something to eat we wont bite. I crossed
the alley and went into their yard. People started to
introduce themselves to me. They seemed like a nice
group of people but my first instinct was always to be
weary . The older woman said where's my manners my
name is Bessie and this is my husband Frank. Nice to meet
you I replied I'm Addie. What a beautiful name she
replied. Come on now get yourself something to eat. She
walked me over to the table that was covered with bowls
and plates of food. Here you go get yourself a plate. It was
almost like she could sense how hungry I was because she
piled the food so high I thought the plate would collapse! I
had never heard of some of the food before but I was
grateful for it ! All of a sudden I thought what am I doing?
What if Esther comes back now? I went into a panic Thank
you so much is it ok if I take this back to my house ? Sure

honey, you're welcome to stay if you want. Thank you but I have to go back home. No problem,well see you again. Everyone said there good byes and I thanked her again and went inside the house , shut the door and cried because I was so overwhelmed !

Here I sat with a plate of food and I was so hungry but I couldn't eat. All I thought about was getting caught. either Bessie would say something to Esther or somehow some way Esther would just know ! She was crazy ,crazy like a fox ! If only she used her mind for good instead of evil .I looked down at the plate of food and all of a sudden realized the smells were filling the room ! On no what have I done? I needed to get rid of the food and air the place out ! I thought about dumping the entire plate in the garbage and taking it out but I wasn't allowed out . How would I explain the empty kitchen can? Then I thought if I'm going to get beat anyway I'm going to enjoy the meal ! I sat down at the kitchen table got a fork and dove in ! There was so much food ! A burger, hot dog, potato and macaroni salad, deviled eggs, and some noodle stuff ! Yes I ate it all ! I went from starving to ready to explode in a matter of a few minutes ! I took the paper plate and folded up as small as I could and put it in a grocery bag. I double bagged that bag and dug the used tea bags out of the kitchen garbage and threw them in the bag. Now to air the house out! Even though I was very full and felt like sleeping I drug out the dreaded lysol soaked a rag and started wiping down everything I could ! If it sat still it got wiped ! By the time I was done I felt like I was going to vomit from the smell but mission accomplished the food smell was gone ! That night as I lay in bed all I could think about was that bag with the crumbled up paper plate. I got out of bed grabbed the bag and went out the kitchen door. I looked around to make sure no one was out and I heaved the bag into Bessie's garbage can and ran back onto my porch as I grabbed the door knob I heard good night Addie ! I spun around and it was Frank, Bessie's husband sitting on his back porch in the dark ! I ran in the house and slammed the door ! How didn't I see him sitting there ?

Chapter 31

I was now on day three of Esther being MIA ! Was it wrong for me to wish she never came back? I cleaned again that morning ,we didn't have a washing machine so we did our clothes in the bathtub. We had a small drying rack we would set up in the bathtub at the other house to hang and dry the clothes . I got it out and washed small things like underwear ,a t shirt and a pair of shorts.. After I was done I looked around proud at what I had gotten done. Knowing if Esther was here she would surely find fault with something. Now what do I do ? I went back downstairs and looked at the tv . It was like it was taunting me , daring me to turn it on . Yeah not gonna happen ! I already broke one of the rules by going out of the house no chance I was going to get caught watching tv ! That day I had two crackers for supper with my tea and went to bed. I woke up did the same thing all over again. By day five of Esther being gone I had my own little routine. Crackers and tea for Breakfast and supper and cleaning in between. Day six I cut a piece of bread in half and ate half saving the other half for supper. On day eight I was so hungry I actually felt sick . I looked around the house again for something to eat just in case I missed something but there was nothing! I was so hungry it was all I could think about ! I opened the fridge and looked at the pack of ground meat, If I was very careful and opened the plastic wrap from the bottom and took the smallest amount I could reshape the meat and wrap it back up. I closed the fridge I couldn't ,what if I got caught ? I went into the living room and sat in the ugly red chair. I give up If I'm not going to eat I'm going to watch tv ! I turned it on and sat down and watched I love Lucy. It instantly became my favorite show. In fairness I didn't have anything to compare it to since I rarely watched tv still I really enjoyed it.

That night I watched tv for hours ! At first I searched the few channels we had looking for something of interest. After a couple of hours I just kept it on for company. The silence was deafening in this house ! I was so lonley on one hand and so thrilled to be free of Esther if only for a few days ! I dozed off watching TV and the room was totally dark except for the glow of the tv. Something caught my eye on the staircase ! I froze ! I saw a black form going down the stairs and landing on the bottom ! This happened over and over again ! It was like I was hypnotized and terrified at the same time! I couldn't unsee it ! I sank deeper into the chair to scared to move ! I slammed my eyes shut and told myself I must be still sleeping when I opened my eyes there it was again ! I jumped up from the chair ,shut the tv off and ran to my bed ! I sat there knees to chest rocking back and forth terrified ! Finally I fell asleep ! The next morning I tip toed into the living room and looked at the stairs there was nothing there ! Was I dreaming ? Did I really see it ? For sanity purposes I convinced myself I was dreaming !

By day 9 Hunger won out over fear I went to the kitchen opened the fridge and took out the ground meat. I opened the pack from the bottom ,careful not to rip the clear wrapping. I took a quarter size piece of ground meat out and broke cardinal number two I turned the stove on ! I sculpted the meat to hide the piece I took and carefully wrapped it back up. I cooked my little beef pattie to what I thought was perfection. I got a plate and glass of water and went into the living room. Everything in me wanted to grab the beef and devour it but I needed to eat it slow! It was all I had and I wanted to make it last as long as I could. I turned on the tv and enjoyed my tiny beef pattie. I wiped my finger along the plate not wanting to waste one drop of the beef juices and licked my finger. In that instant I heard the keys in the back door ! Oh my God Esther was back ! I jumped up ,turned the tv off and shoved my plate under the couch ! All I heard was you fucking bitch and I braced myself for what was coming ! She ran into the living room grabbing me by the hair I dropped to the floor. She drug me by my hair to the kitchen and screamed get up ! I stood up and she grabbed me by the arm and said you touched the ground meat and turned on the stove ! I tried to speak but nothing came out . You better answer me you fucking bitch ! I knew no matter what I said I was going to get beat ! I choose my words carefully. I was so hungry and you were gone so long I ,before I could finish my sentence she looked wild eyed at me and said what else did you do you sneaky bitch ? Nothing I swear I lied ! I can tell by looking at you your lying ! She looked around the kitchen then went into the living room. I was so scared I couldn't remember if I turned the tv off ! I walked into the living room and she went over to the tv looking it up and down and then she touched the back of it ! You mother fucker was all she said and she began to beat on me with such rage ! As she was beating me she said you turned the tv on ? I said nothing I was to busy trying to protect myself from the blows. She stopped I thought it was over but then she reached down and unplugged the extension cord from the tv and said your going to wish you never defied me ! She wrapped part of the cord around her hand and started beating me with it ! With every strike I felt the cord rip my skin open I crawled around the floor trying to get away from her but she wouldn't be stopped ! I cried please I'm sorry , you will be she replied ! All of a sudden there was a knock at the kitchen door ! I heard Bessie scream you leave that child alone or I'm calling the police ! Do you hear me ! Esther spun around and glared at the back door! You fucking bitch you are nothing but trouble ! If she calls the cops you better hope they take me or your dead , do you hear me ?

I laid on the floor neither of us moving and then there was another bang on the door ! Is she ok in there Bessie yelled ! I need to know she's ok or I will call the police ! Do you hear me ? Do you see what you've caused ? Don't move she said as she looked down at me ! She went to the back door , cracked it open, Bessie said I hear what you do in there to that poor child ! I need to know she's alright ! She's fine Esther said , I came home and she ate all my ground meat that I have to stretch for the next week. I just got mad and was yelling at her that's all . What did you expect her to do you were gone for over a week ! She was hungry! Oh God please don't mention the plate of food you gave me please ! If Esther knew I went outside she would surely kill me ! She wasn't hungry I left her plenty of food. She just did it to be spiteful Esther said ! As I laid there in pain I wanted to get up go to that door and beg Bessie to call the cops ! I had to get out of here ! I couldn't take it anymore. I decided this was my shot ! My shot at getting the hell away from Esther ! With this my head spun around toward the kitchen ! She left me enough food ? She left me with cracker and tea and half a loaf of bread ! All of which I was always told never to touch ! I stood up and then heard Bessie say If I hear her scream one more time know I won't warn you before I call the cops ! Esther shut the door and my heart sank ! No! I was to slow I should have gotten up when she came to the door ! Esther came back in the living room and I crawled to the corner, She bent down and got really close to my face and said do you see the fucking mess you caused ? You know this isn't over ,you're going to pay understand? I said nothing . I'm going to bed ,make one sound and I will come down and beat the shit out of you again! ! I waited until I heard her bedroom door close before I stood. I looked at my arms and legs which were covered in red raised welts from the extension cord. They burned like fire . I went into the kitchen and dabbed cold water on my wounds. I could feel the heat from my skin . I slid down to the floor and cried ! I was a kid, my life wasn't supposed to be this hard !

Chapter 32

I laid there that night in bed terrified to sleep ! Esther's words ringing in my head " You know this isn't over ,you're going to pay understand"? She went up to her room early which meant she would be up in the middle of the night ! I sat up , I had to stay awake , I knew she was going to strike tonight ! I sat there anticipating the beating I was sure to get ! My heart was racing , my hands started to sweat ! I stayed awake for a long time then I dozed off . In the middle of the night I was ripped from my bed by my hair and thrown up against the wall ! When I hit it knocked the wind out of me. I was trying to catch my breath and she grabbed me from behind putting her hand over my mouth and hissed in my ear I told you you would pay ! I tried to get away but she gripped my face harder ! You're not going anywhere till I'm done with you she snarled. She started punching me fist over fist ! I could feel her fist strike my body and my body take every blow ! I covered my head with my hands and dropped to the floor ! She jumped on top of me pinning my arms to the floor with her legs and covered my mouth with one hand and beat me with the other! It was getting harder to breath. My nose was filling with snot from crying ! I looked up at her and her eyes were wild ! She was enjoying this ! She had this crazy grin on her face! For a minute I thought of biting her hand. That thought left as soon as it came. If I dared cause her any kind of physical pain I would die right were I laid ! I gave a yell as loud as I could considering my mouth was covered ! She removed her hand from my mouth and grabbed my hair on either side of my head ! She began slamming my head off the floor saying Shut the fuck up over and over again ! I felt everything get fuzzy ,her face was fading , The next thing I remember was waking up with her shaking me saying get the fuck up ! I felt so dizzy , I could hear her but it sounded like she was talking in slow motion ! I said get the fuck up she repeated ! I looked at her and wanted to respond but instead just stared. She was scared ! Did she think she killed me ? I for the first time ever in my life saw panic in her face ! Her mouth was saying get the fuck up but her usually wild eyes were saying please get up ! I sat up and then like a curtain dropping the wild came back in her eyes! She looked down at me seeing that I was coming around and simply walked out of the room !

I slowly got up off the floor. The room was spinning ! Within seconds I ran for the kitchen sink and threw up ! My head was pounding ! I rinsed my mouth and the sink and went and laid on my bed. I had absolutely nothing left ! I hugged my pillow and tried to soothe myself but that wasn't going to happen ! I threw up three more times within the next hour! I went back and laid on my bed. I laid on my side clenching my pillow careful not to move because the slightest movement made me feel nauseous. My head ached and every time I threw up the pain was crippling ! I laid there as minutes turned into hours and soon I could hear Esther's footsteps coming down the stairs ! I tried jump up but my body just wasn't willing! I guess from laying still for hours I stiffened up. She walked passed my room and said don't think you're gonna lay around all day, and went into the kitchen. Slowly I drug myself from the bed. I stood up and literally fell into the wall! I couldn't get my bearings. I was so dizzy and then it hit me! I had to throw up! I knew I'd never make it upstairs and with Esther up I couldn't throw up in the sink so I threw up in the kitchen garbage can ! Esther yelled what the fuck do you think you're doing? I didn't reply I was to busy puking. She asked again, I wanted to say you beat the crap out of me and slammed my head off the floor and now I'm puking! Instead I said I'm sorry I'll clean it up . You're fucking right you will !

That day was pure hell ! I had pain all over my body ! Two lumps on my head . I was vomiting and dizzy. The one constant in my life was Esther being the least maternal human I have ever met. You would think she would find in in herself to give me the day off from chores seeing that she is the one who beat me . Nope there she was chore list in hand when I returned down stairs with the cleaned kitchen garbage can. She handed it to me and I for the first time looked her straight in the eye. She glared back and said you got something you wanna say ? Just like that I retreated to survival mode and put my head down. No I replied. With a laugh she said I didn't think so and drank her tea. She said it's tea and crackers for breakfast today. Wait what she was offering me breakfast ! Was I dying and didn't know it ? She had a open can of evaporated milk on the counter with a sugar bowl. This was new. I watched her pour milk from the can into her tea then add a teaspoon of sugar. She looked at me and said well go on I'm not gonna make it for you. I made tea and got 2 crackers from the sleeve and sat at the table. I didn't have an appetite at all but I didn't want to pass up food I didn't know when I would be eating again. As soon as I sat at the table she looked at me with disgust and left the room. Wow she really couldn't stand the sight of me ! Her hate for me ran deep. I sipped my tea it was amazing with the can milk and sugar! It took my tea that I was always grateful for to the next level. As I ate I looked over the chore list. Everything was blurry. I tried to focus and my headache increased. I felt like I had to throw up again. I chocked it back . Esther was in the next room watching tv and I'm sure her patients with me were running out. There was no way I could stand another beating in the condition I was in. I sat and enjoyed the quiet while it lasted.

I sat as long as I could knowing that any second Esther would bellow for me to get my lazy ass up and get to work. Her shrill voice was more than I could handle with this headache. I started with the kitchen. I filled the bucket with the vile lysol and hot water. I got a rag and wiped the appliances down. Next I cleaned the woodwork. I rinsed my mug out and scrubbed the sink. I emptied the dirty water and was going to put more lysol in the bucket with hot water when Esther came in the kitchen. what are you doing she asked ?I'm going to wash the floor . Don't dillute the lysol pour it straight on the floor so it kills the germs! I never understoof this method ! First of all the smell was smothering ! It was so intense it always gave me a headache. Second of all no matter how much you moped the floor was still sticky and your shoes and feet stuck to it ! I knew better than to protest so I did as I was told !

Before Esther left for work she looked at me and said You know the rules break them and your ass is mine ! Do you understand/ Yes I replied and she was gone. Al I wanted to do was lay down . I couldn't shake this headache. It didn't help that is was so insanely hot in this house! We never opened the windows so there wasn't even a breeze. I looked at my chore list and I had exactly 8 things left to do. I knew Esther would be gone for hours that was her shift so I did the rest of my list as quick as I could ,took a cold bath to cool off and laid down on my bed. all I wanted to do was sleep! I had four more hours until she got home and I would take advantage of the quiet. I must have drifted off almost immediately and woke to the sound of the keys in the back door. I jumped up and straightened my bed so she wouldn't know I was laying down. I quick flip on the light in my room and she walked into the living room. She went directly over to the tv and felt the back of it to see if it was hot from being on. It wasn't I had no intentions of breaking anymore rules. She took one look at me and said I was clean up today so they let us bring home the leftovers from the day. Take one muffin and make tea! I stood there shocked! She offered me breakfast this morning and now she was offering me supper ! This has never happened ! Well what the fuck are you staring at she asked? If you don't want it I'll throw it out. No I want it thank you. Then get in there and eat . I'm going to bed I don't want to hear any noise got it ? Yes I replied as I walked into the kitchen. I was careful not to touch anything but the muffin I was told I could have. I made tea and sat down at the table and ate my supper.

Joe was a distant memory. His visitation visits became further and further apart. Every time he came around Esther would call the cops lying and saying he was abusive. He was alway taken away or told to leave voluntarily or they would arrest him. I guess it just became to much and he gave up ! I understand the hell that was Esther believe me but when he gave up he didn't give up on her he gave up on me ! Esther met a new guy his name was Steven. At this point I didn't get invested . They never stuck around. It was like a revolving door at our house. Esther would date a guy a couple of time and then they would disappear ! Steven was either really in love or totally desperate I couldn't tell which! We were on two months and he was still here this was a record! He was ok ,I mean he tried but it always seem fake for some reason. He was a pothead who smoked a lot ! I laughed to myself thinking maybe thats how he tolerated Esther, he was always high! He had a cigar box he kept under the couch one day when he and Esther were out I looked through it. It was an education to say the least . There were white papers in a pack that read ez papers, a pipe, a baggie with a green dried plant (which I later found out was pot). He had a tiny wire brush ,matches and a couple other things . I quickly put the box back and went to my room. This wasn't the first time Esther was involved with a pothead. It seamed to be a prerequisite to date her . All the men she dated in the last couple of years were drunks and potheads. She would have a bunch of people over the house and I became very familiar with the smell of pot at a young age.

Esther had been switched to the afternoon shift at work and I couldn't have been happier ! I waited every afternoon for 11:30 when she would leave for work. It was the best time of the day ! I would get my chores done and sleep ! I never knew what kind of mood she would be in when she got home from work so I got sleep when I could. If she came home exhausted she would go right to be and it was usually a quiet night. If for whatever reason she had a bad day ,like say the wind blew the wrong way I knew I was in for a beating! Her boss let her bring home the leftovers from work everyday now . It was wonderful because it was a surprise everyday when she'd put the bag on the counter. I was allowed to take one thing for supper. We would put the rest in the fridge for other meals.I would pick the one thing that I thought would fill me because that was it until the next night except for tea and crackers in the morning. Esther's boss knew we had very little money and she was very gracious about it. I honestly thought she switched Esther's shift so she would be a closer and get to take the leftovers home. I never ever begrudged Esther for being poor. What I could never forgive her for was the fact that she blamed me for everything bad in her life and that she stole my childhood !

Chapter 33

It was almost Father's Day and Esther called me into the kitchen. She threw down a paint by numbers kit on the table and said I want you to paint this for Steven . You're going to give it to him for Father's Day and write on the back Happy Father's Day Dad love Addie ! I stared at her in disbelief ! I barely knew this man and she wanted me to call him Dad ! I wouldn't do it ! I didn't say anything but there was no way I was calling him Dad ! She opened the box and got a cup of water and said well sit your ass down and paint ! I had no problem painting the picture but when it can time for me to sign what she wanted I wouldn't do it ! She could beat me if she wanted to ! I started painting and she stood right behind me making me so nervous my hands were shaking ! She slapped me in the back of the head and said stay in the lines you stupid bitch I don't have money to buy another painting ! I continued painting and could feel her breath on me she was so close ! I tried to calm my hands but I was so scared to mess up I couldn't control the shaking and went out of the lines again. She yanked my head back by my hair and then slammed my face into the table saying slow the fuck down and do it right ! I was finally finished and she grabbed it from the table and said you fucking bitch you fucked this up on purpose didn't you ? No I replied my hand was shaking I'm sorry was all I had a chance to say before she slapped me in the face and I fell to the floor ! I crawled backwards trying to get away from her

Summer was almost over and I was thrilled to be going back to school ! I was going to be entering the seventh grade and was thirteen years old because of being left back in the fourth grade. Yes I knew how to survive in my house but with my peers I was years behind.On the Saturday before school was going to start Esther was off of work but she went out. She wasn't gone long and when she came home she called me into the living room and said a boy wants to meet you! I stood there staring at her not knowing what to say ! Oh my God hello are you in there she asked as she poked my shoulder! Yes I replied still not knowing what was going on. Ok here's what you need to do she said. Go upstairs and get washed ,wash really good. Put on clean clothes and come down here so I can do something with that mop on your head. I stood there in utter shock ,A- Esther was being nice to me ,B a boy wanted to meet me? I was never a pretty girl I knew that but I was a nice and kind girl. I did as I was told . I went upstairs and washed and got dressed. I came down with a brush so Esther could fix my hair . She took me in the kitchen and wet my hair from the sink. She brushed it and put it in a ponytail. . I turned around with a smile on my face to look at her and she frowned and said you can polish shit but it's still shit! My heart sank! Why couldn't she ever just be a mother and be kind? She looked at me and said now listen when you go out the front door go two blocks then turn right and go up the hill. when you get to the top of the hill turn left . His house will be the third one in from the corner. Do you think you can handle that without screwing it up ? I stood there ,my mind racing . Wait ,what I said? Are you fucking kidding me Esther said as she repeated the instructions she just told me. Well get going she said as she pushed me toward the front door! I stood at the front door frozen. Holy fuck open the door and go she said as she pushed me out the door. I turned and looked at her with pleading eyes. I wanted to say Please don't make me do this but knew better. I did as I was told.

I followed the directions she gave me and there was a guy waiting on his porch when I got there . He was older than me . He looked to be in his early twenties. I stood there scared to death ! Finally he said hi I replied the same and he asked if I wanted to go for a ride ! My gut clenched , he said come on we'll just go for a little ride! You know that little voice in your head that say run, we'll mine had an evil twin that said Esther sent you here so get in the damn car! I got in the car and immediately regreted my decision. There was something about this guy that wasn't right I could just feel it.I was having flash backs of He glance over at me a couple of times when he was driving and it made me sick to my stomach! He turned of the road into a wooded area and said why don't we take a walk? I could feel my legs shaking as I got out of the car. I shut the door and was frozen with fear! He put his hand out and said come on just a little walk. I felt like was was going to be sick. He walked me deeper into the woods and said let's sit here as he pointed to a log. We sat down and he put his hand on my knee ,I jumped and scooted away. He looked at me and said relax it's ok and kissed me. The smell of him made me nauseous. He smelled like soap and bad cologne. He held the back of my head and pushed his mouth closer to mine forcing his tongue into my mouth ! I jumped up and said I want to go home ! He looked at me and said well this was a big fucking waste of my time ! We walked back to the car neither one of us speaking. He drove back to his house parked the car and said get out! I got out of the car . He went into his house and I just stood there! What just happened? Then all at once it hit me ! I stood in front of his house crying. I ran home . When I opened the door Esther looked at me and said what the hell are you doing back so soon? This was the moment I realized she was the devil ! She sent me up to that mans house for him to have sex with me ! I don't know the sorted details of her little set up ,what price or what her gain was I just know that it was unforgivable! It was depraved enough the way she abused me she didn't have the right to "rent" me out to every creep out there for more abuse ! She looked at me and said you can't do anything fucking right can you? You are totally useless ! Get the fuck out of my sight ! with that I went into my room ,sat on my bed knees to chest rocking back and forth ! As I sat there I was so enraged I knew she was evil and crazy but I on that day was terrified because I realized she had no limits! Would she try this again? Not only did I have to deal with the constant fear of beatings now I had to deal with sexual advances from the likes of the creeps she kept company with !

That night Esther ripped my door open and said where the fuck is it? I stared at her not knowing what she was talking about. She asked again ,where the fuck is it? She said you have 1 minute to give it to me or I will beat the shit out of you! I don't know what you mean , I didn't take anything I replied ! You fucking liar! Steven had a box under the couch and now it's gone ! You're the only one here so give it to me now! I don't have it I repeated ! You fucking bitch , you have ruined my life and I finally found someone that will tolerate you and who hasn't left you aren't going to fuck this up for me ! Give me the fucking box ! She started tearing my room apart flipping things over looking for the box ! Get up she hissed ! I jumped off the bed and she flipped the mattress ! She grabbed me by the hair and got right up against my ear and said give me the fucking box this is the last time I'm going to ask ! I was terrified she had gone to the next level of crazy ! Before I knew it I peed my pants ! This hadn't happened for a long time ! She looked down at the floor and her face turned red! I cried I'm sorry ,I'll clean it up ! She grabbed the back of my head and smashed it to the floor saying you fucking little pig! She was grinding my face into the pee when I heard Steven say I found it from the living room! She let go of my head , I ran to the corner shaking , she walked over to me raised her hand and then stopped! Clean this piss up you fucking pig ! I don't want to see your face for the rest of the night! She slammed my door and I laid on the floor and cried myself to sleep !

Chapter 34

Finally summer was over and it was my first day of seventh grade . I picked out the best of my old shirts and the only pair of jeans I had and got dressed for school. When I came out of my room Esther took one look at me and said wow holy fuck you just get uglier and uglier don't you? I didn't reply. I grabbed my backpack and left for school. It was such a relief to be free of her if only for a couple hours a day ! I looked around and everyone had on new clothes and shoes. I choose a seat in the back of the room to try and hide . I knew it wouldn't be long before the teasing started again. I guess I couldn't blame them I dressed in rags and I did stink ! I did the best I could to wash up but our house stunk and so did my clothes. The bell rang and everyone took their seat. The teacher called roll and when she got to my name a couple of the girls in the front row started laughing. One of them said I thought I smelled something ! I could feel my face burn. The teacher said that will be enough. This year we're going to try something new ., we're going to go around the room and stand and read aloud. We'll start here in the front row. The first row of girls all took their turns,they all were very confident and were great readers. As more and more students read my anxiety was getting worse. I loved to read it was an escape for me .I would pretend I was in the story and get lost in a book. Reading aloud was another story . It was my turn I stood up and started to read, a little louder please the teacher said , the girls in the front row were laughing at me. I could feel the sweat build up on my forehead and my heart started to pound. I continued reading and lost my place a couple of times because my hands were shaking so bad the book was moving. I was never so happy to finish a paragraph in my life. I sat down. One of the mean girls from the front row turned to her friend and said Thank God that tortures over I thought she was going to burst into tears . The teacher said girls this will be the last time I will tell you quiet down ! They both turned and glared at me as if I asked them to make fun of me!

It was time for lunch and I hurried to get to the lunch room so I could find a table by myself . As the kids started to file in sitting alone wasn't a problem , no one sat anywhere near me. When I got home Esther was still at work thankfully. I got changed out of my ratty smelly school clothes and put on my more ratty and smelly house clothes and started my chore list. When Esther got home there was no how was your first day at school honey or did you make any friends? Nope she just thew the bag of leftovers on the counter and said pick one and only one thing from the bag I'm going to bed. I waited until I heard her shut her bedroom door and I peeked in the bag. There wasn't much to choose from tonight but I was grateful there was anything ! I pulled out a small container with mashed potatoes and gravy , placed it on the table and got my cup to make tea. I sat alone and ate my supper. I enjoyed the quiet. I had books to cover for school so I got out the paper grocery bags and got to work. When I was done I crept up the stairs to go to the bathroom careful not to wake Esther because that would surely get me beat. I washed up and went to bed. The first week of school went about the same as the first day. Just when I thought the teasing couldn't get any worse I entered Mr. Harris's classroom.

Mr Harris was a very unpleasant looking man that looked like he hated the world! We all got a seat and he said don't get comfortable I'm going to assign seats . The class groaned. He said oh shut up and stand against the wall in the back of the room. I grabbed my stuff and did as I was told. All of a sudden he said what the hell stinks ! Everyone looked at me! I could feel my face burn ! Oh great I have another stinky kid in class this year he said ! He pulled out a can of air freshener from his top drawer and sprayed it in my direction which made the whole class burst into laughter ! I fought back tears, I wouldn't give him or them the satisfaction of seeing me cry. He began to assign seats and everyone grumbled when they realized they wouldn't be sitting by their friends. He picked up a text book and slammed it on his desk making us all jump. Sit down and shut up. We all did as we were told. My seat was in the row by the window and all the windows were open because it was in the high eighties. He looked right at me and said I made sure to sit you next to the window so if your really smelly I can open the window to air the place out ! The class burst into laughter ! I felt the tears well up but I choked them back. He handed out the textbooks and when he got to me he said damn you really are ripe aren't you ? He turned to the class and said I apologize for ,and he looked down at me and said what's your name ?Addie I relied . I apologize for the smell everyone some people don't have the common sense to bath ! With this the class lost it. Was this really happening? Ok I knew I was the smelly kid, I got that. I did the best I could with what I had. Sometimes we didn't even have soap so water was all I had and it just didn't cut it! He as a teacher ,an adult should he really be the ring leader to my torment? I was unmercifully teased enough by the students I didn't need someone in authority jumping on the bandwagon ! Was he that unhappy in his life that he felt the need to do this to me? The rest of the class was pure hell. It was one mean remark after another from him followed by deafening laughter from the students. I turned my head and stared out the window fighting back the tears wishing I was anywhere but here!

I loved going to school it was my only freedom from Esther ,Mr Harris took that from me. Everyday I would feel sick to my stomach dreading his class. I swear the other kids in the class waited with baited breath for the insults to start. He never disappointed ! From the second he walked in the classroom he was on ! It was like the classroom was his stage . I was helpless , I didn't dare defend myself because I would get in trouble and that would guarantee a beating when Esther found out. There was no sense telling Esther she didn't care. I didn't have any friends so I just took the abuse. The one and only thing I did have control over was my tears. I choked them back everyday I wouldn't give him the satisfaction of letting him see he hurt me. Thankfully his classroom was next door to the bathroom , I would grab my book go into a stall and cry my eyes out after every class! Then I would splash water on my face ,get myself together and go to my next class.. I laid in bed one night and thought about reasons that he would be so cruel to me . What I came up with was that he was very insecure and felt that throwing me to the wolves would take the pressure off of him. He went from being the boring teacher to the "cool" teacher ! The kids in the class were to busy laughing at his rude comments about me to focus on him as a person.

Chapter 35

About a two months into my seventh grade year Esther said well those jeans have seen their last day,talking about my one and only pair of jeans. They were ripped, and to say they were high waters was an understatement. A couple inches more and they would be mid calf! She said lets go you fucking pain in the ass so I can get you a new pair of jeans ! I was so excited I was getting new clothes. I'd been wearing the same jeans for the second year now. We walked to the local thrift store in town. Most kids would have been embarrassed to shop here but not me! Theses clothes may not be new but they would be new to me ! Esther looked at me and said you get one pair of jeans and one top you hear me? Yes I said smiling. She looked down at me and quietly said wipe that stupid smile off your face your at the salvation army not Macy's ! I had no idea what Macy's was and I didn't care. I was getting new clothes ! I picked out a pair of jeans and a sweater. I tried them on and carried my bag home happier than I had been in such a long time! The next day I wore my new outfit to school and I held my head up high when I walked into Mr Harris's class. I had on new clothes he couldn't have anything nasty to say to me today ,right? Yeah well I was wrong ! He took one look at my jeans and started to laugh ! Who the hell sewed your jeans Helen Keller he asked? Why is there a seam stitched down the center of your leg ? I picked these jeans because they were different . I liked unique things but of course Mr Harris felt the need to make them more hideous than unique ! The whole class burst into laughter ! I took my seat and felt my face burn. I sat there as I did everyday staring out the window in humiliation. ! After class I went into the bathroom had my daily cry and went to my next class .

I thought that was it for my humiliation for the day boy
was I wrong! A group of girls were gathered in the hall at
there lockers and started to laugh as I walked by. This was
nothing new they laughed at me everyday! Then they
started to follow me down the hall. Nice sweater the one
girl said . I turned around and said thank you. Where did
you get it she asked. I knew I couldn't say I bought it at
the thrift store so I lied and said my Aunt bought it for me.
Huh do you know where she got it one of the girls asked?
No I don't I replied. She said well I know where you got it !
I felt sick, I said nothing. Let me see the cuff on your right
arm. She grabbed my arm and twisted it over and said yep
there it is just like I said! Your a scummy little liar ! This
was my sweater I got bleach on the cuff so I donated it to
the poor at the local thrift store! Are you freaking kidding
me I thought to myself ! Out of all the sweaters in the
store I have to choose the one that the meanest girl in
school donated ! Seriously ,come on what are the odds
of that ? At that moment I felt like I was cursed ! Why did
everything go wrong in my life. All the girls stood there
laughing at me. Not only are you poor but your a filthy
little liar too ! Well I guess I earned the liar part ! I hated
lying and liars but I just wanted them to like me. I put my
head down and walked to my next class.

When I got home that day Esther was still at work. I
changed and threw my new clothes in a heap on the floor!
I laid on my bed and cried myself to sleep ! I woke up to

Esther grabbing me by the hair screaming it must be fucking nice I'm working my ass off and your sleeping! She pushed me against the way , things are getting a little to relaxed around here . What the fuck are your new clothes doing on the floor ? I quickly scooped them up and as I stood she slapped me across the face and said you ungrateful bitch ! That's the way you take care of new clothes? I'm sorry I said as I folded them and put the at the foot of my bed. Ungrateful bitches go to bed without supper ,and she walked out of the room ! I grabbed my chore list and got to work. When I went into the kitchen to do the dishes Esther was just finishing her supper. I kept my head down and went right to the sink and started the dishes. She walked by and dropped her dish in the sink and said boy that was good ! She laughed and went up to her room. I finished cleaning the kitchen and for once I wasn't hungry. I went upstairs washed up and went to bed.I woke up and looked in the archway Esther was shadowed in light . I sat up quickly and grabbed my blanket close to me. I couldn't see her face just her outline. She stood there for another minute and then just walked away! That was enough to scare to crap out of me. I laid there for the rest of the night staring at that archway praying she didn't come back !

When it was time for me to get up I was exhausted. I still couldn't get that creepy vision of Esther watching me sleep out of my head ! I walked into the kitchen to get a glass of water since I assumed the food ban was still on and Esther looked at me and said well hurry your ass up and make your tea before your late ! I grabbed my mug ,teabag and the pot on the stove with the hot water . I went to the table and put sugar and canned milk in my tea. Everything from the smell to the way this tea filled my belly was complete comfort. I finished,rinsed my cup out and went upstairs to get washed for school. When I came down I stared at my jeans and sweater that laid on the bed. I loved them so much when I got them now I wanted to light them on fire and watch them burn. Instead I got dressed and walked to school.

When I got there I seriously thought of not going in! What would happen if I just kept walking? Anywhere had to be better than here I thought ! Just like that I snapped back to reality and walked up the stairs to the front door. When I got to the top of the stairs this boy I had seen in class but had never spoken to came up to me and pushed me down the stairs ! I caught the banaster not before I smacked my knee off the concrete step ! I looked up and he stood there laughing with a group of kids I recognized from Mr Harris's class. He said smelly scum bag how bout you take a bath once in awhile ! They all laughed and went inside . I gathered my books ,holding back tears I walked to class. When I got there I noticed my knee was bleading through my jeans. At this point I didn't even care. As I sat there in class I thought of how easy it was for that boy to push me down the stairs ! He didn't even know me and he had such hate for me ! What had I done to him? Better question was what was done to him that he had such rage for a complete stranger ? This made me see we are all dysfunctional in our own way! Some of us have been the victim and some are victimizers. We can let our past define us or we can become a person who despite all odds is kind and caring . Class was over and I went to the bathroom to clean up my knee. By this time the blood had dried to my jeans and the cut was ripped open again when I pull my jeans from it . It began to bleed all over again . I took a paper towel from the bathroom and folded it ,placing it on my knee I pulled up my jeans. This will have to do. As if my day was horrible enough already my next class was Mr. Harris's ! I walked into the room and the same kids I saw outside were laughing at me Hey stinky did you have a nice fall ? I put my head down and went to my desk. I sat looking out the window until Mr Harris came in. Like clock work he started right in on me. See you liked that outfit so much you wore it again today Addie. I didn't reply. Wanna crack that window so we can get the stink out ? I raised the window and class started. I had no idea what class was about I mentally checked out. That seemed to be the theme for every class for the rest of the year! I just didn't care anymore! What was the difference what I did in class I would still be the smelly kid who got teased my both students and Mr Harris !

Chapter 36

The last day of the year came and what I feared was my reality! I flunked seventh grade ! I had given up! One person could only take so much before they loose hope . I stood outside the school watching all the kids laughing and making plans for the summer. Seeing their smiles reminded me that in a few minutes I would be getting the beating of my life for being left back . I was both terrified to go home and numb at the same time. I knew I wasn't doing the work required of me in class . In the back of my mind I knew this was coming and a part of me didn't care. My life was shit ,no matter how you looked at it ! At home I was abused in school I was bullied . I had no break and it was just to much ! No matter what I did Esther would never love or be proud of me! The only reason she wanted me around was to beat me! She got a perverse thrill out of it ! When she wasn't beating me she would verbally tear me down so there wasn't a day I didn't feel worthless. I walked home and there she was waiting for me smiling ! It was like she knew before I gave her my report card! She snatched it from my hand and smiled ! Oh you really fucked up this time and lunged at me but this time I didn't resist. I took the blows I didn't try to defend myself. She drug me down the hall to my room and started to punch me like it was her job. I felt almost like I had left my body I felt the pain of every strike but I had nothing left to fight back with ! I just didn't care anymore! She stopped hitting me and grabbed me by the hair and shook me! So now your not even going to fight back she hissed! I didn't replied she pushed me to the floor and said your even more pathetic than I imagined ! She walked out of my room and slammed the door! I laid there on the floor for what seemed like hours. I stared at a crack in the floor and just wanted to disappear. I could feel the oh to familiar pain and stiffness starting to set in that happened after every beating. I didn't even attempt getting off the floor. Why bother the pain would be just as bad laying on my bed.

It was some time in the middle of the night Esther stormed into my room and crouched down on the floor and hissed did you really think I was done with you you stupid bitch ? I'm gonna make you wish you were never born ! To late I thought but I didn't reply. She said get your ass up and go take a piss and get right back here! I did as I was told. When I came back into the room she smiled her creepy smile and said I have a surprise for you . Now she got my attention ! I honestly thought she was going to kill me! She went into the kitchen and came back with four pieces of thick rope ! Oh my God she is going to kill me! I looked past her to the door! Go ahead make a run for it she said ! I dare you ! I stood there frozen in fear ! She pushed me on the bed and grabbed my left arm and tied it to the metal headboard! Please no I'm sorry don't I begged ! Shut the fuck up you stupid piece of shit ! She grabbed my other arm ,this time I fought back . I ripped my arm from her grasp and she laughed ! Go ahead and fight I love a challenge ! She yanked my arm back and tied it like the left. I squirmed trying to get free. I thought I was going to loose my mind! All I could think of is when she would sit on my chest and cover my mouth when she was beating me so the neighbors wouldn't hear me cry.. The weight of her body made it so hard to breath. From that point on the mere thought of being restrained sent me into panic! She went to the foot of the bed and grabbed my left leg ,please I'll do better I promise please let me go I begged ! She laughed and said you won't be doing anything for awhile ! I fought like I never fought before as she tied both my legs to the foot board ! She looked at me and said well get comfortable because you'll be there for awhile and walked out of the room. I tried to wiggle my limbs free but nothing worked ! I yanked so hard I had welts forming on my wrist ! I started crying and for the first time since I was very little I went against the ruled and started screaming ! One way or another I was going to get untied ! I couldn't take being restrained. My heart was pounding out of my chest . Esther ripped my door open and jumped on my bed covering my mouth to shut me up ! This was my breaking point I couldn't fight anymore ! She looked me straight in the eye and said if you scream again I will cover your mouth until you stop breathing got it ? I shook my head yes , I would have agreed to just about anything to breath ! She removed her hand and I felt myself get dizzy . I was choking on my own snot . Since I was laying on my back everything was running down my throat. I tried to keep my voice calm and I begged please untie me . Esther glared down at me and said Fuck you and walked out of the room !

As soon as she left the room I turned my head and tried to let the drool run out of my mouth onto the bed. My throat was still thick with snot , it was so hard to breath. I kept telling myself that soon this would be over. She had to untie me sometime, right ? Then it hit me , Steven would be coming over soon! He was always here now! She would have to let me go . How would she explain me being tied to the bed ? A short while later I heard the front door close . He was here ! This was my chance, my chance to get free ! I was just about to yell Help me please I'm tied to the bed when my door opened. Esther was standing in the doorway and said under no circumstances do you untie her ! I saw Steven look into the room and I thought surely he would think this was barbaric and he would untie me ! Instead he looked at me one more time and walked into the kitchen ! Are you freaking kidding me you spineless piece of crap ! You're not going to do anything I thought !Esther looked at me smiking and said get comfortable, see you later and walked toward the kitchen !

I could hear the dishes clanking , were they really eating in the next room knowing I was tied to a bed ! What kind of animals were these people ? Steven walked passed my room again and looked at me. I didn't say a word but gave him a look that said Please help me. He turned and went down the hall to the living room ! A few minutes later I smelled the oh so familiar smell of pot waifing in the air ! Esther poked her head in my room and said I'm going to untie you so you can piss then your going right back do you hear me ? I shook my head yes but thought like hell I'll go back ! As soon as she unties me I'm making a run for the door ! I wouldn't be tied up again ! I'll turn her in ! She untied me and grabbed me by the arm walked me to the bathroom and pushed me into the room. She came in and shut the door. well hurry up take a piss. As I sat down to pee my mind was racing ! How would I get passed her ? The only way was to charge her! I got up , blew my nose and washed my hands. I turned in her direction ready to charge and she grabbed my arm. There was no way I was going willingly. I fought every step of the way ! We got to my room and she pushed me on the bed. She was going to have to knock me out if she wanted to tie me up again ! She grabbed me by the throat and slammed me onto the mattress ! She knocked the wind right out of me ! She sat on my chest and tied my left arm ! I flailed my right arm around ,she smiled down at me and said do you really think you're going to win this fight ? I may not win but I was going to go down fighting . Finally she got a hold of my arm and tied it to the headboard. She grabbed my left leg and I thought well this was it and I kicked her as hard as I could hitting her square in the shoulder ! The blow knocked her backwards into the door ! You little fucker you'll pay for that she said as she tied my left leg to the foot board ! She yanked my right leg so hard I felt the pain in my hip ! She straddled me on the bed then dropped down on my chest ! Hope that kick was worth it she said as she covered my mouth ! Between the weight of her on my chest and her hand over my mouth it was getting harder and harder to breath ! I started to feel dizzy and for a minute thought what would happen if I just didn't fight it ? I tried I really did but shear panic took over and I started to squirm, trying to get her off me! She started to laugh looking directly into my eyes and I stopped squirming ! The fight was giving her to much pleasure, maybe if I didn't fight she would loose interest ! Sure enough she got off my chest, I gasped for air ! She looked down at me and said you ever try shit like that again and they'll find you dead got it ? I shook my head yes and she walked out of the room !

As I laid there tied to my bed unimaginable terror ran through my mind. I tried to think of anything other than what was happening to me. There were so any times during horrific beatings that I would just repeat over and over again in my head in a few minutes this wont be your present it will be your past. You've gotten through it before and you can do it again. It had worked in the past but the panic of being tied up ran to deep. I started to beg please untie me please I'm sorry I yelled into the hall. Esther came running up the hall and got right in my face and said one more fucking word and I promise you you will regret it ! She glared down at me with that icy stare and I could feel a small amount of pee coming out! I have to pee please I begged ! Tough and she walked out of the room! I had dealt with so much in my short life and somehow gotten through it but this was to much I had to get untied! I played out several scenarios in my head. Would I fight her to get free? Hell yes I was I was terrified but anything was better than this . I was about to call her and try and beg again for her to untie me when she came into the room . You have ten minutes go piss and there's tea on the table then your coming right back in here! The hell I am I thought ! There's no way on this earth I'm going to let her tie me up again ! I got up to walk and my legs felt like they couldn't support me! The pain in my hip was excruciating . Get your ass moving Esther snarled! My hip still hurt from when she yanked my leg . It was painful to walk. If you don't walk faster you can forget going to the bathroom! I pushed through the pain and sat down to pee . She stood there in the bathroom blocking the door ! I felt like a caged animal ! I got up washed my hands and looked at my reflection in the mirror . Hollow scared eyes stared back at me. My mind raced , I had to get away. I swear I would plow her down and run out the front door if given the chance ! I wasn't going back to that bed ! I stood at the table to drink my tea. It hurt my hip to sit down. Let's go I don't have all day she said ! I drank my tea and looked past her figuring out my escape route. She leaned into me and said I dare you to run ! Please run because I will have so much fun kicking your ass ! Damn It's like she was in my head ! I began to beg Please don't tie me back up ! I'll clean the whole apartment. I'll do anything you want. You'll clean the whole apartment anyway she replied ! Please I'll do better in school. You stupid dumb bitch you'll never do better ! I swear I'll study harder ,I'll get good grades I replied ! Get the fuck in your room I don't have time for this shit ! There was no way I was going without a fight. I stood my ground. You move or I'll move you she said ! I was terrified to defy her but the fear of being tied up again out weighed that ! She grabbed me by my hair and drug me to my room. I fought with all I had but she tied me to the bed! She got right up against my face and said remember this day I told you you will never win against me and walked out of my room !

Panic set in , I started to freak out ! My heart was racing , I broke into a sweat ! It felt like I couldn't breath , I had to get untied ! I yanked my wrist back and forth until there were little blood marks on them ! I kept pulling hoping my old rickety headboard would give way and I could get free

but nothing worked ! I tried to calm myself down ! I
thought of my Grandparents ,Joe, Maria and Harriet . I
tried to detach myself and take my mind away from what
I was going through! I thought of my Grandparents house,
the one place I felt safe. How I wish I was there now ! I
thought about Maria , what was her life like now? Did she
miss me as much as I missed her ? I thought about Joe
would I ever see him again? Harriet how was she doing ? I
hope her life had gotten better ! About Max I hope he had
a life of love and freedom ! I could hear Esther and Steven
laughing in the livingr oom In that moment I realized what
a coward Steven was ! How could he be in the same
apartment where a child was tied to a bed and beaten
and not step in and do something ? It would be one thing
to know about it but he had walked past my room ,saw
me tied to the bed and kept walking ! I realized he didn't
love me , I was no one to him but at some point human
kindness should have kicked in at the very least !

I was kept tied up to the bed for five days total ! Being left
up only to pee and have some tea ! As fast as it started it
ended ! Esther walked into my room ,untied me and
walked out ! I crawled out of the bed and tried to stand . I
still had so much pain in my hip from when Esther yanked
my leg . It was hard to bear weight on it ! I hobbled
around my room so glad to be untied ! I turned and stared
at my bed which had been my prison for the last five days
and I felt sick to my stomach . I turned away, I couldn't

look at that bed one more second ! Esther ripped my bedroom door open and I went to run to the corner and tripped and fell ! I crawled the rest of the way placing my back against the wall . I brought my knees up against my chest bracing for whatever was coming next ! She stood there staring down at me which such joy ! How could she look at her child and know that she has caused so much mental and physical pain and smile ? She said get some shoes on and go across the street and get milk ! What the hell was wrong with her ? I stood there filthy because I hadn't bathed in five days. My hair so greasy, I stunk and my hip was killing me but I did what I was told . I looked around my floor for my shoes but didn't see them. Hurry the fuck up let's go she said ! I grabbed my brown plastic winter boots and put there on with no socks . I went to walk passed Esther and she laughed , you dumb bitch it's eighty five degrees out and you have boots on ! You re so fucking stupid it hurts she said ! I thought these boots are the least of my problems , but I said nothing ! She handed me what looked like paper money and I stared down at it . Well what the hell are you looking at get going ! I held the "paper money" in my hand and looked back up at her . It's a food stamp you dumb bitch ! I get food stamps to take care of your sorry ass now get moving. I headed for the door and when I got to the living room I turned and saw Steven laying on the couch watching tv ! He looked up and said hi , I kept on walking ! What a piece of crap he was ! I went across the street to the small gas station that had a few grocery item,like milk, bread and such . I got the milk out of the cooler and placed it on the counter. The guy behind the counter gave me a sympathetic head tilt look like damn you are a mess ! I felt my face burning and placed the food stamp on the counter. He picked it up and held it to the light ,checking it over and gave me change. You want a bag he asked? No thank you I replied and walked out . I stood there for a second and thought what would happen if I went to the police station and told them everything ? Would they help me ? I was about nine blocks from the station I could easily make it there. I was going to go for it ! I turned to start up the hill and that's when I heard Esther's shrill voice yell for me from the porch ! Let's go get up here! I'm dead , she saw me , how was I going to explain why I was going up the hill ?

Chapter 37

I took as long as I physically could going up the stairs to the apartment. I was trying to think of a excuse to tell Esther why I was going to go up the hill but I couldn't think of anything ! When I got to the door she looked me straight in the eye and said It would be the worst mistake of your life ! We both knew that she knew what I was about to do !. Nothing else was said about it .With that I became even more introverted if that's possible! I resolved myself to the fact that Esther did in fact own me and it was in my best interest to do as I was told.

Summer was hell! Filled with chores ,random beatings when it was just Esther and me, more mind games and very little food ! I was so happy when it was time for school to start ! Oh lucky me the dreaded Jeans that I got so teased about still fit me and guess what I got to wear the first day ? Yep , well my life was nothing if not consistent! I knew a couple things for certain , I would get teased unmercifully by students , I was still the smelly kid and oh yes for an added bonus I was going to have to endure the constant humiliation of Mr Harris . I couldn't believe I had to go through him tearing me apart again this year but that's what I get for being left back I guess ! I knew one thing for sure I was going to do everything in my power to get good grades ! I would never be a A student because in my opinion my home life wasn't conducive to it ! I was so stressed out all the time at school because of the bullying and the anticipation of going home and when I got home the beatings and the overall horrific environment left little time for studying.! I would do the best that I could.

The first day of school was like every other . Laughter and talking behind my back when I walked by. Isolation with no friends but it was my norm so I had to get used to it ! First period the teacher assigned seats and one of the girls made a comment immediately when her desk was next to mine ! Oh no I'm not sitting next to smelly , and the class erupted into laughter ! I looked down at my desk and could feel my face burning ! Ok that's enough the teacher said , go sit down now or go to the principles office ! The girl reluctantly sat down. I could feel her glare even though I didn't look up ! My strategy this year was to not engage ! I would keep my head down. focus on my school work and basically just get through the day ! My bright spot was lunch ! I got free lunch and so I was guaranteed a meal everyday. It was a nice change from the random feedings I got at home ! The downside was free lunch kids got a special color ticket in the morning in homeroom so just another thing to be teased about ! Oh well I was teased anyway at least I wouldn't be hungry. I would of course would sit by myself but we got to check out book in library so I would eat my lunch and then read. I was obsessed with it. I would get so engrossed that sometimes I wouldn't hear the bell letting us know lunch was over . A teacher who would monitor the lunchroom would blow her whistle and yell get a move on lunch is over! I would snap back to reality and get to my next class!

Mr Harris's class was still torture! I swear he spent his summer coming up with new material on how to humiliate me in front of everyone ! One day about three weeks into the year he was tearing me up as he usually did and he said aren't we all happy we got the smelly kid in class this year and the kids started laughing ! I just sat there with my head down. He called on a girl in the second row and said aren't you glad and I couldn't believe what came out of her mouth ! She said why don't you stop picking on her, maybe it's not her fault ! The class went silent! Excuse me Mr Harris said !She repeated herself and said I don't think it's right the way you make fun of her all the time ! I looked at her out of the corner of my eye and then at Mr Harris. His face was red and he looked so furious ! How dare she ruin his little script of insults by throwing a wrench into all the verbal digs by saying something nice ! It's like he didn't know what to do ! Who was he if not the teacher who ridiculed a student getting the other students to think he's cool ! Becky was the girl who spoke up and she at that moment was my hero ! He said well since you have no issue with the smell maybe you wouldn't mind sitting next to her he said ! I thought ok well it was nice while it lasted ! Surely Becky would back down so she didn't have to sit by me but she did something that shocked me ! She said sure ,grabbed her books and switched seats with the girl next to me ! I sat there ,mouth hanging open not believing what just happened ! She looked over at me and said Hi I'm Becky and you need to stand up for yourself ! What he's doing is wrong ! I looked at her and felt tears well up in my eyes ! Hi I'm Addie and I'll work on that I replied ! For the first time I smiled in Mr Harris's class and lifted my head. He glared back at me and I swore to myself No more ! I wouldn't let him torture me anymore ! It was a very freeing feeling and I would be forever thankful to Becky for standing up for me when no one else did !

Chapter 38

For the first time ever I walked out of Mr Harris's class and I didn't have to run to the bathroom to cry. I always got all my books for the day in the morning because my locker was by Mr Harris's room and I stayed clear of that hallway. That day I walked to my locker and put the books I didn't need inside. I turned and there was Mr Harris glaring at me from his doorway. Part of me was scared to see what he would do tomorrow since Becky stood up to him but today I wouldn't let that ruin this feeling of pure bliss ! I walked to lunch and when I got there Becky said hey Addie you wanna sit with us? I turned and looked behind me because no one had ever asked me to sit with them in my life ! Well do you wanna she asked again? Yes ,Yes I would thank you I replied loudly and a few people turned around ! I sat down and Becky said this is Ellie,Stacey and Patti pointing to the other girls at the table . Hi I said ,face burning. They all said hi and didn't make a huge deal about it and started talking about their day. I sat there listening. This is what it was like to talk to peers. They talked about their classes, boys and home. I took it all in. Ellie said hey Addie what are you doing this weekend? Knowing I wasn't ever allowed out I lied and said I had to go visit family. Oh bummer we were all going to hang out. I wanted to hang out more than anything I ever wanted in my life but knew I would never be able to. Maybe next time she said. Yeah maybe next time I replied. Everyone was so nice . Was this really happening ? The lunch bell rang and I didn't want it to end. Becky got up and said see you tomorrow Addie . I waved and said good bye to the rest of the girls and floated to my next class.

I had Becky in Mr Harris's Class and Patti in my English class.I never would have known because I never looked up from my desk. from that day forward we ate lunch together everyday . I had to keep bowing out every time they asked me to do something after school because I wasn't allowed out of the house. I devised a plan , if I worked really hard and got good grades I would ask if I could go out with friends. My study skills and retention where horrible. No matter how many times I read something it just didn't stick. I wouldn't give up. I took really good notes in class. When the teacher would say something I would reword it in my notes in a way that made sense to me. I had library two times a week and I studied ,really studied my notes and for the first time in my life I felt confident taking a test. It was test day in Mr Harris's class I had studied really hard . When I was done with the test I was amazed that I breezed through it ! I lacked confidence in myself and allowed self doubt in making me feel I flunked the test. The next day we got our test back and Mr Harris wrote in big red letters See e after class on my test ! I waited after class and he glared down at me and said clearly you cheated on this test so I'm giving you detention ! I stood there in disbelief, so this is what I got for studying ? He said you can go now! I turned to walk out of the room and turned back and said I studied and I did not cheat . I 'm going to the Principals office because you have done nothing but humiliate me since the first day I had your class last year . I may have flunked every one of your test up to this point but I studied for this one. What your doing is very unfair and I don't deserve it! I was walking out of the classroom and he said ok I'll ask you four questions pertaining to the chapter and if you know them I will give you a C . No thank you I knew the material and I know my grade had to be better than a C. I'm going to the principle . I was shaking as I walked to the door. I felt like I had to throw up. He called me back into the classroom and said sit down I will retest you . I told him I had lunch next and he said you want to retake the test or not? I sat down and retook the test. He watched me like a hawk. I placed my test on his desk and he graded it. Oh my God I got every one right ! My first A in my life ! I know this is childish but the A was so much sweeter because it was in Mr Harris's class ! He pushed the test toward me and said get out of my room ! I thought my heart would explode I was so happy !

The next day in class Becky took her seat right next to me. I couldn't believe it I had a friend. She leaned over and said now listen defend yourself! Mr Harris is a bully and he picks on you because you take it! Stand up for yourself and I gaurantee you he'll stop ! Class started and Mr Harris walked into the room It's gonna be a hot one today, someone open the window to get the stink out of here. Watch this Becky said ! Did you bring a tuna sandwich again for lunch Mr Harris Becky said. The class roared! See beat him to the punch line ,it through him off. Mr Harris stood there glaring at Becky ! Don't call out in my class again or your going to the principles office got it ? Yes Becky replied ! Class went on and he didn't harass me at all ! For the first time ever he didn't make jokes at my expense! Becky looked at me and said your not such an easy target now that you have me in your corner ! Thank you so much I replied ! No problem he's a jerk and what he's doing is wrong! See you at lunch she said. I was gathering my books to leave the class and Mr Harris come over to my desk and said you think your so cool because someone stuck up for you well your not! I kept hearing Becky in my head saying stand up for yourself ! Shaking I looked up at him and said I don't know what happened to you to make you so mean but if you continue harassing me in your class I'm going to the principle and letting him know what you've been saying. He stood there glaring at me and said like he would believe you over me! Like you said I have someone standing up for me and I'm sure she would back me up. He glared at me and said get out of my room ! I could barely feel my legs I was shaking so bad but I grabbed my books,went to the bathroom and threw up ! I did it I stood up for myself ! I went to lunch and told Becky what happened and she laughed he knows his comic days are coming to an end! Now he'll actually have to teach the class and everyone will see what a dork he really is ! We both laughed and ate our lunches.

Patti sat next to me in English and I thought can this really be happening am I making friends ! I found out Patti lived about 6 blocks from me. I never realized . She said hey wanna walk home with me? I stood there staring at her , hello earth to Addie you in there she laughed ! Yeah ,Yes I'll walk home with you I replied . Ok see you after school. We walked home together. My houses was first on the way home . Pattie said wanna walk to school in the morning ? Yes I said just a little to excited and she laughed ok see you then. Bye I replied and watched her walk up the street. I walked onto my porch stood there at the door and cried. I had friends ! Honest to goodness friends !Was this what it was like to be a normal kid? I opened the door and snapped back to reality. There was Esther glaring at me. What the fuck are you looking at she said.

Nothing I'm sorry I replied. Get your ass in the kitchen and get it cleaned up I'm going out. I won't be back tonight, bed at nine got it? Yes I replied and walked into the kitchen with a smile on my face! I made friends at school and Esther is leaving for the night it felt like Christmas ! I heard Esther leave and I spun around the kitchen I couldn't remember being this happy in a long time ! Esther bought a second hand radio at the thrift store and I turned it on ,oh how I loved music! I danced around the kitchen as I did my chores. Things were looking up it was tea and a cheese sandwich for supper ! This was a great day. I thought about my new friends, what were they doing right now? I went up to the bathroom and grabbed my jeans and sweater and scrubbed them on the scrub board in the tub with the fels naptha soap. I rung them out as hard as I could and hung them on the line in the backroom . I looked around the bathroom to see if there was soap other than the fels I needed to do something about my hygien. Sadly there wasn't any so I filled the tub with water and scrubbed my body like I never scrubbed before. Washing every square inch of myself. I got out of the tub , put my Pajamas on , got my library book and read laying on my bed. From now on I was going to make sure I didn't stink. I couldn't expect people to want to be friends with me if I was the smelly kid !

Chapter 39

I loved school now I had friends and when I had Mr Harris's class I walked in with my head up and looked him straight in the eye. He preyed on me because I was weak and I took it I wouldn't be the victim anymore. Some of the kids in the class tried to get him to start with me again but he redirected their attention to our studies ! I was amazed , just like that I stood up for myself and he left me alone. All it took was this little bit of confidence and I felt my world shift ever so slightly ! These were my people! I finally fit in ! My friends meant the world to me ! About a month later Patti was waiting for me after school and we walked home together. she was a real chatter box ! I loved to hear her stories about her day. As we were walking she stopped and looked at me . I stopped and asked if she was ok. She said can I ask you a question? Sure I replied, what is it? She stood there and I could tell it was hard for her to ask me whatever it was. Finally she said Um does your mother beat you ? My heart started to pound and my ears were ringing. I froze ! I immediately froze she said I'm sorry , it's non of my business! I stood there , what do I do ? Do I feel safe enough to tell the truth? Do I lie? I looked at Patti and I could tell she was asking out of concern I started to cry I put my head down and shook my head yes! Just like that all the years of pain and beatings flooded out of my eyes! I couldn't stop crying ! Patti looked at me with such sympathy ! I said its ok but couldn't seem to stop crying ! It's like everything I held in for all these years just came to the surface at once ! Patti reached over and hugged me which made me cry even harder ! We stood there on that sidewalk and I sobbed ! I sobbed for my stolen childhood, for missing my Grandparents, Maria , Joe , Harriet and Max ! For all the beatings I endured ! Finally I pulled away from Patti and apologized for crying like a baby ! Patti looked at me and said don't ever apologize for feeling ! I stared at her , this is what it was like to have a genuin friend that cared for you ! We started to walk again and I said how did you know, about my mother I mean? What she said next almost knocked me off my feet ! She said this is a small town and people talk . Not to be rude but just about everyone in town know s your mother is crazy and beats on you !

Wait what I said ? Patti said her parents were talking about this lady one day and how crazy she was and her poor daughter . How she beats on her and how her daughters never aloud out of the house ! They didn't mention any names at first but it wasn't hard to put two and two together she said. Being such a small town everyone knows everyone and I could tell by the way they were talking it wasn't a local. You and your mother were new to town so ... People know this and no one tried to help me ! I wasn't mad at Patti she was just a kid but why didn't a adult step in and help me ? I turned to her with tears in my eyes and asked why no one did anything to help me ? She hung her head in shame, No I don't mean you I mean the adults,why didn't anyone call the cops ? I overheard my parent's saying your mother runs with a rough crowd and they were afraid of retaliation. . I wiped my face and looked her right in the eye ,Patti who else knows this? . Do the girls know I asked ? Yes they know that's why Becky stood up for you in class! She told us you take enough crap at home and you shouldn't have to put up with it at school too ! I will never be able to thank Becky enough for standing up for me in Mr Harris's class or for you girls being my friends. Would you all still be my friends if you didn't feel sorry for me ? I held my breath while she answered ! Yes of course was her reply ! To be very honest when we heard your story we knew we had to do something ! Becky made the first move by standing up for you and introducing us all to you ! After we all got a chance to get to know you we all knew we would be friends ! She hugged me again and we continued walking. For the first time in a long time my heart was full ! I had true friends ! We were approaching my house ,I have to get in before I get in trouble ! I'll see you in the morning. Will you be ok she asked me? Yes thank you I said as I walked onto my porch I turned and waved and said I see you in the morning.

The first thing I saw when I walked through the door was Esther. Who the fuck was that you were talking to ? Just some girl from school I replied afraid to tell her the truth ! If she thought I was making friends she might do something to jeopardize it ! If I had to lie to protect those girls I would. They befriended me when no one else would . Well get your ass changed and start on the chores! I'm going out . with that she slammed the front door behind her and was gone. I sat down on my bed and processed what Patti just told me . People knew about Esther and how she abused me ! No one did anything ! Then I thought people knew my secret hell ! I was both embarrassed and relieved at the same time ! My whole life I lived in this violent prison and now I felt maybe just maybe there was light at the end of the tunnel ! If people knew could they help me ? As I did my chores it was all I could think about ! I found strength in the fact that my life was no longer a secret ! Then I remembered what Patti said " her parents heard Esther ran with a tough crowd and they feared retaliation if they did anything." . My heart dropped, would their fear prevent anyone from helping me ? Suddenly I became very sad ! was I right back where I started from ? It would only take one person to be brave enough to step forward , That's all I needed was one!

The next day I felt so uncomfortable knowing the girls knew about my abuse at home. Now not only was I the poor smelly kid I was the abused kid too ! Becky could tell something was wrong and asked me if I was alright. I told her that Patti told me that people knew about my home life ! She looked me straight in the eye and said " listen you were dealt a crap hand in life don't let it be all your gonna be" ! Her words were profound ! We both looked at each other and no more words were needed ! Maybe just maybe I was going to be ok ! My friendship with the girls grew stronger everyday. I still got bullied at school but when I was with my girls people just seemed to leave me alone. Bullies only preyed on the weak and when someone was alone. I made sure whenever possible I was with a least one other person. I was doing better in school .I took better notes and used every library period to study. I would go to the back of the library, where it was the quietest and not lift my head from my studies until the bell rang for the change of classes. It was paying off ! I went from all D's & F's to four high C's and one B ! I was so proud of my report card I ran home I couldn't wait to show Esther ! Maybe just maybe after she saw how hard I was working she would let me out with my friends ! When I got home there she stood ,hand out well let's see your report card she demanded ! I smiled and handed it to her. She stood there speechless then finally looked up at me and said well you finally learned to cheat so you could get better grades ! She dropped my report card at my feet and walked away ! I picked it up and thought no way I worked my butt off and I'm going to tell her ! I followed her down the hall and she spun around, glaring at me I gathered my courage and said I studied really hard I didn't cheat ! She stood there looking at me then laughed, you studied really hard and all you got were C's and a B you are retarded aren't you. With that she stepped to me I flinched and step back. She said you every step to me like that again and I'll kick you're ass got it ? Yes I replied. Get change and get your chores done she said as she slammed the door to her room !

I felt so defeated I thought surely she would be proud of me when I got better grades and I could ask I could hand out with my friends for just one night. She made it seem like no big deal but instead of giving up I worked harder. I wasn't going to go back to all F's I had a system of study ing that worked and I knew if I stuck with it I could get better grades.

Chapter 40

It was about this time that our school started a Friday night program. The school provided transportation to a youth center about a half hour away. There was a indoor roller skating rink ,game room and basketball court. All you had to do was register every Friday and be at the school at five p.m. for pick up. I knew I'd never be able to go so I didn't even bother mentioning it to Esther. I didn't have to lie about why because they knew about Esther. I simply told them I'm not aloud out sorry. ll worried all the time that the girls would get tired of me never being able to hang out ! I couldn't bear losing them as friends! To my amazement they always responded that's ok maybe another time. Yeah I said maybe another time .

It was parent teacher night at our school and for the first time I was excited ! I had improved in all my classes and maybe with the teachers telling Esther this she would see how hard I was working. We went in one at a time with our parents for the teacher and parent to meet .After the initial meeting the teacher would include us in the meeting to ask if we had any questions. Esther was less than pleased to have to attend but it was required. On the walk to the school she made sure I knew how she felt. You just never stop being a pain in my ass do you she snarled ! Right before we walked in she said sit down shut your mouth so we can get this the fuck over with got it ? Yes I replied and we went in. Esther had met all of my teacher and it was going well then it was time to meet Mr Harris . We walked in and I had to give him credit he didn't try to put on a show and act as if he was a decent human being. He was direct , no small talk and very abrasive. After he was done talking Esther looked at him and said wow that was so informative with a snide tone! You could tell he got that she was being sarcastic and raised a eyebrow ! I thought oh please say something cocky to her you wont know what hit you ! It was like he sensed she would have the last word and he said nothing. As soon as we got out of his class but were still in ear shot of him Esther said what a dick under her breath and I turned to see the look of shock on his face ! I never thought it possible but it was the one time that I agreed with Esther !

All in all it was a very good night! My teachers praised me for how hard I had been working to raise my grades making me very proud. Of course Esther used her fake voice and said Oh I'm so proud of you honey , great work !Then we got outside the school and Esther burst my happy bubble saying boy your teachers are a bunch of stupid assholes ! Like I give a shit about what they're saying ! It's seventh grade for fucks sake not college you should be doing good ! And there it was the reminder that no matter what I did I would always look like nothing in Esther's eyes!

Against all odds Esther and Steven were still dating ! I don't know what kind of lottery hell he won to be dating her but... He would always try to make conversation I talked to him but I would never forgive him for not doing something when I was tied to the bed ! I knew better than to be rude to him so I kept our conversations polite and short. ! Was his life that empty and pathetic that Esther seemed like a good choice in a mate ? Well one benefits was that Esther beat me less when he was around so I was thankful for that. Esther informed me we were moving again ! I was in a panic oh God please don't let us be moving out of my school district . I couldn't bear to loose my friends ! I was thrilled to find out we were only moving one town away which was literally half a mile from where we currently lived . I could stay in my same school and would still have my friends. This time we packed everything we owned and moved to our new apartment. This apartment was on the third floor. The landlords lived on site and were a very nice older couple. I was getting good grades and my friendship with my girls was growing stronger everyday.

I still wasn't allowed to go out but that was all about to change. Esther was still waitressing and Connie, her boss asked her to bring me in since she hadn't seen me in awhile. I was telling the girls at lunch my plans for stopping in at Esther's job and Becky said I have a plan ! A plan for what I asked ? Don't worry just show up and I'll handle the rest she said. I became very nervous, things were going better and the last thing I wanted to do was to make Esther mad. Not knowing what Becky's plan was I asked again and she insisted she keep it a secret and it would all work out. I protested and told her Esther didn't like to be messed with and this plan whatever it was was sure to back fire. She again insisted it was genius and fail proof . Telling me not to worry ! That afternoon as I walked to the restaurant I felt sick ! Why hadn't I insisted

Becky not go ahead with this plan ? What was I thinking ? I walked in and there was Esther using her fake voice saying here's my Addie now ! Reaching down and hugging me . Her touch made me recoil ! I knew if anyone saw any resistance and commented on it I would get beat so I smiled and leaned into the hug! Let me tell you being embraced by all that evil was horrible and the fake sugary way Esther was talking it was a wonder her teeth didn't rot out of her mouth !

Connie came over and hugged me and said we insisted your Mom have you stop in since we haven't seen you in so long. Me remembering my manners replied with so nice to see you again. With that her Connie hugged me again saying aren't you the sweetest . I smiled and could feel my face burning ! I wasn't used to so much positive attention. She said you sit right up here and I'll get you something to eat. I sat at the counter and she said what will it be ? I'll just have a soda I replied . Nonsense I feed people it's what I do I can't have you leaving here hungry now can I ? Tell you what I'll surprise you she said as she walked back to the kitchen. Esther came over and under her breath said be polite, eat and then get the hell out ! Then she reached over and gave me another fake hug while smiling and saying how was school honey ? Her words creeped me out I know what she really wanted to say was I wish you were never born but I played along. School was good thanks I said with a smile. Connie walked out of the kitchen with the tallest sandwich I had ever seen. She placed it in front of me and said here you go sweetie a BLT club with fries and a cola. I looked at it and replied oh thank you it looks amazing . She pinched my cheek and said you need to come around more often you make my day . Now eat up . I bit into the club sandwich and was in heaven ! It tasted as good as it looked. I was so hungry but slowed down so not to draw attention to myself. I picked up my napkin to wipe my face and I heard the door open I turned to look and in walked Becky ! My heart just about stopped !

I was sick to my stomach when I saw Becky ! What was her plan ? Before I had a chance to run the different scenarios in my head she walked over to me and said hey Addie ! I didn't know you'd be here. Esther was waiting on a table and spun around glaring in my direction. I saw the look in her eyes and put my head down staring my sandwich ! Hi Becky I replied so low that is was almost silent. Hey Connie, Becky said as she set next to me at the counter ! Becky sweetie how are you ? Good thanks . Your moms not working today Connie said as she walked over to Becky to give her a hug. Becky's mom was a waitress too. Oh I know I wanted to ask you if I could put up this poster in your window it's for school. Our school runs a bus every Friday night to a youth center a couple of towns away so we kids have something to do. Sure honey go put it in the window. Becky turns to me and says Addie how

come you never go to any after school activities. I froze ,
like a puma Esther was at my side! Oh Addie doesn't know
anyone , she's shy and felt uncomfortable going to a after
school event alone. Becky didn't miss a beat and said oh
you must be Addie's mom hi I'm Becky. Esther said hi nice
to meet you in her fake voice. Well problem solved Becky
said because Addie knows me and I go to all the after
school activities. She's more than welcome to go with me
and my group of girls. We'll introduce her to other kids.
You have a great daughter Becky said looking straight into
Esther's eyes. It was then that I saw Esther's expression
change. She knew she was being handled and didn't like
it. Thank you Esther said as she glared down at Becky.
Becky didn't waiver she stared right back at Esther.

Connie came over and said well isn't this perfect. Good
thing you stopped into today when Addie was here . Now
she'll have someone to go to all the school events with !
Isn't that great Esther Connie asked? Oh yes it was perfect
timing that Becky here came in just when Addie stopped
in. Then I knew a beating was in my future! The gig was up
Esther knew we planned this "chance" meeting. Becky
was quick on her feet and said I was last in class today and
our homeroom teacher reminded us about the Friday trip
to the youth center. She had the posters on her desk I
asked if I could take one to hang it here where my mom
works because so many kids stop here after school. She
said it was a great idea so here I am she said smiling at

Esther. Then Becky starts talking about gym class and I thought where's she going with this ? She said you know tomorrow we're getting uniforms for gym ? They said it's better that everyone dresses the same that way no one gets made fun of for not having popular gear . Oh I didn't hear anything about it I replied. Yep no more taking gym class in our regular clothes now we have to change in the locker room before gym . This got Esther attention and I knew why, I had bruises on my body that if seen would surely send up red flags. Ok I thought enough Esther has a short fuse and it looked like she reached her breaking point. As if Becky sensed what I was thinking she said well I have to get home for supper . See you in school tomorrow Addie. She looked at Esther and said nice meeting you ,Esther gave that look like she knew exactly what just went down and said nice meeting you too dear ! Holy Crap I was in so much trouble! Connie came over to say good bye and Becky was gone !

Chapter 41

Since our move I had a half mile walk home. Connie said do you want me to give you a ride home. No I replied it's not far at all and I love to walk. Ok see you again she said as she wiped the counter. Esther said I'll be right back I'm going to walk Addie out. With that she followed me out the door and I could feel the rage permeating off her body as she followed me. When we got outside she looked me right in the eye and said I hope you enjoyed your little play you little fucker ! You and that little bitch Becky were so subtle ! I just stood there saying nothing ! You two think you're so smart don't you ? You forget who your fucking with she asked ? I'll deal with you when I get home ! As far as that little sneaky bitch Becky I don't want you to so much as look at her anymore you understand? I began to cry and said she's my friend I can't stop talking to her ! She looked down at me and said the only thing that preventing me from kicking your fucking as right now is that were in public and I would be arrested ! I said stay away from her and that's what I mean got it ? Now give me a hug because they are watching through the window ! As she hugged me she hissed in my ear I can't wait to beat your ass when I get home ! With that I turned the corner and headed to home !

I was so terrified I didn't want to go home ! This had to stop I had to tell someone! I continued walking in a daze. I was almost to our house. Thoughts ran through my head of going to the police station,to a church, hell into a grocery store anywhere there were people ! There had to be someone in this world that would help me ! According to the girls "the town" knew ! Why wasn't someone helping me ? Fear won out as I walked on my porch and went into the house ! I got in and right away started to pace the floor ! I tried to come up with a reason any reason for Becky's performance . I would never rat her out she was my friend. Do I dare tell Esther that people in the town knew she beat me ? No because if I did that she would make us move again and I would loose my friends.I felt a wave of nausea hit me and I ran to the kitchen sink and got sick.I seriously didn't know how much more I could take ! The tick of the clock on the kitchen wall was deafening. With every second that passed I was closer to my next beating. I should have know better than to think I could have friends, that I could have a normal life ! I sat on my bed ,knees to chest rocking back and forth and I heard Esther's keys in the back door.

My heart started to race , she stormed through the door and made a beeline right to my room. She was a women on a mission . All she had to do is look at me and all I could say was I'm sorry over and over again. Oh you will be she replied ! She slapped me across the face knocking me to the floor! So you and your little bitch friend think your so smart ! No I'm sorry I said again. So what was the plan she was going to come in and I would let you go hang out ? No she's just a friend from school that's all. You're a piece of shit you don't have friends ! At that moment my fear took a turn and all I could hear in my head was Becky saying you have to stand up for yourself ! I looked Esther in the eye and said your wrong I do have friends ! Esther looked at me and for a minute she was frozen ! Then she laughed and said no one would ever want to be friends

with you ! They probably pity your pathetic ass that's all !
No they are my friends I stood my ground ,shaking inside
but I did it. She said look around where are your so called
friends ? Are they going to protect you from the beating
your gonna get ? With that she ripped me from the floor
by my hair and started wiping the floor with me. She drug
me back and forth . I was running trying to lesson the
tension on my hair and she kicked my feet out from under
me ! I landed on the floor with a thud ! As soon as I did
she started kicking me ! I crawled to the corner of the
room and covered my head with my arms ! I braced
myself for her next strike and there was nothing ! I
peeked out from behind my arms and I saw her turn and
walk out of the room ! Was she done? Was she coming
back ? I sat there to scared to move for the rest of the
night ! I must have dozed off at some point because I
woke up with this jarring pain in my leg ! I slowly stood up
feeling the oh so familair after a beating stiffness all over
my body !

It was a school day , I had to pee so bad but didn't dare go
upstairs for fear of waking Esther. I went into the kitchen
and wet my head in the sink pulling my hair back into a
ponytail . I splashed my face with cold water and went
and got dressed. As soon as I got to school Becky was
waiting for me . So how did you like she started to say and
stopped Oh my God what happened to you she said as
she grabbed me by the arm and led me to the bathroom.

Wait what's wrong I asked as she stood me in front of the mirror ? I looked in horror at my reflection and saw I had blood on the corner of my mouth and a huge black and blue on my face! I freaked out ! I didn't go upstairs this morning because Esther was sleeping . I should have gone up and looked in the mirror . What am I gonna do now I said in panic to Becky ? You're gonna march your ass down to the principles office and tell the exactly what happened she replied. I can't you don't understand I said standing up to Mr Harris was one thing but Esther was a whole different kind of monster ! She owns me I said defeated ! Becky looked at me and the sadness in her eyes was more than I could bear I had to look away ! I have to come up with a story about these marks in case anyone asks. In case anyone asks Becky said in disbelief ! You look like you were jumped believe me people are going to ask. Please I said please help me come up with something I don't want to have to move again ! Wait what Becky said looking confused ? Every time a neighbor or anyone starts to figure out that Ether beats me we move! Most times in the middle of the night! I can't bear loosing you and the girls. You're my friend. Becky looked at me with tears in her eyes. She spoke softly Addie aren't you tired making excuses for that monster ? Yes I'm exhausted but it's my life what am I supposed to do ! I've seen her go up again so many people and win everyt ime. I have no more fight left in me ! Please Becky if you're my friend please help me come up with a reason I look like this!

Together we made up a story that the kitchen floor was wet and I fell last night hitting my face on the table! Becky said know that I will not be a part of this next time ! You need to tell someone ! The bell rang and we had to get to class. I hate lying and was so anxious for the rest of the day thinking someone was going to ask what happened to my face. I was relieved and saddened at the same time when it was time to go home and not one person asked me what happened or if I was ok ! Is it any wonder Esther had gotten away with abusing me for so long when everyone was to busy with their own lives or turned a blind eye to what was right in front of them ! That afternoon when I got to the home I knew I had 3 hours until Esther got home from work so I rushed through my chores so I could lay down. The stress of the day had really gotten to me .All I wanted to do was sleep. It felt like I had just laid down when I heard Ethers keys turn in the back door ! I jumped up and straightened my bed , grabbing the dust rag I left on the foot of my bed and pretended I was dusting. As always her first stop was my room. She took one look at me and said holy fuck did you go to school with your face looking like that . Yes I replied , She looked at me and said did anyone say anything? No I said with my head down! Huh and you said you had friends! They didn't even care enough to ask if you were ok ! I told you no one gives a shit about you. The sooner you realize that the better off you'll be! The bags on the counter with the leftovers,take one thing then finish your chores and go to bed ! I'm going up to bed now make a sound and wake me up and I'll beat your ass ! I headed to the kitchen. As I sat there eating my supper alone a sadness came over me that made me burst into tears. My life was shit plan and simple !

Chapter 42

It was Saturday morning which was just another day in my house but there was a bright spot this Saturday. Esther got a call asking if she could do a double because one of the waitresses had called off sick. In her sickening sweet fake voice she said sure no problem. As soon as she hung up the phone she said mother fucker lazy bitch called off again now I have to go work a double ! I didn't realize that I had a huge smile on my face until Esther slapped me saying what the fuck you smiling at you dumb bitch ? I put my head down but didn't reply . This place better be spotless when I get home you hear. Yes I replied as I watched Esther leave ! I was thrilled a whole day just to myself ! No threat of beatings ,no being made to feel worthless and I could even take a nap if I wanted to ! This was a good day and boy did I need it.

I wanted to get my chores out of the way first then I would have the rest of the day to myself. I started in the kitchen and made my way around the house I was done everything in two hours I Next I would take a bath and scrub the crud of cleaning from my body. I'd been doing my best to not stink when I went to school. I wish I had something besides phels napta but I used what I had. After my bath I went downstairs t the kitchen and made a cup of tea and some saltines. I had two library books I checked out this week that I wanted to read so I curled up on my bed and began to read. I drifted off to sleep and must have been out for awhile because when I woke up it was dark out ! I jumped up in a panic ,I was so confused I didn't know what time it was ! I ran to the kitchen and looked at the clock on the wall and thankfully I still had forty five minutes until Esther would be home from work. I ran through the house again just to make sure all my chores were done and decided to scrub my school clothes in the bathtub on the washboard. I rung them out and hung them up in the back room to dry. I went back downstairs and waited for Esther to get home . I knew she would be exhausted after working a double so I did my best to stay out of her way . As soon as she got home she looked around trying to find something out of place or that I forgot to clean but to my surprise she didn't find anything ! She threw the bag of leftovers on the counter and said you know the drill take one thing and don't make any noise I'm going to bed. Ok I replied and she went up to her room.

I looked in the bag and there was a burger on a bun ,a couple of muffins, some mashed potatoes and a few pieces of chicken. I knew better than to touch the meat. That was a unwritten rule that was always Esthers. So I decided on the mashed potatoes and a cup of tea . I sat at the kitchen table with my book and enjoyed my supper .

By Monday morning my black and blues were turning yellow . Still visible but I guess I was invisible . No on inquired about what happened! Which only reinforced my belief that there was no way out for me as far as Esther's prison ! I mean it was one thing if people didn't know what abuse happened behind closed doors but a totally different situation when they saw a child who was neglected and now showing up with blood and black and blues on her face and they did nothing.

Becky came over to me first thing Monday morning and asked how my weekend was . Ok I guess you know my normal I replied ! Listen Becky I have to tell you something Esther said I'm not allowed to talk to you anymore ! Wait what the hell Addie She said sounding mad and rightfully so ! I know she seems threatened by you I said . Well she should feel threatened by me she beats the shit out of my friend and I'm not going to stand for it ! Know that I'm still going to talk to you in school

Becky and since I'm not aloud to hang out nothing is really changing ! That's bullshit Addie not only does she physically abuse you but now she's trying to isolate you from your friends ! Well guess what that shit doesn't fly with me ! You have to stand up for yourself and tell her that you aren't going to be her punching bag anymore ! Becky don't you think I want to I asked ? It's not like I've enjoyed the beatings over the year but what can I do she's a monster and she owns me ! That's just it she doesn't own you she's your mother and a damn horrible one at that ! I know but look at my face you can see the black and blues and have any of the teachers so much as asked me what happened? Becky went silent and looked at me with such pain in her eyes , bowing her head she replied no they haven't! Well that's exactly my point , I'm so thankful for you and the girls you all mean the world to me ! You're all I have ! If I make waves I get beat or even worse if Esther thinks anyone is on to her then we have to move again ! I honestly don't know what I would do without my friends so please just hang in there a little longer and maybe it will all work out ! The bell rang for first class so we grabbed our books and started our day

Chapter 43

Steven was at our apartment just about everyday now slowly moving his stuff in or casually leaving it behind.

One day when I got home from school both Esther and Steven were there. I felt sick what was going on? Steven said I have something to ask you ,how would you feel about me moving in here with you and your mother. Esther was standing behind him making her eyes huge and glaring at me so I knew what I was expected to say. Sure that would be great I replied and a smile spread across his face. I'm so happy your ok with it he said and walked over and hugged me. I recoiled but then saw Esther glaring at me so I leaned in and let him hug me ! That weekend he got a couple of buddies to help him move his stuff in. He only had a few pieces of furniture, kitchen stuff and his clothes. By the end of that day he was totally moved in. Let's celebrate by ordering pizza. What do you like on your pizza he asked both of us. Whatever you like was Esther's reply ! I almost fell over Esther wouldn't even let me decide which way the toilet paper should hang , I liked it over and she slapped me and said never put it over alway under got it ? Yes I replied lesson learned! Now she was letting someone decide what she was going to eat ! Maybe Steven had tamed the Beast I thought and laughed to myself !

When Steven left to pick up the pizza Esther grabbed me by the arm listen you little fucker this guy could be our meal ticket don't fuck it up you understand ? Yes I replied . Silly me I thought maybe just maybe she cared for the guy but she was just using him ! Even though he left me tied to the bed I sort of felt bad for him. We were all just pawns that she used in her life! My mistake to think that her empty cavity of a body contained a heart and soul ! Things changed for the better after Steven moved in . While sitting in my room I overheard him say to Esther she needs to be able to go out with her friends. She never leaves the house or sees anyone ! I was so thankful that he was pleading my case but all I could think was tread lightly because you don't want her to go to the dark side ! Esther may have hit her head or gotten beat with a kind stick because she said your right I'm going to let her go to this thing her school has on Friday nights. We have a poster hanging at work . It's a weekly trip to a youth center were the kids all hang out and it's chaperoned ! My heart stopped , oh please don't be lying about letting me go I thought ! Why don't we tell her together that she can go Steven said I know she'll be excited . I held my breath waiting for Esther's answer ! They came to my room and I had to pretend I didn't hear the conversation. Addie how would you like to go with your friends on Friday to the youth center Steven asked ? My heart pounding I said oh I would love that ! Esther stood behind him glaring at me I put my head down. Well it's settled you can go ! Please be careful stay with your friends and don't do anything your not supposed to do! I promise I won't I said with tears in my eyes. Thank you I said looking directly at Esther. I'll be good Thank you ! They went back into the living room and I sat on my bed crying ! I was going on a after school trip with my friends Esther free ! I couldn't wait to tell the girls !

As soon as I got to school the next day I ran to find the girls ! You won't believe this I can go to the youth center Friday night ! You're shitting me Becky said staring at me ! No I'm serious, Steven , Esther's boyfriend pleaded my case and she said yes ! We all screamed with excitement so loud that one of the teacher's walking through the halls said girls let's keep it down ! We giggled as he walked by. We'll talk at lunch we all agreed and I went to my first class ! I felt like I was gliding through the halls all day long ! I was going to be able to hang out with my friends ! I still couldn't believe it ! When I got home that afternoon from school I walked into the apartment and I could hear clanking coming from the kitchen ! I timidly walked down the hall and poked my head into the kitchen and saw Steven at the stove! I stood there in amazement ! Our stove rarely got turned on , and I can't remember ever coming home from school and seeing our kitchen so alive ! Steven turned around to dump a steaming pot of something in the sink and jumped when he saw me ! Addie you scared me I didn't know you were there ! I'm sorry I said said thinking I was in trouble ! It's ok no big deal. Yes I replied I love it ! Wanna help make the salad , I stood there in shock we were having pasta and salad ! Is this a dream ? I'm used to saltines and tea for supper ! Yes

I'll help make the salad I said in delight ! Ok go wash your hands and I'll get the stuff out of the fridge. I ran to the bathroom with excitement . I was going to have a real supper just like normal kids ! I went back into the kitchen and helped with the salad. Steven said sorry I cheat when It comes to sauce it's out of a jar! It smells great I said as it was warming in a pot on the stove. I heard the front door Esther was home. Please let her be in a good mood I thought . She walked into the kitchen and I held my breath . She looked around and said wow you cook to Steven and he said yep and Addie helped .

Esther hugged Steven from behind and turned to look at me with a cold icy stare in her fake voice she said that great . I quickly looked down at the floor. He said hey Addie you want to set the table? We only had two plates , did this mean I wasn't going to be able to eat ? Steven said I put my plates from my apartment in the cabinet I hope that ok . I set them on the table , he pulled open our silverware draw which usually had barley anything in it but now was jammed full of utensils ! Here you go he said as he handed me three forks . We all sat down to eat and it was delicious. He got up to put the leftovers in a container and Esther shot me another death look. I jumped up and said I'll do the dishes ! Oh that's ok Addie you go do your homework I got them. I stood there not moving, I could feel Esther's stare through the back of my head. Oh it's no problem , you cooked I can clean up. He turned to me and said now that I live here I can help out. Your a kid and I'm sure you have homework to do so go ahead. Thanks for helping me make supper.. When I turned around there was Esther looking at me like she wanted to eat my soul. I immediately looked down at the floor. Go ahead Addie and do your homework she said as she clenched the back of my neck squeezing it so hard I almost screamed ! I went into my room and for the first time I could ever remember was able to do my homework without doing hours of chores first !

That week every afternoon I came home from school there was Steven in the kitchen rattling pots making supper ! I found myself rushing home for the first time in my life. As I helped him with dinner's my mind went back to when he saw me tied to the bed and did nothing ! This Steven was so different from that one ! A part of me wanted to ask how could he have left me in that condition but a bigger part of me didn't want this to end. I wasn't getting beaten because Esther was never alone with me. Sure she would still shot me her death looks and occasionally pinch me , squeeze my neck or yank my hair but that was it ! I guess I had to let it go , maybe Steven was really high that day being he did smoke pot . I just can't imagine being that altered that seeing a child tied to a bed wouldn't make you spring into action but that's me. One thing that concerned me was that Esther was storing up rage ! It's a sick thing to say but she used her beating me almost like a workout ! Some of the worst beatings I got were when she hadn't beaten me for a day or two then she would unload on my like a craze animal. I made sure when she shot me her looks I always looked at the floor. I never tried to test her or forget that somehow someway she would find a way to get to me.

 The big day was here it was Friday and at five o'clock I would be getting on the bus the go to the youth center with my friends ! Now all I had to do was go home help with supper, and pray Esther didn't change her mind. Esther came home and I held my breath. What kind of mood was she in? Would she say I couldn't go? I couldn't believe it after supper she said go get washed up and we'll give you a rude to the school. I ran to the bathroom and stood there for a minute still not believing this was happening ! I washed really good and wished I had different clothes to wear but ... When I came out of the bathroom Esther was in the living room, Steven said here's two dollars buy yourself a soda or something. Oh I can't but thank you . Go ahead and take it it's ok. I looked down the hall to see if Esther was coming, I was to scared to take it . Thanks anyway I said. It's like he realized I was scared and put it back in his pocket. When he got to the living room he pulled it back out of his pocket and said like it was the first time here Addie here's some spending money . I froze ,Esther stared at me and finally said go ahead it's ok. I reached out and took the money and said thank you very much. Esther was standing behind Steven and glared at me. I made a decision right there that I wouldn't spend any of the money I would bring it home . That way Esther couldn't be mad at me.

We got to the school and the kids were all waiting on the steps for the bus. Right away I saw my friends ,Oh no what was Esther going to say when she saw Becky ? I felt sick I was told to stay away from her and there she was ! We got out of the car and all of a sudden I hear a woman say hey Esther how you doing ? She was a pretty woman with dark hair. Esther in her fake voice said hi Barbara I'm ok how about you? Doing good, this must be Addie I've been hearing so much about she said with a smile. I still had no idea who this woman was then Becky came over and said mom can I have a couple of dollars to play the games in the game room. Sure honey , she dug around in her purse and gave the money to Becky. So this was Becky's mom and she worked with Esther maybe things would work out. Barbara looked down at me and said the girls are so happy you're going tonight. I smiled and said I'm excited too . Barbara said Esther would it be ok if Addie came over one day after school to our house? Becky has the girls over just about everyday and they have a snack and do their homework. They stay at the house,I'm always there she said. No ! holy crap Esther's gonna flip out, grab me and drag me back to the car ! Sure Esther said let me know when ! What the hell , did she just say sure ? I spun around so quickly I must have drew attention to myself because everyone looked over at me. Oh no one of the rules is to never ever draw attention to yourself! I'm in so much trouble! The bus pulled up and I thought for sure I wouldn't be able to get on. We all got on the bus and the parents waved good bye to their kids including Esther ! Was this really happening ? Just like that we were on our way !

The bus ride to the youth center was more than I could ever imagine ! We all talked what seemed to be normal teen stuff but it was all new to me. Clothes ,make up and boys. I sat back and listened. I didn't care that I had nothing to contribute to the conversation I was just happy to be there with my friends. Becky opened her purse and pulled out some make up , Addie let me do you make up ! I knew if Esther even saw the smallest trace of make up on me I would never be able to leave the house again. No that's ok maybe next time I said. Ok Becky replied seeming to know the reason why . We got to the youth center and the chaperone said under no circumstances do you leave the building . We're leaving at nine sharp, don't make me have to come looking for you ! Everyone understand The bus erupted with a resounding yes and were all go off the bus! I was so excited my heart felt like it was going to pound out of my chest.

Once inside we decided to hit the game room first . Next the girls wanted to roller skate. I had never touched a pair of roller skates in my life . They all said come on you'll be fine I laced up my skate and stood up and as quick as I stood up I went down ! I sat there on the floor for a minute then got up. After falling more times than I could count I managed to stay on my feet. We skated to the blaring music which was accompanied by a light show and my heart soared ! This was what it was like to be a normal kid ! I may have to go back to Esther in a few hours but for right now I was free and I was going to enjoy every second of it ! Before we knew it it was time to go . That's when the depression became so real for me. I had a little taste of freedom now I had to go back to my prison I could feel the tears welling up in my eyes . I tried to choke them back but the flood gates opened.I quickly ran to the bathroom because I felt like such a baby! I knew I only had a few minutes before we had to get on the bus so I dried my eyes, got myself together and got on the bus with my friends.

On the ride home all the girls except for me and Becky feel asleep. Becky looked at me and said my mom knows! I spun around and looked at her and said your mom knows what ? Everything, she knows everything ! You told her ? I didn't know she already knew about Esther beating you ! I told you it's a small town and people talk ! She told me she's known for a long time now and when Esther came in for the interview word got out around town and so many people came up to her and said how can you work with that monster? I sat there with my mouth hanging open. My mother said she told them you get more flies wit honey than with vinegar ! My mom said she would act nice to Esther knowing you and me were friends so that you might be able to come over to my house and she could make sure your safe if only for a short time! I was speechless. Then I started to cry again. What's wrong Becky asked? Nothing these are happy tears, before you all I was alone now I have people who care and I've waited so long for this .

When I got back to the school Steven and Esther were there to pick me up. How was it he asked I downplayed everything because I knew if I said I had to much fun Esther wouldn't let me go again. It was fun was all I said. I was quiet the rest of the ride home. When we got home Esther said Steven got called into work tomorrow for overtime looks like it's just me and you until I have to go to work. I froze where I stood Steven said yeah I got the call tonight but I'll be home at three and we can make supper. There was Esther standing behind him with that look that I knew all to well. I was going to get a beating tomorrow I could just tell. She's been holding in her rage for over a week now and beating me would be her release! I'm really tired is it ok if I go to bed now I asked. Sure Esther said and the look she gave me sent chills down my spine ! She actually looked excited I know she was thinking about beating me ! I've seen that look to many times before to be mistaken !

Chapter 44

I went into my room , closed the door and started pacing back and forth I knew what would happen the minute Steven went to work! I laid in my bed that night to terrified to sleep ! finally drifted off to sleep only to be ripped from my bed in the morning by my hair! Esther's eyes were wild ! She started swinging me back and forth on the ground by my hair! What did I do I'm sorry I begged ! Shut the fuck up you piece of shit ! No I swear I didn't do anything. You and that little bitch friend think you can out smart me ? No we didn't do anything . I have to go along with you hanging out with that little fuck because I work with her mom and I need my job but just know your life will be hell because of it ! I won't hang out with her I'm sorry I pleaded ! To fucking late for that isn't it ! She yanked me up to my feet and then slammed me against the wall knocking the wind out of me. I dropped to the floor and crawled to the corner covering my head with my arms. Please I'm sorry , the room was silent . I peeked out from behind my arms and she had left the room! I could hear her in the kitchen filling the tea kettle ! I sat there in agony ! My back hurt when I breathed where I hit the wall. My head ached from having her drag me around by my hair ! I was terrified to move ! There I sat in the corner of the room in my all to familiar position knees to chest rocking back and forth .

As I sat there I heard her go about her day . She made herself breakfast , took a shower, walked past my room and looked right through me as if I didn't exist! She went into her room got dressed and left for work ! I slowly got up from the floor and went to the window to make sure she was walking up the street and she spun around and glared at my window ! The look on her face was that of pure evil ! I dropped to the floor! I waited a few minutes and timidly looked out the window again. I knew she had to be gone now if she intended on being at work on time. I peaked my head out of my room ,looking up and down the hallway. Even though I knew she was physically gone she was still in my head ! I went into the bathroom and looked at myself in the mirror . Every time I saw my reflection after a beating I recognized myself less and less ! The eyes staring back at me were those of a scared little girl. A girl that never knew a normal childhood . A girl that had so many fears . A girl that felt helpless and forgotten. I often had a dream I was screaming for help at the top of my lungs and no sound came out and no one came to save me !

I shook my self back to reality I had exactly two hours until Steven got home from work. In that time I had to perform the magic act I had perfected over the years of making the beating I just went through seem like it never happened. I showered, and gingerly put my hair up in a ponytail. My head throbbed but I managed to hide the spot where my head had tiny red blood dots from my hair being pulled out ! I got dressed and made some toast and tea. Now that Steven lived there Esther no longer rationed the food. After eating all I wanted to do was lay down. I knew I had to wash the dishes and tidy up the kitchen first . When I was done I went into my room and laid down . I just needed a few minutes to rest . I dozed off and when I woke up I could hear Steven in the kitchen making supper. I jumped up and ran to the kitchen. If Esther found out I was sleeping in the middle of the day and not helping with supper I would be in so much trouble !

Steve looked at me and said hey sleepy head ,how was your nap ? I'm sorry I didn't mean to fall asleep I replied ! I can help you now, what do you need done. Well I'll let you in on a little secret I know how to make about five things so tonight were dining on grilled cheese and tomato soup ! How's that sound ? It sounds amazing . I'll get the bowls. He looked at me and said you know you apologize to much. I'm sorry I don't mean to . I think you're owed a few apologies if you ask me and he looked at me and it was like I fully understood what he was trying to say. I think it was his way of apologizing for not doing anything when I was tied to the bed. I saw sincere remorse in his eyes. Sometimes adults do really stupid thing they wish they could take back . You know what I mean he asked? Well the way I figure if they are truly sorry and they act better the next time then I think they've become a better person. I hope you're right he replied. We just had a moment. I can forgive him because I feel he was genuinely sorry. All of a sudden I heard Esther coming in the front door. . You ok he asked? Yeah I'm fine looking around the kitchen making sure everything was in order.

Esther entered the kitchen and said wow something smells great ! She walked over and hugged Steven then said hi Addie how was your day ? What I felt like saying was well it was ok minus the part when you beat the crap out of me but what I said instead was it was good. We sat down and ate supper . I couldn't shake my headache and said I'll clean the dishes and then I'm going to go to bed. Oh that's ok Addie I'll get the dishes Steven said. Esther shot me a look. You cooked I'll wash the dishes. You two can go watch tv. Ok if you insist,goodnight in case I don't see you later. Good night I replied and started to clean the kitchen. They both started to go into the living room and Esther said I have to go to the bathroom I'll be right in. Ok I'll find something to watch on TV Steven said as he headed to the living room. Esther doubled back into the kitchen and grabbed me by the back of the neck. I saw you watching me out the window when I left for work still a sneaky little bitch huh ? No I'm sorry I won't do it again. Listen fuck face you better not ruin what I got going on here you hear me? We have food and can pay our bills since Steven's here you better not fuck it up she said as she slapped me in the back of the head. I won't I replied looking down at the floor. Finish the dishes and get your ass to bed.

I got done cleaning the kitchen turned the light off and went into the bathroom. . As I was walking to my room I could smell pot and incense coming from the living room.Maybe Esther would get so high she would pass out for the night and I could sleep. That's exactly what happened. I slept through the entire night . When I woke up I quietly went to the bathroom then back to my room. I got out my library book and laid on my bed reading. About and hour later Steven walked passed my room . You like eggs and toast he asked? Yes love them I replied. Ok give me a few minutes to shower and I'll start breakfast. I heard him go into the bathroom and like a puma Esther was in my room. He's only being nice to you because he has to she whispered to me. Don't think he gives a shit because he doesn't. Ok I replied. We want to do something today just the two of us say you have homework or some stupid kid thing . I don't want you tagging along got it. Yes I said looking at the floor. She tip toed back to her room and waited a few minutes after he came out of the bathroom and walked passed my room into the kitchen. Oh I didn't realize you were up already she lied as she said good morning to Steven. Wow she lied with such ease it was scary !

Chapter 45

As we were eating breakfast Steven said you up for a hike today Addie? I already knew what I was supposed to say. I have lots of homework to do maybe next time. Ok maybe next time he said and Esther went to get ready. They said good bye and I was happy to have the apartment to myself. I knew better than to just hang out without cleaning first . After I got the cleaning out of the way I took a bath. Now that Steven lived with us we had honest to goodness real soap and shampoo it wash heaven ! I remember the first bath I took with "real " soap I was so dirty I actually left a ring of filth around the bathtub when I let the water out ! We had a old claw foot tub . I ran the water nice and hot and sank into it letting the water soothe me. I grabbed the shampoo and lathered up my hair making sure to get it nice and clean.I sank down into the tub laying flat on the bottom rinsing the shampoo out of my hair and listing to the complete silence. I got a wash cloth and washed every square inch of my body. It felt amazing actually using soap and getting clean. As I stepped out of the tub I thought as soon as I'm legally allowed to leave I will get a job and a apartment . I will take nice long warm baths and I will have large cozy towels to dry off with . I got dressed then got my library book out and started reading.

 I loved reading I used my imagination to take me away from my world and pretend I was a character in the story . Reading was very soothing to me . If Esther wasn't around and the apartment was calm I usually drifted off to sleep. I'm not sure how long I was sleeping but I woke up when I heard the front door open. I quickly jumped up and got my school books out to make it look like I was doing homework . Esther came passed my room and said in her fake voice we're back as she glared at me. Joe walked passed my room door carrying grocery bags. I hope you're hungry I'm making burgers and fries for supper. That sounds wonderful I replied . Do you need any help? Sure come on in the kitchen and I'll give you something to do. I went onto the kitchen and Steven said as his back was to us it's so nice that you always want to help. Esther said with her fake voice that's my Addie as she pinched me so hard on the back of my arm it brought tears to my eyes !

Have you ever had a California burger he asked ? No I replied . Do you like lettuce , tomato and mayo ? Yes , yes and yes I replied. Ok he laughed can you cut the tomato when I make the burgers ? Yes I can and I got to work. Esther got the fries out and put them on a cookie sheet in the oven. This was a first , making a meal all three of us in the kitchen working together it was almost normal. Then Esther grabbed the back of my neck and squeezed it when Steven was at the stove frying the burgers. Are you finished all your homework yet Addie? well there it was normal moment over as I knew to make my exit out of the kitchen !

After we ate supper I stacked the plates in the sink and wiped the table. You going to youth center this Friday Steven asked me? Right away my stomach hurt ! I don't think so I replied , remembering the beating I got just the day before for hanging with Becky ! Why not he asked me ? You are a kid you should be hanging out with friends not home all the time . Esther chimed in with I think you should go ! You're only young once , right ? Ok she is definitely bat shit crazy ! I sat there frozen not knowing the right answer ! I knew Esther was baiting me to say yeah sure I'll go so she would have a reason to beat the crap out of me when Steven wasn't around for going. Esther said well then it's decided you'll go ! With my head down I replied ok. I'll wash the dishes I said and both Steven and Esther agreed . Ok thanks Steven said ,we'll be in the living room if you want to come watch tv. I could feel Esther's eye's burning a hole through my head as she stood behind me . No thanks but I'm in the middle of a book I got at the library and I think I'll go in my room and finish it so I can check another one out on Tuesday. Ok then see you in the morning he said . Ok see you in the morning I replied as they both walked down the hall toward the living room. I washed the dishes and made sure the kitchen was in order , went to the bathroom and went onto my room. I closed the door and sat on my bed.

So this is how it was going to be. Esther would agree I should go to the youth center then beat me for going ! Well if nothing else she was consistent, consistently crazy ! I was so excited to go to the youth center on Friday no I was dreading it . I knew the whole time I was there I would be thinking of the beating I was going to get as soon as Steven wasn't around. That was Esther's sick plan. She'd fix me for wanting to hang out with friends. She would get in my head so that I couldn't even enjoy my time out then in her demented mind she would feel justified in having a reason for beating the crap out of me !

Monday morning at school the girls were so excited that I was aloud to go to the youth center again. I smiled along with them thinking of what was waiting for me when Esther got her chance to pounce on me ! That Friday came and off we all went to the center. I tried to have a good time I really did but all the time all I thought about was my next beating ! I was so tired , so worn out from all the pain ! On the ride home Becky said ok what's up ? Nothing I said with my fake smile! Listen you might be able to fool other people but not me so let's hear it. I sat there for a minute and debated on weather I should tell her what Esther had planned for me and I decided to tell her !

After I was done she had this look of rage on her face ! Ok what the hell Addie , this shit has to stop ! I know I agreed but what do I do I asked ? You stand up for your God damn self that's what you do she said in a voice loud enough to make some of the kids on the bus look our way ! Becky I'm not strong like you ! You don't understand how evil she is ! She's only evil because you take it she replied ! Stop letting her shit on you ! Oh how I wish I had half the fight Becky had ! I was beaten into submission so many times that I was weak ! You need to stop letting her do this do you understand Becky asked ? Yes please don't say anything to anyone including your mother I begged ! You know you can always trust me, but know if she does this again I'll tell her exactly what I think of her and let her know that I will tell anyone with ears what a piece of shit she really is ! Becky please no don't ! If you do that she'll make us move again ! Fine but you need to stand up to her you hear me ? Yes was all I said. We pulled up to the school and all the parents were there . We stood to get off the bus and Becky looked at Esther and turned to me and said look at that Son of Bitch standing there like mother of the year ! Becky please I begged ! Yeah I know ,

I won't say anything. Becky got off the bus and went right up to her mom and gave her a hug. I love you mom she said ! Her mom had tears in her eye and replied I love you to honey ! I got in the car with Steven and Esther and went home.

As soon as we got home I asked Steven if he had to work overtime the next day . To my relief he had off !! I was elated, that meant I could sleep in peace tonight because Esther couldn't beat me when he was home ! I got home and said my good nights and went to bed. I wonder if Steven knew every night he went to sleep with the devil laying right beside him !I hugged my blanket close to me and drifted off to sleep . Monday rolled around and I went off to school. When I go there Becky asked well what happened? Nothing Steven didn't have to work so I was safe .

Chapter 46

One of our teachers made a announcement before class that he was chartering a bus and planning a trip to Disneyland when school let out for summer break . He handed out fliers with all the info and said the first thirty kids to pay and have permission slips signed could go . The class was buzzing with excitement. I folded the paper and stuck it in the back of my textbook. There was no chance I would ever show this to Esther. Everyday another kid would bring their money in for the trip and the teacher would give us a countdown of how many spots were still open. .There were two spots left four days before the trip deadline and the teacher said Addie I still don't have you permission slip for the trip. I looked up from my desk knowing he must be mistaken. Timidly I said I'm not going on the trip. Yes you are your parents already paid. I sat there confused! I walked up to the desk and quietly said I think you have me mixed up with someone else I'm not going on the trip. Addie I think your confused your mother Esther paid and your going. I literally had to hold onto the desk because I felt like I was going to fall over ! Here's another permission slip have it signed before the end of the week. Ok I said still in denial as I walked back to my seat !

When I got home that afternoon Steven was cooking in the kitchen. I debated on asking him about the Disney trip but decided to wait until Esther got home and ask them together. That night when we were eating supper I gathered my nerve and said Um did you pay for a trip to Disney my teacher was running ? They both looked up and said yes ! I was in such shock I dropped my fork ! I can go , to Disneyland I asked? Disneyland in Florida I said? Yes they both replied ! I started crying ! What's the matter Addie , Steven asked , don't you want to go ? Oh yes I want to go so bad I replied ! How did you even find out about the trip I asked ? I never brought home the trip info. That's not important he said but you're going ! Thank you , Thank you I kept saying over and over with so much excitement I started to cry again. I looked past Steven to see Esther's expression and she was giving me her cold stare ! I immediately thought this must be one of her sick tricks !

School let out and I passed seventh grade with four B's and one high C. I was very proud of myself! The day of the trip was in two days ! Steven said to me at supper we have to take you shopping for a few things to take on your trip . Oh thank you but I don't need anything I can use what I already have. We'll just get you a couple of pair of shorts , t shirts , a bathing suit and toiletries. What are toiletries I asked. Like shampoo, deodorant and toothpaste. Oh that will be to much money I replied. I can go without them. Nonsense, we'll get the travel sizes they are all cheap. Thank you so much I said as I stood up and hugged Steven. I jumped back as soon as I hugged him ! I'm sorry I said ! Sorry for what he asked ? I just stood there not knowing what to say ! We didn't hug in our house and I thought I crossed the line. You're fine Addie stop apologizing all the time for things you shouldn't ok I'm sorry I said then laughed. It was habit I was alway apologizing. Esther gave me her icy stare. I'll do the dishes and clean the apartment the whole summer to pay you both back for letting me go. That's not necessary Addie.

I'll make up a chore list and stick to it all summer I replied. Ok if that's what you want he said.

The next day we went to a store a real store not a salvation army for my clothes for the trip. Then we went to a drug store for my toiletries! I couldn't believe it I was really going ! I was going to be free of Esther for a entire week but why did I keep thinking somehow Esther would ruin it for me? Steven came passed my room the day before the trip and said here's a duffel bag so you can pack for the trip ! Sorry it's not a new one but it will work just the same he said. It's a great bag thank you. Do you need help packing he asked ? No, I can do it but thank you. He left the room and I had my new clothes folded on the bed. I got four pair of short and four t shirts, one sweatshirt and one pair of jeans and my first ever bathing suit! I got underwear and my sneakers out of my closet and laid everything out on the bed. I would have to wear a couple outfits more than once because I would be gone for seven day but who cares. I've wore my clothes over and over my whole life now I had options! I dumped the bag of toiletries on my bed. My first ever deodorant ,I was so excited ! A travel bar of soap and shampoo ! I packed my clothes and toiletries in the bag Steven had given me and stood back and looked at it. I still couldn't believe this was happening ! I sat on my bed and started crying ! Maybe just maybe my life was going to change!

Esther walked passed my room and I jumped off my bed. I knew she hated me sitting around . I looked at her and said I'll go clean up the kitchen and bathroom and ran passed her to start. She said nothing just gave her usual I'll eat you heart for dinner stare ! I cleaned the kitchen and was moving on the clean the bathroom . Steven said sit down and take a break , the bathroom isn't going anywhere ! Esther came up the hallway behind him and gave me a look which I knew meant get your ass in gear! I said that's ok I like to clean and besides I want to do it to pay you both back for letting me go on my trip ! Steven said that really isn't necessary, you do so much around here your just a kid! He turned to walk toward the living room and jumped when he saw Esther right behind him ! I thought to myself yeah I totally get it she freaks me out too ! I giggled to myself ! Damn Esther you always seem to sneak up on me he said ! I thought tread lightly Steven you don't want to make her mad ! Esther smiled and said I just wanted to see what we're doing for supper.

As we ate supper that night Esther and Steven said now stay with your teacher,never go anywhere alone, and be polite . I will I replied. Steven said we got you this fanny pack to take with you . Your meals are included but were giving your teacher a little spending money for you to buy a few small things. You can wear it in the park if you want soda or snack money. I don't need any extra money but thank you I replied. It's not much and if you don't use it you can always bring it home Steven said with a smile. There was no way I was spending that money I appreciated being able to go more than he would ever know. I would definitely bring the money home.

The day of the trip was finally here ! I couldn't shake the feeling that Esther was going to stop me from going ! As I laid there in my bed I could hear movement in the kitchen. I got out of bed and stood by my bedroom door trying to hear if it was Steven or Esther in the kitchen. I could smell food cooking so I knew it had to be Steven! I tip toed out of my room and up the hallway to the kitchen and saw it was indeed Steven, I was so releaved ! Hey there you ready for your big day he asked me ? Yes I'm so excited ! You go get a shower and get dressed I'm making breakfast . I looked toward the hallway and he seemed to sense what I was thinking . Your mother isn't up yet I let her sleep in. I ran to my room and got my clothes and towel and took a shower. As soon as I got out of the shower I could hear Esther in the kitchen ! My heart sank ! I got dressed and stood by the closed bathroom door listening to what she was saying to Steven trying to gauge what kind of mood she was in. All of a sudden I heard her say Addie let's go you're going to be late ! I prayed please just let me get on that bus and get the heck out of here as I walked out of the bathroom !

After breakfast Esther said to me come on I'll double check your bag and make sure you have everything ! There it was her chance to get me alone ! I walked behind her to my room Steven was cleaning up the kitchen. Sure enough as soon as she got me alone she grabbed me by the back of the neck and squeezed hard. Listen you little bitch you better appreciate this trip and know that when you get home you better clean this apartment every single day till it's spotless got it ? Yes I replied ! Don't think for one second that I still don't own you she hissed into my ear ! As she heard Steven coming down the hallway she released me from her grip and hurried over to the bag which was on the bed. She opened it pretending to take inventory of it's contents. Looks like you got everything, you ready to go she asked? Yes I said as I grabbed my bag and we were off .

When I got there there were some kids already there with their parents. Steven went over to my teacher who was running the trip and handed him a envelope, I'm guessing with my spending money in it. As I looked around I recognized some of the kids but didn't really know them. What if I got bullied ? I could handle it I was going to Disney and I would be Esther free for seven whole days ! Steven came back over to us and said it won't be long now ! Have a wonderful time ! Thank you again for letting me go I said looking in their direction but more so at Steven ! Esther glared down at me and with her fake voice said

Have a great time honey ! The bus arrived and the teacher said time to go everyone. All the parents hugged there kids and said good bye and I held my breath still terrified that Esther would pull a Esther and at the last minute say I couldn't go . I grabbed my bag from the ground and said ok see you when I get back. I walked toward the bus and could feel Esther stare piercing my back ! Just keep walking I told myself, just keep walking you're almost on the bus ! At one point I picked up the pace so much I was almost running ! My Teacher said slow down there's a seat for everyone ! I'm sorry I replied ! He stuck his head on the bus and said pick a seat and sit down to everyone. I picked a seat on the opposite side of where Esther was standing . Come on I said to myself hurry up everyone get on the bus let's get out of here ! When the kids were all on the teacher gave us the rules ! No running around the bus , No screaming, you're responsible for your own stuff you have on the bus so keep it with you ! He told us it would take about fifteen hours to get to Disney and that we would stop half way for something to eat. You're all in seventh grade now let's act like ! Now wave good bye to your parents were going to leave ! Go please just go I thought ! I looked over where Steven and Esther were standing and they were gone !

Did she leave ? Could it be possible I Was really going ? Then I sat down in my seat with such a feeling of peace and relief until I looked out my window and jumped in horror ! Esther and Steven had walked around the bus to the side I was on so they could wave good bye ! Steven was waving like he was in a parade all happy and smiles and Esther held her hand up and glared at me . I waved timidly and thought let's get the hell out of here ! The bus started to pull out , here we go the teacher said and my heart leaped with joy ! I turned and watched as Esther faded further and further away ! Oh what a feeling of complete joy and yet a feeling of fear ! I was so thrilled to be on the bus but a small part of me couldn't help but think Esther's just crazy enough to follow the bus, make it stop and rip me off of it . I sat there looking out the window as the miles passed , get me as far away from her as possible !

About an hour into the bus ride our teacher said ok you're going to be four to a room in the hotel when we get there . Listen up to who you'll be rooming with ! Oh my God , I never thought this far ahead, I have to sleep with other people in the room. People I don't know ! No one's going to want to room with the smelly kid ! Since Steven moved in we've had soap and shampoo and I've not had the odor problem but my past is well known. Before he read off the list he said and no switching rooms ! I will check every room every night and God help the person who I find in the wrong room ! He started reading off the list and I waited for my name to be called with a pain in my stomach ! He called my name with three other girls I

vaguely knew from school . I waited for the protest of I'm
not sharing a room with the stinky girl but heard nothing
! I had visions of them locking me out of the room or
making me sleep on the floor ! I wouldn't let it ruin my
trip !

A few minutes passed and a girl came up to me and said
hey your sharing a room with us as she pointed to the girls
all sitting together on the bus . Want to sit with is for the
rest of the way ? I just stared at her > I had a very hard
time with trust and thought that she was doing this to
play some kind of trick on me . Hello she said laughing ,
you want to sit with us she asked again? Timidly I said yes
thank you and walked back to where the other girls were
sitting. They all introduced themselves . There was Lori,
she was the girl who asked me to sit with them, Cindy ,
Brenda and Megan. Lori looked at me and said I'm friends
with Becky ! I stared at her ! Did Becky tell her my past I
wondered? Anyone gives you any crap you tell me ! Was
this happening ? Were thee girls befriending me ? They all
started talking about what they were going to do when
we got to Disney. I sat and listened with such joy ! Lori
said Addie chime in , what do you want to do when we get
there ? I'm fine with anything I replied ! Nope she said we
all have to have input. I sat there I'd never been on a trip
so I had no idea what to say . They started including me in
the conversation and I was so nervous my hands started
to sweat ! I was trying to respond but was so afraid I

would say the wrong thing I almost couldn't speak ! Lori looked at me and said listen everyone here's cool feel free to jump in . so I slowly started to be part of the planning !

We stopped about three hours into the trip to stretch our legs and the teacher said come over and get your hoagie and drink. I didn't want to spend the money I was given so I hung back and Lori said come on Addie. I reluctantly walked over to the teacher and said excuse me Steven gave you my money can you take it out of that for the hoagie? The teacher said me and my wife paid for the hoagies they're free he laughed. Oh ok thank you I said as I took the hoagie and drink. I went over to the picnic table to join the girls. We ate and planned more for what we were going to do on our trip . We all went to use the bathrooms before we got back o the bus . We all went in and after everyone washed their hands they all stood in front of the mirror applying lip gloss and brushing their hair. I stood back and watched them . I watched how they talked to each other smiling , applied their lip gloss, flipped their heads upside down and brushed their hair. They were all naturally confident, pretty girls. Lori looked at me and said do you need to get in here to apply your gloss ? No that's ok I replied, knowing I didn't have any. Come on get in here, she pulled me up to the mirror. I stood there starting to panic , here use mine she said as she handed me her lip gloss. oh that's ok I said , don't be a dork here take it Lori said. I took it in my shaking hand and tried to apply it. I was so nervous I almost missed my mouth. Here like this she said as the other girl continued to groom themselves. Now do this she said as she sucked her lips in and rubbed them together . I did as she did and she said look how pretty you look and spun me around facing the mirror. Pretty was never a word that anyone had ever used in describing me . Tears came to my eyes as I looked at my reflection. Lori looked at the other girls and said hey we'll meet you out there in a minute.

The other girls went back outside and she turned to me and said listen please don't be made at Becky but she told me your story. I think you are one of the strongest kids I've ever met and you got dealt a shit hand as far as your home life ! I just stood there not knowing what to say ! Becky asked me to look out for you on this trip and that's what I'm gonna do ok? I shook my head yes and she said we better get back out there before the teacher flips on us . I wiped my face and headed back outside with her. So nice of you girls to join us the teacher said as we got on the bus , we giggled and took our seats. He said I'm going to call your name answer when I do. After he took roll we were on our way. The teacher and his wife sat in the front of the bus and every once in awhile would say ok keep it down when the volume got to loud.This time we drove for a longer time. Finally we got out at another roadside rest and the teacher said come on over and get your mac and cheese and drinks . When your done use the bathroom and get back on the bus. We all did as we were told and we were off again !

By this time we were all tired . Most of us fell asleep. we awoke with the teacher yelling we're here ! My heart just about burst trying to take everything in. Never have I seen so many colors . The trees were so different and boy was it hot ! Our teacher said now we're going inside the hotel lobby , you represent our school so don't act like fools ! We all filed off the bus and the excitement level was over the top ! We were all small town kids and this was Disney world ! We waited in a group until our teacher and his wife came back with our hotel room keys. Here's how it's going to work he said. Everyone grab your bags , find your rooms and rest for one hour. Everyone moaned, the teacher shut it down immediately, cut the crap and listen he continued. After the hour is up I will come to every room and tell you your instructions for the day . Do not leave until I talk to your group personally understood ? Yes we all replied and went on the hunt for our rooms. We found ours right away and Lori said four to room two beds me and Addie will take one bed and you two can take the other is that ok? Sure Cindy said. We all unpacked and took turns taking a shower. There was a knock on the door. It was our teacher, he said ok here's the deal your going to be in eighth grade in September so I'm allowing everyone to go with their friends. Stay with a buddy, never ever go anywhere alone ! Be back at the hotel at eight p.m. sharp ! Don't make me regret giving you all freedom ! We all looked at each other giddy with excitement. Now go have fun he said and went on to the next room !

I couldn't believe it he was setting us loose in Disneyland with no adult supervision ! Oh Esther would freak if she knew this ! Lori kind of assumed the leader role in the group . Ok guys do we want to all stick together or break off into pairs. I stood there thinking oh please someone come with me ! Brenda said I'm good with going all four of us together ,Cindy agree,Lori said that's got my vote and I was thrilled I said sounds great to me . We grabbed our hotel key and we were off ! I can honestly say I had never been more excited in my life ! We were all so amazed at the sights, the characters and the huge volume of tourist ! Lori had a disposable camera and we took pictures with the characters , and of each other on rides and walked until our feet hurt. Our first day went by so quickly. It was time to report back to the hotel. We went back to our room and waited for our teacher to take roll. Ok girls you're free to roam the hotel until eleven then back to your room. Under no circumstances do you leave this hotel tonight ! Ok we all said as we left to go get something to eat. Our stay included two meals a day from the hotel cafe . We were all starving ! We ate and talked about what we were going to do the next day. At one point I just sat back and watched the girls interact. Was this my life now ? When I returned home would I have more freedom ? You know what I would deal with that when I got home for now I would enjoy every second !

That night as I laid there in bed I started worrying as I always did at night. I finally dozed off and woke up to Lori shaking me ! I jumped up in the bed grabbing the sheet ! What's wrong I asked ? You were screaming in your sleep are you ok ? I'm sorry I didn't realize I was . Don't apologize I just wanted to make sure you were ok . I'm fine thanks, sorry if I woke you up ! You apologize to much Addie you need to stop that . It was a hard habi t to break . we better get some sleep so we're not tired in the morning . Ok Lori said as long as you're ok. I'm good thanks I replied and we both laid down and went back to sleep.

The next morning we all got showers and waited for our teacher to take role. It was eight in the morning. He said ok girls go have breakfast and see you back here at eight p.m. ! We all just looked at each other ! He was giving us the entire day this time to roam the park ! We grabbed our key and we were off ! We came back to the room about two in the afternoon to take a nap ! We were exhausted ! About and hour later we were off again. This went on until the night before our last day there. Somehow we had gotten lost in one of the parks and didn't make it back in time for curfew ! We got back to our room at eight forty five and our teacher was furious ! Where were you girls he screamed ? We got lost , were sorry we told him ! I don't want to hear sorry get something to eat and back to this room ,you have thirty minutes ! When you get back you all are to stay in this room all night and not leave he said as he slammed the door to our room. We all knew we screwed up but we honestly did get lost. We hurried and got something to eat and went back to our room. We watched tv and hung out for the rest of the night before going to sleep ! Tomorrow would be our last day here and we wanted to enjoy every second of it ! Before we knew it it was time to pack and get back on the bus ! I didn't want to go home but what choice did I have. We were all sad to be leaving ! Disney is definitely the happiest place on earth and I would carry the memories of this trip with me forever !

Depression started to set in the closer we got to home! A lot of the kids were sleeping on the bus but I couldn't stop thinking what I was going back to! The mere thought of Esther made me feel like I had to get sick I put my head against the cool bus window and watched the trees go by each one bringing me closer to my life of constant fear. Lori was sleeping in the seat next to me and I wasn't aware she woke up . You ok she asked ? Yeah I'm good thanks. In a low voice she said you know you can report your mother for all that's she's done ! If only it was that easy I thought ! You don't know my mother I said sadly !

No one wins against her , I've seen it over and over again. Just when I she's gonna get caught or someone is going to figure out what a monster she is nothing happens. It's almost like she's above the law ! She's crazy like a fox ! She knows just what to say, just how to act to get the attention off of her and I'm back to square one ! There has to be something you can do , she has to be stopped ! I shook my head and leaned back on the window. We got to our first roadside rest stop , got out got something to eat and went to the restrooms. As soon as I got in the stall and closed the door burst into tears ! I dreaded going back so much that I almost told my teacher what was going on then I thought back to all the times I was going to say something and I could hear Esther's voice in my head ! Go ahead say something no one will help you and when they leave I'll beat the shit out of you !

As the bus was pulling into our small town I felt sick. I started to shake and feel nauseous. We rolled into our school parking lot and all of the parents were there waiting to welcome their kids back. I scanned the lot and I saw Esther and Steven ! My eyes locked with hers and my insides started to shake. The teacher said make sure you grab all your stuff and I hope you all had a great trip ! We filed off the bus and I hung back and watched parents hug their kids and didn't want to move because the minute I went over to Esther I was officially back . I took a few steps and Lori came over and hugged me. When she did she whispered in my ear are you sure you don't want to tell someone. Yes I replied and she squeezed my hand and went back to her parents. Esther and Steven walked over to me and he said welcome back . Did you have a great time ? Yes it was amazing. Esther hung behind him as she always, she glared at me and if looks could kill my life would have ended in that very moment ! My teacher came over and handed Steven the envelope with spending money he had given me . I asked Addie a couple of times if she wanted any of her spending money but she said no so here it is. Ok thank Steven replied. See you in school in September Addie he said . See you I replied as I walked back to the car with Esther and Steven.

Chapter 47

Tell us all about it Steven said. I talked about the hotel, the parks , but left out the part about all the freedom we had roaming the parks everyday. As we pulled up to our apartment a sadness fell over me that was almost crippling . I grabbed my bag and went in. You hungry at all Steven asked? No thanks we stopped on the way home and ate. Is it ok if I go unpack ? Sure when your done come on out into the living room we have something to tell you. My head shot in their direction. I can wait to unpack if you like . No that's ok we can talk when your done Esther said. I walked to my room with a knot on the pit of my stomach ! Oh please don't let them tell me we're moving ! I can take just about anything except that ! I quickly unpacked and put all my dirty clothes in a pile on my bed until we went to the laundromat and went to the living room.

Come on over and sit down Steven said. I waited to hear what was going on. When you were gone he said we had a lot of time to talk and , he stopped and looked at Esther, Well I'll just say it, We would like to get married ! We wanted to talk to you first and make sure you were ok with it. I was in shock ! Married was he insane ? Did he realize he was marrying the devil ? Then I thought if they married he would be here all the time and Esther wouldn't ave a chance to beat me . That sounds wonderful I replied ! Oh I'm so glad you're ok with it he said ! Will we be staying here . I mean are we going to have to move ? No not for now , this apartment is close to my and your mother's work and your school so we'll be staying. I breathed a sigh of relief, I think it's a wonderful idea. I know without saying Steven has been trying to make up for that day that he did nothing when I was tied to the bed. I'm not sure what made him not react or how he didn't realize that a sane person wouldn't tie their child to a bed but he had been nothing but kind to me since so I was trying to just let it go.

While I was gone Esther was switched back to day shift at work . She and Steve had talked about it many times at supper and he said are you able to get day shift so our schedules would be more compatible ? Esther said she would look into it and I guess they worked it out because the day after I got home from Disney both she and Steven left together in the morning to go to work ! I was in heaven ! With the two of them being on the same shift there wasn't a time Esther was alone with me! I kept my promise and cleaned every day to repay them for letting me go on my trip. I would turn on the music and clean and think about what a great time I had on my vacation ! The night were usually the same . Steven would pick up Esther from work and we would make supper together . This went on for about two weeks and every once in awhile I would catch Esther glaring at me so intently I would have to look away. Then one day Steven had to go out of town to see his family and I knew this was the window Esther had been waiting for.

Steven said his good byes and left and Esther pounced on me like a rabid dog ! She grabbed me by the hair and said oh you don't know how long I've been waiting for this ! She started shaking me back and forth by my hair and hissing so fuck face, that being her pet name for me , did you have a good time at Disney ? Little fucking Princess thinks she deserves a vacation ! No I'm sorry I thought you wanted me to go I'm sorry ! Oh you will be she hissed !

With that she started punching and slapping me with such rage that I dropped to the floor and crawled to the corner of the living room ! Get the fuck up you pussy she screamed at me ! I didn't move ! Bitch you better get the fuck up when I tell you to ! I slowly stood up only to be knocked to the floor again. Get up she shrieked ! I stood up this time she took both her hands and pushed me into the wall knocking the wind out of me ! I fell to the floor trying to catch my breath ! Just remember just because he's here doesn't mean I won't get my hands on you ! He has to leave sometime and when he does your ass is mine Got it ? Yes I said , looking down. I have to get ready for work . Get your ass up and start cleaning ! I did as I was told.

When Esther left for work I laid on my bed and cried ! When in the hell would this stop ! I had to find the strength to stand up to her ! I wouldn't deal with this anymore ! I got a shower and started cleaning. About and hour later there was a knock on the door. I froze , we never got company. I peeked own the hallway and there was another knock this time it was louder ! I crept down the hallway and peeked out the living room curtain and couldn't believe my eyes it was Becky and Lori !

I wasn't allowed to open the door for anyone when Esther was gone. Becky said Addie I know your in there and I know Esther is at work . Open the door please . I stood there debating what to do then Becky said we're not leaving until we talk to you ! I went over and cracked the door open just wide enough to see out and said I'm not aloud to open the door when Esther isn't here ! Becky said Addie please open the door I just want to make sure you're ok ! I'm ok I replied . Addie open the God damn door before I kick it in ! I opened the door and Becky pulled me into a hug . Are you ok ? Yes I'm fine . Lori hugged me and I winced . What's wrong she said nothing I'm fine . Addie you're not fine what's wrong ? Did that son of a bitch hit you again ? Turn around she said ! Why I asked just turn around . I did and Becky lifted my shirt ! Hey what are you doing I protested ? That bitch Becky said as Lori gasped ! I swung back around facing them ! You have marks all over your back ! I'm fine it wasn't bad I said ! Are you fucking kidding me you're defending her Becky screamed ? No I'm not I replied and please keep your voice down if the neighbors hear you they'll say something to Esther ! well for fuck's sake Addie someone should say something to that bitch ! Becky please keep your voice down !

Lori stood there with tears in her eyes and I found myself consoling her. It will be ok Lori don't cry ! Lori looked at me with such pity that I couldn't stand it ! You two have to go if Esther finds out you were here I'll be in so much trouble ! I feel like walking right into the restaurant and calling Esther out for the piece of shit she is Becky said enraged ! Please don't say anything ! She and Steven are getting married and things should get better I said ! Yeah things look real good now don't they Becky asked with disgust ? I'm doing the best I can , I said as I started to cry ! Lori hugged me and said we 're just worried about you Addie that's all . I know and you'll never know what you girls mean to me ! There are times you're the only thing that keeps me going ! Just give me a little more time and I swear I'll work it out. Ok Becky said hugging me , you better or I'm gonna let the world know exactly what a evil bitch Esther really is ! They left and as I walked back into the apartment I knew I had to figure this out ! I wasn't put on this earth to be Esther's personal punching bag. One way or another I would put a stop to her taking all her rage out on me !

Steven came back from visiting his family and was oblivious to the beating I got when he was gone ! mean how would he have any idea it happened ? Esther had become a expert at hitting me only where the wounds would be covered now that I was school age and people would figure out my truth ! The summer went on with both of them leaving and getting home the same time from work . Esther still got her rage out on me but it was only when Steven ran to the store or was in the shower so they weren't full on beatings they were like mini beatings. Funny what you are grateful for ! Soon school would be starting and I'd be in the eighth grade and be able to see my friends ! I couldn't wait !

Chapter 48

About a week before school started Steven said you have to go shopping for school clothes . Oh that's ok I 'm good I don't need anything . You wear the same thing all the time ! We'll take you to the store and get you a couple of outfits. I can go to the salvation army and get some stuff cheaper. No we'll take you to a real store and get you some stuff . Esther said thank you Steven that would be very nice. Thank you so much I'll take very good care of the clothes. I know you will . We'll go tomorrow morning. We got to the store and he said go pick five tops and three pair of jeans. Oh I don't need that many things. Get on now go pick them out. I looked at all the prices of the shirts and picked the cheapest ones . Then I went over to the jeans and did the same .Next he took me to the shoe department and got me a pair of sneakers. I couldn't believe all the stuff I got ! When we got home Esther said go hang up your new clothes and we'll get supper ready .

I laid all my new clothes on the bed and stared at them ! They were beautiful ! I couldn't believe they were mine ! I picked out what I was going to wear the first day of school and folded together and paired the other items into outfits. Now that Steven lived here we went to the laundromat to wash our clothes instead of washing them in the bathtub. Steven used fancy detergent and fabric softener which made our clothes smell amazing. It was official when I went back to school I wouldn't be the smelly kid anymore. The first day of school was here I was so excited to see my friends and wear my new clothes. All I had to do was avoid Esther as long as I could so I could get out the door without her saying some God awful thing to me that would just make me insecure. I took a shower and put on my new clothes. I brushed my hair and decided to wear it up in a ponytail. I looked at myself in the mirror and all I could hear in my head was Esther laughing and saying no matter how long you look you'll still be ugly! I knew I wasn't a pretty girl but I swore to myself everyday I would be the nice girl! I would always remember what it feels like to be put down,picked on and made to feel worthless ! I would always fight for the underdog and be kind. I walked out of the bathroom and Steven said well look at you , you look great ! Thank you I said as Esther stood glaring at me behind him. I shot my head down looking at the floor . All I wanted was to get out the door and catch the bus to school.

When I got to the bus stop I stood by myself avoiding the cliques . Only a few short minutes and I would be with my friends. The bus finally arrived and I waited for everyone to get on . The cool kids sat in the back of the bus and the rest of the kids filled in the seats remaining. I sat in the front of the bus with the kids that were basically the "leftovers" . We didn't fit in the popular, jocks or preps groups . We finally got to school and right away I saw Becky ! What a sight for sore eyes ! She came right over to me and gave me a hug . Look at you girl , you look great ! Thanks so do you I replied. How was the rest of your summer I asked her ? Fine how are you doing ? Better things seem to be calming down . That's fantastic Addie ! Well let's get inside , being eighth graders we run the school this year ! I don't want to miss a second of it ! We both went to homeroom where they announced there would be a brief assembly in the gym first thing this morning. We all groaned knowing how boring the assembles were but we had no choice so off we went to the gym.

When we got there the principle said everyone stand against the walls please do not take a seat. Ok this was new what was going on? He then instructed all fouth graders to take a seat in the back rows. The followed with the fifth graders in front of them , then sixth , then seventh. He then said all eighth graders you take the front rows you've earned them . There was hooting from all us eight graders as we took our seats ! Now as eight graders you're responsibility is to remember how it felt being the fourth grader coming to a new school and be kind to your underclassmen ! I don't want to see any bullying ! There will be a zero tolerance for it ! Everyone got that . we all responded and he shared a few things that would be happening this school year and dismissed us. As soon as we got out of assembly Becky said oh go figure as soon as we become eight graders they implement the zero tolerance rule ! Where the hell was it when we were fourth graders ? Well I have to be a little mean to a couple of the underclassmen just to keep them in line. I turned to her and said Becky you're one of the kindest people I know you couldn't be mean even if you tried. She looked at me and smiled bumping me with her hip . Come on lets get to first period.

On the way we had to pass Mr Harris's class ! The sight of the room brought back so many horrible memories of how he unmercifully bullied me. Maybe the principle should have that zero tolerance talk with him so no other poor student will have to endure his humiliation ! He had two doors to his room ,one at the front of the room and one at the rear. As we walked by my hands started to sweat. We got to the door at the front of the room and there he was standing so smug in the hallway looking down his nose at all the students. I put my head down just wanting to get passed him before he saw me and Becky said don't you dare ! You hold your head up and walk past him like he never had any affect on you at all ! You hear me she said? I knew she was right and I had to reclaim my dignity. I raised my head and walked right passed him ! I gave him a side glance and out of the corner of my eye I saw him recognize me and I almost caved but I held strong and walked on ! What a rush I was giddy ! Becky looked at me and said how great did that feel ? Amazing I replied as we went to class !

I decided right away I was going to study hard and get good grades. I had to work twice as hard as some of the students to retain the information we were taught in class ! No matter how much I listened in class it was like the lessons wouldn't stick ! I took a lot of notes and rewrote them over and over again so I could pass tests . It was time for parent teacher night. I went with Esther to school and she met all my teachers using her fake voice of course. We got to my reading teachers class and we went in and he asked me to sit in my assigned seat I had in class when he spoke to Esther. I did as I was told . I could still hear every word they were saying. Esther asked the standard questions. Was I behaving in class? How were my grades ? Then the teacher said well the only issue is Addie doesn't participate in class voluntarily. If I call on her she won't make eye contact. I think she has a bit of a crush he said . My head shot up ! I don't make eye contact because I was trained my whole life not to . Oh God does he mean he thinks I have a crush on him ? Eww definitely not ! I didn't mean to be rude but he was a man and a extremely hairy man at that ! I cringed at the thought. Why was it that not one of the teachers thought hmm this child is very thin and up to this year always had very poor hygiene and can't make eye contact with anyone maybe she's abused ! Were they all so wrapped up in their own lives they didn't see the obvious clues ? By the way how conceited was this teacher anyway ? His first thought was I had a crush !

Esther told the teacher I was always shy and that was my nature . That was the reason for not making eye contact. On our ride home she said what the fuck is wrong with you ? Why don't you look at people when they talk to you? You're drawing attention to yourself ,haven't you learned anything ? Ok did she really just ask me why I don't look at people when they talk to me ! Maybe because for my whole life I was trained to look at the floor ! I mean come on was she serious with that question ? From now on when a teacher asks you a question you better look directly at them and have the answer got it ? Yes I replied. When we got home Steven asked how it went and Esther said she's doing good in all her classes but her reading teacher thinks she has a crush on him because she won't make eye contact ! What a ego maniac Steven said ! Maybe she just doesn't want to look at him . Did he ever think of that ? I laughed and Esther shot me a look. Steven don't encourage her ! Ut oh did she just reprimand Steven ? That was a first ! Up to this point she agreed with everything he ever said to his face but I knew her better than anyone and I know her views are totally different from Steven's. Steven looked at her and said I wasn't encouraging anything I was simply making a statement ! I had to shut this down quick before it became a argument ! Oddly enough they never fought and I remember the constant fighting when Joe lived with us and I would avoid that at all cost.

I got a B on my history test today I said trying to lighten the mood ! That's great Steven said and Esther was silent. We all just stood there and finally Steven said I have to go make my lunch for work tomorrow and walked up the hall to the kitchen. Esther cleared the living room in seconds ! She grabbed me by the back of the neck and hissed in my ear you little mother fucker do you see what you did ? If you ruin this for me I swear to you you will pay ! She gave my neck one more hard squeeze and said get the fuck in your room and don't come out for the rest of the night ! I did what I was told ! That night I smelled pot and incense like every other night but tonight I heard the muffled sounds of a fight ! I sat in my bed knees to chest rocking back and forth . If this didn't get worked out Steven would leave and I would be back to constant beatings ! I couldn't go through that again ! I had to do something to smooth this over!

Chapter 49

It was two days since Esther and Steven had a fight and you could cut the tension with a knife. Since they rode to and from work together I couldn't get Steven alone to try and talk to him and stop this from getting any worse .Friday night when we were eating supper Steven said he had to work overtime the next day . I dropped my fork, I'm sorry I said it slipped ! I was going to get the beating of a lifetime when he left for work in the morning ! Esther blamed me for the fight and she beat the crap out of me for no reason all the time now in her eyes she had a reason. I could feel the tears welling up and knew if I cried I would get it twice as bad tomorrow ! I choked them back and said I'll do the dishes as I stood up from the table . Steven said thanks I'm going to bed ! Esther looked at me with such hatred it almost stopped my heart ! When Steven left the room Esther grabbed me by the hair and said I'm going to kick the shit out of you in the morning and went into the living room. That night Esther slept on the couch for the first time since she and Steven started dating.I went into the bathroom and threw up! The fear that was building in my was crippling ! I stood in the bathroom for a long time deciding what I should do ! I honestly thought of running away ! Where would I go ? I had no money and Esther would beat the life out of me when I had to return home !I brushed my teeth and quietly went to my room. I crawled into my bed and sat up against the headboard, clutching my blanket rocking back and forth staring at the door ! That's the way I stayed the entire night drifting in and out of light sleep.

At six a m I heard Steven go out the front door and shoot out of bed ! Esther wasted no time she ripped my door open and glared at me and said I'm going to enjoy this more than you know ! She grabbed me and started to full on punch me in the stomach ! I dropped to the floor and without a word she ripped me up by my hair and started punching me again . I tried to get away and she cornered me against the wall and started coming at me her hands were moving like a windmill ! . All her punches landed on my upper body. In true Esther fashion she was careful not to punch me in the face because how would she explain that ? I dropped to the floor again and this time she started kicking me right where I lay! I put my hands up to defend myself and she hissed you dared to raise a hand to me ? Are you freaking kidding me , I was just trying to block to kicks ! She came at me and pulled my up by my hair again and said you better fix this ! With that she walked out of the room !

I heard her go in the shower . I stood where she left me frozen in fear ! She came out of the bathroom ,looked in my room and said fix this ! She got ready for work and I heard her leave. with the sound of the door closing I dropped to the floor , only then realizing I had peed my pants ! I laid there and cried . Finally I gathered myself up and went to the bathroom . I looked in the mirror and my hair looked like I had been in a wind tunnel, going every

which way. My head ached, I had extreme pain in my
midsection . Every time I moved a certain way or inhaled
the pain intensified ! I took my clothes of and looked at
my body . From my neck down I was covered in huge red
marks some of which looked more like burns than just
red. I filled the tub with warm water and tried to sit but
my mid section hurt so much ! I pushed through it and
sank to the bottom of the tub. The water burned my skin
like fire even though it was just warm ! I hugged my knees
and cried.

Steven came home and I came out of my room looking for
Esther . He said your mother has a double today she won't
be home until later tonight. How convenient I thought !
She made herself scarce so I could"fix it " Steven I'm sorry
of I cause trouble . It was all my fault . You should be mad
at me not my mother I said choking on the words. He
looked at me and said Addie you didn't do anything , she
made the comment and scolded me like I was a child !
What I wouldn't give if she just scolded me instead of
using me as her personal punching bag I thought ! Then I
lied and said ok she'll probably be mad at me for telling
you this but she seems to really love you , although I knew
for fact Esther wasn't capable of love! She seems happy
with you , another lie I thought to myself. I felt I was
setting the poor guy up for the slaughter ! Then I
remembered him seeing me tied to a bed and doing
nothing, and he was an adult after all. How did he justify

seeing that ? How could he live with that monster and not know what was going on ? Then I thought of all the nice things he has done for me since and I felt horribly guilty. He stood there looking at me. The way he was looking at me almost seemed he could hear my thoughts. I had to say something. Please don't tell her I said anything I shouldn't have gotten involved. You two just seem good together and I hope you can work through this. Thanks Addie he said then asked me if I wanted to help him make supper. I told him yes and that I would be right back. I went into the bathroom my body was stiffening like it did after every beating and my pain was so intense! When I was cleaning the other day I saw that Steven had bought Tylenol . In all my years I had never taken as much as an aspirin but I had to do something for this pain. I ran the water in the sink so Steven couldn't hear me opening the pill bottle , read the back and it said take two so that's what I did . I went back out into the kitchen to help Steven with supper doing the best I could not to show how much pain I was in.

Esther got home from work and I prayed what I said "fixed it" She laid her purse on the counter and looked at Steven, he looked at her and I felt so guilty for what happened next ! He went over and hugged her and the look in his eyes was genuine love ! I guess what they say is true there's someone for everyone even Satan ! Can you watch supper Addie he asked ? Just stir the pasta every few minutes . I want to talk to your mom in the living room. He smiled at me as they left the kitchen. I could hear some of the conversation from the kitchen but not all of it. It sounded like they were working it out and he didn't mention that I talked to him at all. I ran the water in the kitchen and made extra noise when I was digging in the cabinet for the colander so they wouldn't think I was listening. I stirred the pasta and set the table. I didn't want to listen to anymore of their conversation. Knowing they were working it out was all I needed to know . A part of me would never forgive Steven for not coming to my rescue when he could have but I had to give him respect for stepping in and helping support and raise someone else's child and never laying a hand on me. I never saw Joe again and Steven stepped in and took over his role. We ate supper and everyone seemed to be getting along. I went to bed that night in pain but knowing I wouldn't be ripped from my bed in the middle of the night because Steven was there.

The following Thursday I came home from school and both Esther and Steven were there ! I walked through the door and they both looked at me and smiled . Steven's smile I had seen before but a smile, a true smile on Esther's face was very foreign ! Drop your books in your room we're going out to dinner Steven said ! I stood there looking at the two of them wondering ok what's going on .Steven looked t me and said do you notice anything different ? I looked around the living room, no I replied. They both held out their hands and he said guess what we did this afternoon? They were both wearing wedding rings ! Oh you poor fool I thought looking at Steven but what I said was congratulations ! He came over to me holding Esther's hand embracing me into a group hug . I cringed when Esther's arm wrapped around me ! I waited for the pain from her squeezing my neck or pinching me but it didn't come ! Let's go get in the car we're going to supper to celebrate. We went to a Italian restaurant a town away and had a great meal. That night when he was in the bathroom Esther came in my room I ran to the corner ! You're gonna call him dad now that we're married she said ! I knew I was taking my life in my hands but my response shot out of my mouth before I could stop it ! No was all I said ! Both she and I were shocked by my statement ! She stepped toward me with rage in her eyes but just then Steven came out of the bathroom and she said ok get ready for bed Addie in her fake voice and left the room !

That night as I laid in bed all I could think of was her telling me I was going to call Steven dad now ! I may have not stood up to her before but there was no way in hell I was calling him Dad ! No disrespect to him but I had a father, although he abandoned me I still had a father ! I wouldn't do it ! She could beat me if she wanted to but I wouldn't change my mind ! The next morning they were

both getting ready for work and Steven was truly happy !
He thought he had just made the best decision of his life !
Little did he know he was on borrowed time ! I could see
right through Esther ! She was going to take this poor soul
to the cleaners ! She saw dollar signs when she married
him where he saw and felt love ! I truly felt sorry for him !

When I got to school that day I told the girls the news !
Becky said you're shitting me he married satan ? Yep I
replied ! He must be insane she said ! I told her I felt sorry
for him ! She said you need to worry about you ! Who's
feeling sorry for you ? He's an adult , he can take care of
himself she said ! This much was true but I still felt sorry
for him ! Once Esther took up residency in your head you
never got her out ! When I got home that afternoon
Steven was cooking supper and Esther was at the
laundromat. Steven said hey how was school ? Good I said
with a smile. Go change, wash up and you can help with
supper . By the way when your mother gets home we
have a surprise for you ! I spun around, a surprise ? Yep
but you have to wait until she gets home to find out ! My
stomach sank ! If Esther had anything to do with it it
wouldn't be good ! Can you just tell me what it is I don't
like surprised I told him ! Nope sorry you have to wait !
Hurry back so you can help with supper. What bomb was
she going to drop on me now ? I was in the kitchen
helping with supper when I heard the front door open and
I braced myself for Esther's "surprise" !

Esther came into the kitchen and said something smells great what are you cooking tonight ? Taco's Steven replied , there almost ready . Addie can you set the table ? Ok enough with the polite banter I thought tell me what the surprise was ! I sat at the table for what seemed like forever then Esther said we have a surprise ! I wanted to hear this for the past hour then all of a sudden I didn't want to know ! What if they were planning on moving ? I would loose my friends and have to change schools! The tension was building ! All of a sudden Steven said if you could go one place in the world where would it be ? I sat there staring at him thinking just tell me already ! He said get some sleep tonight because tomorrow morning where going to your grandparents house ! What I screamed so loud Steven jumped ! Yep ! I looked back and fourth at both of them if this was a joke it was beyond cruel ! Seriously I asked ? Yep I'm going there so they can meet me ! I jumped up from the table in tears ! I haven't seen them in so long ! Thank you I said as I started crying harder. I'm going to pick out a outfit for tomorrow and I ran to my room.

I hardly slept at all that night I was to excited ! We got on the road by nine am . We had to stop for gas and I wanted to go in with Steven to pay for the gas because I knew Esther was dying to get me alone to make sure I knew the rules once we got to my Granparents house ! I opened my door in the backseat and Esther said Addie stay with me and there it was ! As soon as Steven shut his door Esther turned to me from the front seat and said Listen you know the rules, go in say hi then sit your ass down and shut up ! You are not aloud to be alone with them and under no circumstances to do you say one fucking word about what happens in our house ! Do you understand ? Yes I replied with my head down just in time for Steven to open the drivers side door and say were off ! I was stupid to think that this might be a normal trip where I could actually talk to my Grandparents like a normal grandchild ! I loved them so much but never got a chance to get close to them because of Esther ! They were my Grandparents but they didn't really know me ! How could they when I was never allowed to talk to them ! I wouldn't let this ruin my day ! I was going to see my Grandparents for the first time since we moved out of state ! we pulled up to their house and I could feel the tears welling up in my eyes ! I missed them so much. I wanted to run from the car and into their house but Esther immediately gave me that look . I walked up behind them to the porch . Esther rang the doorbell and my Grandmother answered the door and immediately the tears came ! I tried so hard to choke them back but there was no use ! we went in and I pretended to cough so I could wipe my face before Esther saw me crying ! My Grandparents asked how I was and it was apparent to me now that we were like strangers ! I never blamed them , you can't bond with someone you never see. They hugged me but everything seemed awkward. As a child I never picked up on this but now it was very apparent. My Aunt Linda was there with her family which made Esther beyond mad ! They still after all these years couldn't get along. and I didn't see that changing anytime soon !

My Grandmother made a delicious meal and I was forced to hang back and barley speak as per Esther's rules ! I knew it was Esther's way of preventing me and my Grandparents from bonding but I also knew that if I didn't do as I was told I may not ever see them again ! They met Steven and seemed to like him but I could see they were on their guard because Esther had a way of attracting let's just say less than desirable men . I hated the way Esther called my Grandmother mother ! It was more the loathing tone in which she said it ! My Grandfather seemed to have Esther's number meaning he knew she was trouble and he never let his guard down. I'm positive he had no idea that she beat me ! My Grandmother on the other hand seemed to at times feel sympathy for Esther ! No matter how many crazy things she would do my Grandmother always seemed to give her the benefit of the doubt which drove my Aunt Linda insane! It was time for us to go and I said I had to use the bathroom before the drive home . I went into the bathroom and sobbed ! I got myself together and came out and gave one last look at everything . I ran my hand over the dinning table and chairs , my Grandfather's recliner and my Grandmother's rocker as we headed to the door . I held my hand that I had touched everything with as if to put those memories deep in my heart so when times were bad I could look back on them with love ! I turned one last time to take it all in and then we were back in the car !

Depression set in deep on the ride home ! I leaned my head on the window and watched as we drove further and further from my Grandparents house. That night I cried myself to sleep wondering if and when I would see them again ! Back at school on Monday I let the girls know Esther and Steven made up so the house was calmer again ! Steven had applied for a better job and got it ! It would mean a huge pay hike for him. When he told Esther she was almost giddy ! I know it wasn't so much joy for him but more money for her to get her hands on ! We went out to eat to celebrate . Then he dropped the bomb , he had to swing shifts ! He had to work all three shifts switching every week ! I went into full blown panic ! That meant I would have to endure more of Esther's beatings ! When he announced this Esther looked directly at me with this gleam in her eye that I knew all to well ! I could see her chomping at the bit waiting for her first chance to get a hold of me ! A week after getting his new job Steven said he heard of a house for rent ! NO ! I thought , please I can't move ! He said the great thing is it's only five blocks from here and Addie can stay in her same school ! I was thrilled , not about moving but that I wouldn't have to leave my friends ! We went to see the house and it was very nice ! Probably the nicest house we've ever lived in ! We did a walk through and decided to take it. We packed up the apartment and moved the following weekend !

Chapter 50

Steven's first shift change was coming up and my stomach hurt just thinking about it ! I was deciding on weather to stand up to Esther or tell someone what was going on .Either way I was terrified ! Steven's first shift change was from days to second shift ! As soon as I got home from school I wanted to run to my room and barricade myself in so Esther couldn't get me but I knew that wasn't an option! That afternoon when she got home from work she walked passed my room glaring in but didn't do anything ! Ok I knew her she was psyching me out ! She wanted to give me that false sense of security and then pounce ! She's done it so many times before ! She walked by my room again and said I have people coming over get out here and clean everything up , I'm going to lay down for a little bit ,. I stood there staring at her ! What the fuck is wrong with you she asked ? Nothing I'm sorry I'll go clean . She slapped me in the head as she walked by and said it better be cleaned right or when I wake up I'll kick your ass ! Her having friends coming over always astonished me that anyone would be friends with Esther ! I mean I had to be around her but some people actually choose to ! By the way as soon as they get here I want you in your room. I'm cooking for them but you tell them you already ate if anyone asks got it ? Yes I said with my head down afraid to make eye contact not wanting to tick her off ! I wasn't going to get beat and all I had to do was clean ! I'll take that any day of the week ! Oh and don't let e see you in the refrigerator , I hope you ate at school she said with a smile as she went to her room !

So were back to rationing food ! Before Steven came we were dirt poor so it almost made sense to ration food but Esther did it with extra evilness ! Now that Steven lived with us we weren't rich by any means but we had food , electricity and heat. Maybe she was to tired to beat me and as sick as it sounds maybe she choose a nap over it . Who cares I wasn't getting beat ! I cleaned and although I was hungry I didn't touch any food. I went to the bathroom and went to my room. About two hours later I heard Esther get up I had my room door closed and held my breath as she stopped in front of it then started walking again down the stairs. Then I waited to hear her bellow, saying I didn't clean good enough but nothing happened ! I was in shock but thrilled ! A little while latter I heard the doorbell ring and people arriving ! A little while longer and the smell of something cooking waifed up the stairs. I was hungry but I've been way more hungry I'd live ! I wasn't getting beat ! Suddenly I heard footsteps on the stairs I froze ! Then whoever it was bypassed me and went to the bathroom and shut the door ! I breathed a sigh of relief ! So far so good no crazies ! As the night went on I could smell the oh to familiar sent of pot and incense . What a shocker these people were stoners too ! I didn't have a clock in my room so I had no idea what time it was but I was starting to get tired. I didn't trust that someone wouldn't try to come in my room so I took my pillow and blanket and laid on the floor in front of the door . This way if someone did try and get in I would know immediately !

I must have dozed off because when I woke up it was morning ! I got up got a shower and got ready for school ! I crept down the stairs to see if the coast was clear and there laying on our living room floor were Esther's stoner friends ! There were about fifteen of them ! What the hell ! Didn't these people have jobs ? The living room was a mess with plates and beer bottles everywhere. Not my problem I thought as I opened the door and went to catch the bus to school ! when I got home the mess was still there with a note ! Clean this mess up was all it said ! Steven had already left for work so there was no supper tonight ! I grabbed a garbage bag and headed to the living room ! I grabbed all the beer bottle first . Most of them had some liquid in them with cigarette butts floating in them ! The smell was disgusting ! Then I scraped all the plates into the bag and stacked the plates on the coffee table ! After taking the trash out I went into the kitchen to tackle the dishes, clean up the dishes,sweep the floor and vacuum the living room . Everything was in order and I was ready to go to my room when I heard the front door open ! Esther was home I froze ! She was carrying grocery bags . Well don't just stand they like a idiot grab a bag ! I did as I was told and carried the bags to the kitchen. I saw Esther looking around checking to see if everything was clean enough to meet her standards and waited for her to flip out but all she said was I'm taking a nap. I have friends coming over stay in your room ! This was my new norm ! I'll take it I wasn't getting beat !

The next morning I came down to the same stoners and trashed living room ! I walked past it all and went to school. When I got home it was a repeat of the day before ! I cleaned up the mess and went to my room ! what was Steven's opinion of coming home after a work at eleven at night and finding all the stoners both men and women laying all over the living room floor? After all he was paying a majority of the rent! He would be switching to night shift the following week . I wonder what will happen when he won't be there to monitor the party ? As I suspected without Steven coming home at eleven the partying lasted longer than usual ! The smell of pot and incense waifed up the stairs from the living room. I could hear laughter and music well into the night ! When I came down the stairs to go to school and looked into the living room I was shocked at the amount of people laying in the living room ! The number of stoners had just about doubled ! I closed the door and went to school ! When I got home I made sure to be quiet because Steven was sleeping because he had to leave at ten thirty at night when he was on night shift in order to get to work on time . I went into the kitchen to get a garbage bag and saw a note on the table. Addie there's a plate for you in the fridge, Steven. I took the plate out of the fridge and was very grateful for the grilled cheese and tomato soup he left me.

After cleaning up all the party mess I headed up to my room .I heard Esther open the front door and I closed my bedroom door and got my home worrk out. I was so tired because the partying kept me up the night before but I had a history test to study for so I pushed on ! I heard a knock on my door, I jumped off the bed and opened the door. It was Steven ! Hey how have you been he asked ? Ok how's work ? Going good but it's hard getting used to swing shifts ! I bet your happy your day shift next week ! I can't wait , I'll feel human again he said. Did you get the plate I left you in the fridge ? I was just about to answer him when Esther came up the stairs ! She hugged Steven and glared at me over his shoulder ! I knew she wasn't happy that he left a plate for me . Well I better get back to studying I have a history test tomorrow . Ok he said we'll make supper together when I'm day shift . Ok I closed my bedroom door !

I'd been telling Becky that the beatings just stopped ! She was thrilled ! Maybe she's to stoned , Becky said since she knew about the party's every night at my house ! I don't care what the reason is I'm just thrilled I'm not getting beat ! As I was saying the words to Becky I knew that I could never let my guard down when it came to Esther ! The following week when Steven was day shift I helped him make Supper after school . When I would leave in the morning the stoners were all over the living room floor laying am amongst the party debris . when I got home the mess was cleaned up . Steven came home from work evryday , cleaned the party mess, did the wash and made supper ! Esther had quite the little set up going ! Both Steven and I were her maids ! I wanted to see how the party situation went once Steven was day shift ! Sadly we ate supper and Esther would get me alone and tell me to go to my room and stay there with a oh so familiar squeeze to the back of my neck ! I'd go to the bathroom , since I wasn't allowed to come out at all when the stoners were there and I'd head to my room for the night ! I thought for sure Steven would object to me staying in my room all night but he didn't . I would hear him come up the stairs to go to bed while the partying was still going on. He would stop at my closed bedroom door for a minute then just go on to his room and go to bed.

Every night when we were making supper that week I wanted to say something about the partying but then I thought about it and remembered I wasn't getting beat so let them party ! His swing shifts had gone full circle and he was on second shift again three to eleven at night . I would soon find out that was when Esther would once again take up pouncing on me ! His first day of second shift I came home from school and did the party clean up and dishes and Esther came home and I tried to hurry up the stairs to get out of her way . She grabbed me on the staircase by the hair and started shaking me back and forth ! What did I do I screamed ! Shut the fuck up she hissed ! You didn't clean this house good enough and I have friends coming over ! I'll clean it again I said , even though I knew it was clean ! Get your ass down there and get it done. I hurried down the stairs tripping on the last step and falling on the floor! Esther stood there laughing you are the dumbest bitch I think I ever met she said as she drew back and kicked me in the thigh ! Pain shot up my leg and I crawled to the corner ! Get the fuck up and get this place cleaned she said as she slapped me across the face ! I dropped to the floor ! I assumed the "protection curl" where I would sit in the corner protecting my back with wall and protect my head with my arms ! For as long as I could remember my forearms always has black and blue, defensive marks on them and no one ever inquired how I got them ! She went up to her room for her nap and I cleaned the downstairs again !

 When I was done I quietly went to the bathroom to brushed my teeth and peed ! ! I sat there on my bed listening to her downstairs in the kitchen clanking pots and making food for her pot smoking friends as if she just didn't kick the crap out of me ! I heard the door bell and then heard all the stoners filed in. Every night it seemed like the crowd grew ! I laid on the floor right in front of the door to go to sleep. For the remainder of Steven's second shift week Esther would take joy in knocking me around ! Sometimes giving me a reason. Like I missed something when doing the dishes and other times there was no reason at all . She did it for her sheer pleasure !

The weeks went on much like the previous then I started to see financial problems slowly happening ! Steven was making almost double what he was when Esther first met him but she was spending it faster than he could make it ! Every night she would cook for a larger and larger crowds. She made meals not just snacks ! Then there was the alcohol, the beer distributor delivered once a week right to our house ! I know she got a lot because I always had to help carry it in . Our house became the home for wayward drunks and stoners ! Hell at one point she could have charged a cover and paid out rent and all utilities but for whatever reason she decided that Steven footing the bill was the way she wanted to go ! Steven and Esther began to fight on a regular basis ! We were renting the house and he kept saying the landlord can kick us out the large parties need to stop ! Esther started to show her dark side and verbally attack Steven every chance she got ! I was terrified that Steven like Joe would finally have enough and leave! The one night they had a huge fight and Steven left , Esther walked right up to my room and beat me so severely that I was afraid I would have to go the hospital ! Careful to keep al my bruises from my neck down so they weren't visible ! She went as far as to give me a note to be excused from gym for two weeks after keeping me home the first week so my black and blues would heel . We had gym once a week and when I handed my gym teacher the note to excuse me from two gym classes she informed me that if I missed another one I would have to get a Dr's note. I did some quick thinking on my feet and said can you send a note home with me for my mother so she knows to make a Dr's appointment if I miss another class ? Sure she said , I hoped when Esther saw the note it would be a deterrent for her beating the crap put of me !

When I brought the note home Esther read it and slapped me across the face ! Who the fuck does this teacher think she is she asked? I stood in silence ! I'm not making any doctors appointment ! She'll make me change for gym in the locker room and .... before I had a chance to finish my sentence she had slapped me to the floor ! I don't give a fuck , and she walked out of the room !

The fighting escalated between Esther and Steven ! He put his foot down and said I will get a separate checking account and you won't have access to my money ! That sent Esther over the edge ! She started screaming and throwing things ! I sat on my bed knees to chest ,rocking back and forth and knew that she would come for me as soon as she was done with him ! He kept saying calm the hell down you sound like a phychopath ! Ah now your getting it I thought ! What the hell took you so long to realize what she really is ? Esther let out this bloodcurdling scream and then there was silence ! Truth be told I was more frightened by the silence ! Did she kill Steven ? I was to terrified to move ! I sat there listening , please let there be some kind of sound I thought ! Then all of a sudden I heard Steven say you're fucking nuts and the front door slammed ! I heard Esther's footsteps on the stairs , Oh my God she was coming for me ! When she was just about to the top of the stairs the door bell rang ! Esther froze on the steps ! Then there was a loud pounding on the door, open up it's the police ! Holy crap she did it now ! This was my ticket out of here ! I would knock her over if I had to to get the the door and beg the policeman on the other side to get me the hell out of here ! I got up off my bed and she ripped my door open , don't you fucking move she said as she looked at me like a caged animal ! All of my plans to dart left me ! Whenever she glared at me like that I reverted back to that scared little girl the first time I got beat ! I stood there frozen ! The police banged on the door again this time much louder ! We got a disturbance call for this address , please open the door so that we can see everyone's ok the officer said !I could see Esther's wheels turning in her head , she finally realized she had to answer the door. You come down with me and don't do anything stupid got it ? I shook my head yes i reply !

Esther opened the door and there were two male police officers on our porch. We received a disturbance call for this address one of the officers said to Esther. Is everyone ok ? Yes she said and I thought here we go she's going to say Steven hit her like she did with Joe but unlike the day with Joe she didn't have any marks. She said can I talk to you outside I don't want my daughter to be subjected to this ! Are you freaking kidding me I thought ! You have subjected me to a lifetime of fear and pain but this is when you choose to shield me ? What a load of crap ! Sure thing just let me make sure your daughter is ok first . The officer stepped in our house and looked at me and said are you ok ? Are you hurt ? Do it say please take her to jail she beats me I thought but instead I said I'm not hurt . Ok he said we're just going to talk to your mom out here on the porch she'll be right on . Ok I said disgusted with myself for not having more of a backbone ! Ok I still had a chance . They were cops they were trained to see crazies right ? Wrong within a few minutes Esther was back in the house smiling and so proud of herself ! Damn bastards wouldn't know their asses from a hole in the ground ! It empowered her , at this point she felt invincible and sadly I believed she was ! She came at me not missing a beat and a few minutes later I was in my room feeling this would be my life forever !

We hadn't heard from Steven for over a week ! Not so much as a phone call ! Esther started to show a human side , she was scared ! Scared her meal ticket was gone ! I heard her at night calling around asking if people had seen him with no luck ! Finally after two weeks she tracked him down at work ! She brought me along for the sympathy play ! On the ride over she said tell him you miss him and give him a hug when you see him ! You remember what it was like before he was in the picture ? She didn't even wait for me to respond . Well that will be your life again ? She pulled up right when he was getting off of work . All his co workers were in the parking lot heading to their cars . They were all like Oh someones in trouble and you're gonna get it now! Laughing at Steven's expense ! Esther what the hell are you doing here ? I need to talk to you she said ! You're crazy stay away from me ! Hi Addie ,how are you doing ? This was my que , I miss you Steven I said and really meant it ! He was the only normalcy I had in my life ! Even though it was true I felt horrible ambushing him like this ! I know Addie I miss you too. Can you come home I asked ? Me and your mom have to work some stuff out , I might not be home for awhile he said. I ran over and hugged him, please come home , she's sorry. I turned to Esther and said tell him you're sorry ! She shoot me a look and I turned away from her stare. I'm sorry if you want the parties to stop they will. If you want to handle the money and have a separate checking account let's do it! Holy crap she was scared I thought ! You lost your shit the other day Esther ! I know I'm sorry , I was tired from work and I know what you said was true I guess I just had to have time to process it. Please come home she said. He stood there , staring at both of us and finally said I'll follow you home. First I have to stop at my friend house to get my stuff. Addie why don't you ride with Steven ? Ok I said and stood beside him.

Both Steven and I knew the real reason Esther wanted me to go with Steven is so I could report back to her where he had been staying when he was gone . He pulled up to a house which I had never seen before and said I'll be right out . Ok I replied as I relaxed in the seat.He was gone for about fifteen minutes when a friend walked him out on the porch and said dude you're making a mistake ! I have to try and save my marriage don't I. She's a crazy bitch ,get out while you can the friend said. Steven shot him a look and nudged his head in my direction letting his friend know I was within ear shot ! Not that I didn't totally agree with the friends opinion of Esther ! Oh sorry dude the friend replied as he waved to me ! Steven threw his bag in the back seat and we drove back to the house. Butter could have melted in Esther's mouth she was being so sickening sweet ! I made myself scarce figuring they needed to talk . As I was walking up the stairs Steven said hey Addie give us a minute and then you can help me make supper . Esther said sheepishly um there's nothing here you'll have to go to the store before we make supper ! Ok let's talk first then I grab a few things at the store he said . They were talking in the living room and I went into my room and laid on my bed. I was so tired ! The last two weeks were hell ! I become Esther's personal aggression release , more than usual and it had taken it's toll. All I wanted to do was sleep.

I heard the front door close and I jumped up from my bed as I heard Esther take the steps in lighting speed ! She ripped my door open and hissed who's house was he staying at ? I had know Idea who the friend was, but knew I better come up with something. I don't know who the guy was , he came out on the porch to say good bye . He had dark longer hair and he was thin . He lived up by the old park with the swings. Son of a bitch that's Larry , Esther said ! He's a worthless piece of shit ! I thought well he thinks the same of you but kept my mouth shut ! What did Steven say on the ride back she asked ? Nothing just asked me how school was going that's all . You eat supper then get your ass back in your room hear me ? Yes I replied . Now get your ass downstairs and make sure every things cleaned up ! Can I go tot the bathroom I asked hurry up I need to get in there she said . I went into the bathroom and lifted the lid to the toilet knocking a box off the back of the toilet onto the floor. I picked it up looking at it not sure what it was. Esther barged right into the bathroom and snatched the box from my hands. I guess I must have look confused looking at the box and she looked at me holding the box up saying if you want to use it you have to clean it ! I was so naive I had no idea what she was talking about but later found out it was a douche I Ok way to much information ! What a classy thing to say to your daughter !

When Steven got back from the store you could cut the tension with a knife ! You could tell that he was conflicted , should he have come back or should he file for divorce ! Esther was turning on the chram so heavy I thought she'd break something ! He was unimpressed ! How about we all watch a movie tonight he said , I think mainly because he didn't want to be alone with Esther ! I have homework to do , I said as I was heading up the stairs I turned and said it's nice to have you back Steven. He smiled , Thanks Addie . I went up and closed the door to my room. I was so tired . All I wanted to do was sleep ! I grabbed my pillow and laid on the floor in front of the door. Just in case something went wrong and Esther decided to come after me . I must have dozed right off, I woke up ad it was morning ! I listened for any sound of movement , there was none. I grabbed my clothes and headed to the bathroom to take a shower. I turned on the shower and waited for the water to get hot but it didn't . There was a knock on the door it was Esther we're out of oil looks like it's a cold shower for you today ! So it began ! We were right back to where we were when I was very young ! No hot water, which always followed by no heat and no electricity ! Luckily it was May so a cold shower was fine ! I got dressed and left for school. When I got there I told Becky the news that Steven was back but he didn't seem happy about it ! Her only comment was that dumb bastard had a out and he jumped back into the fire ! My thought were selfish but I was so glad he was back , it meant less beatings for me !

Chapter 51

That day in school the teacher said I have papers up here for summer employment. You have to meet income requirements . Please see me after class if you would like an application ! A job , I could have a job ? I could hardly wait , as soon as class was over I went up to the teachers desk and said May I have a job application ? Sure Addie fill it out and have your parents fill out the income section and bring it back to school. Thank you I said as I almost floated out of the classroom ! I wanted this job so badly! I brought the application home and Steven took a look at it .Don't you want to spend your last summer before high school hanging out with your friends ? Sure I want to hang out with them but this will be from seven in the morning to three in the afternoon . Can you fill it out I asked ? I think we better wait for your mom to get home and see what she says. He must have seen the disappointment in my face because he said wanting a job shows you have great character ! Thank, I really do want it . I'm not even sure what the job is but I'm a hard worker and I'll take any job they'll give me. Steven smiled , you are a very hard worker and a sweet kid Addie ! I heard the keys in the door and grabbed the application and slipped it into my History book. Steven looked puzzled at me. I'll wait until after supper to show it to her I said . I set the table ,

Esther came in still in her Suzy sunshine phase. How's everyone doing she asked? I wondered how long she could keep up this act before her fangs came out ! Steven said Addie where did your application go ? I froze , what the hell ? I spun around and looked at him in disbelief ! Esther broke character for a minute and said what application in her natural evil voice ! Steven said they passed out forms for summer jobs in school today and Addie brought one home ! I told her that's wonderful don't you think Esther ? He turned and winked at me ! Oh ok I see what he did ! I thought he ratted me out when in fact he brought up the subject knowing Esther would be more likely to agree to it if it came from him ! You know what Addie we'll fill that whole thing out after supper so you can hand it in tomorrow morning at school . Thank you I said smiling, until I looked at Esther who knew she just got played ! There was nothing she could do because she had to keep up her performance if she wanted to convince Steven to stay. After supper we filled out the application and the next morning I left a few minutes early so I didn't run into Esther . I knew she would try and rip up the application !

When I got to school I handed in the application and right before last period my name got called with five other students to come down to the office ! I felt sick , I knew I didn't do anything but when your a kid and get called to the principles office it's just the natural response . When we got to the office the secretary said take a seat he'll be with you in a minute. A few minutes later he called us in as a group . Ok students your here because you filled out paperwork for summer employment . Are you all still interested ? Yes we all said . Now that I looked at the other students with me I should have figured out why we were all here earlier ! We were the poorest of the poor so we all qualified for this summer program. After all it was set up for low income. I took the liberty of setting up your assignments. Take a look and please let me know if there's a issue for any of you. Your assignments are all in your hometowns so you won't have any trouble getting to work. You are to show up the Monday after school lets out . It's imperative that you be on time. You are representing the school. If you are late two times you will be let go. Ok that's all Have a great summer and good luck with your jobs. Thank you I said so loud that everyone turned to me and laughed . Sorry I said red faced ! Not a problem it's nice to see you so enthusiastic about your job. Everyone go back to class.

I was so excited I got a nurses aide position for our local hospital. As soon as I got off the bus I ran all the way home . I forgot Steven was switching shifts today and he was working nights. My heart sank. Esther would be home in a few minutes and I already knew what that meant. She had be playing the happy routine now for almost a week and today she got to drop the act because Steven wouldn't be around. I ran up to my room to hide my work assignment paper and I heard her come home . As predicted she cleared the steps like a cougar and pounced on me in record time ! You thought you were so smart last night with your little work performance didn't you ? Then this morning you ran out of the house early so I couldn't rip the paper up ! No I wanted to get there early to hand it in. It was first come first serve I lied ! You little bitch , she said slapping me over and over again in the face . I dropped to the floor . She drug me up by the hair ! So you want a job ? Yes I said through tears I do ! Fine get a fucking job , the sooner you have one the sooner you can work on moving the fuck out you ungrateful bitch ! With that she waked out of the room ! Ungrateful ! Is she freaking kidding me ? What do I have to be grateful for ? The fact that she has beat the crap out of me since I can remember or the fact that she has made me feel so worthless I sometimes question my existence ! I'd show her , I'd do a great job at work and prove her wrong I wasn't worthless !

I was both sad and happy when my eigth grade school year was over. I would miss my friends terribly but I was so excited to start my new job. I said good bye to my friends and Becky made me promise I would ask to hang out with them this summer ! Stacey said I'm going to stop at your house this summer to see if you can hang out ! Don't worry I won't let on that I know anything. Ok I said regretting my comment as soon as she walked away ! Esther would know ,Esther always knew ! I was starting my new job after the weekend and I couldn't be more thrilled ! When I got home I went straight up to my room. I waited for Esther to get home . She had to be proud of me I got all B's on my report card ! She came home and said your up in your room so your report card has to be horrible ! Get down here and let me see it ! I walked down and handed it to her. She look at it and then at me and said oh now I guess you want me to say something fucking stupid like good job ? Well guess what it's eighth grade not rocket science ! Get your ass up to your room! I have friends coming over tonight and I don't want to hear anything out of you , you understand ? Yes I said as I went up the stairs ! would it have killed her to say something encouraging about my report card ? By the way why were people coming over ? She and Steven discussed stopping the parties ! She just got him back and already she's back to her old self ! Oh well not my problem ! All I knew is that I would have a night of peace ! I went to the bathroom and brushed my teeth then headed to my room. Steven had bought me three books that I was looking forward to reading . I dropped my pillow on the floor ,leaning against the door and started to read the first one.

As always when I read I drifted off to sleep . I was awaken by Esther plowing through my door ! What the fuck she said as my door didn't open all the way because I was laying on the floor ! Get the fuck up ! I jumped up and she said get your ass downstairs and help me clean . Steven will be home in one hour and I have to clean up the party mess so he doesn't realize I had people over ! I must have looked at her like are you kidding me because she slapped me across the face ! Do you ever look at me like that again you little fucker ! I make the rules around here not you ! Get your ass moving ! I ran down the stairs and grabbed all the empty beer bottles and paper plates. I took the trash out and then ran the vacuum . Hurry the fuck up , your moving slow as shit Esther screamed. I checked the living room again to make sure I didn't leave a trace of her stoner friends being here then sprayed air freshener. Esther came out of the kitchen and said what the fuck did you spray that for ? It smelled like , I was going to say pot but instead said cigarette smoke . Get your ass in the kitchen and make some toast , make sure you burn it ! I looked at her , the burnt toast will cover the smell of the air freshener ! Don't question what I say just get your ass in there and do it ! I did as I was told . Steven came through the door and the whole downstairs smelled like burnt toast ! I had to give it to Esther she new her stuff !

Steven looked around and right away knew it was way to clean ! I didn't want them to start fighting again so I said hey do you want to see my report card ? Sure he said . I'll run up and get it , I'll be right back. I sprinted up the stairs and sprinted back down . I handed him the report card. Addie this is wonderful , way to go ! Yeah that's what I told her Esther said ! I just ignored the lie ! Are you hungry Steven I asked? No I'm really tired. I think I'll go up to bed. well I have to go to work so I'll see you all when I get back Esther said as she headed out the door. Steven turned to go up the stairs and I said I got my working papers today ! I start on Monday , I'm going to be a nursing assistant on the geriatric floor ! That's wonderful Addie Congratulations ! I'm going to bed now but I'll be up to make supper we can talk more then . Ok good night .

Monday morning bright and early I was up, showered and ready for my first day at work. We still had no hot water so it was a quick shower ! I was so nervous ! All I wanted was to excel at my job. When I got to the hospital I was surprised to see my old neighbor was going to be my supervisor. Addie how are you she said as she gave me the oh to familiar head tilt of pity I usually got from neighbors in my small town that knew Esther! Oh how I wish one , just one of them wouldn't feel pity for me but would have stepped in and reported Esther ! I'm good thank you I replied ! Well you'll be working with Alice today. Just shadow her and she'll show you the ropes. Ok thank you . Alice was a very nice middle aged woman who was grateful for the help. Ok in the morning the first thing we do is knock on the door announce ourselves and see if the residents need anything. The ones that are ambulatory we set up with their basins , towel and toiletries so they can get washed. The ones that need more help we bath. Ok I replied. They get showers twice a week, the list of showers is on the desk. It was so sad to me that you live your entire life and you are resorted to a hospital room which was minimally decorated and you bathed out of a basin and only showered twice a week ! They were all taken care of here but it seemed to me that we should be doing more for our elderly.

As we went into every room Alice introduced me and informed the residence that I would be working on their floor for the summer. Oh how I loved working with the elderly ! It sparked something in me , I think I had found my passion and what I wanted to do for a career. After a couple of rooms Alice said do you think you can handle this one on your own. I'll give it a try . Alice came in the room with me but hung back to observe. I went in and made sure I followed all the steps she had taught me from the previous rooms. When I walked out of the room she said wow you're a natural at this ! Thank you I said beaming ! We finished our morning rounds and reported back to the nurses desk ! How did it go the supervisor asked ? Great Alice replied this girl right here is a gem , she said patting me on the back ! I knew she would be my supervisor said ! We continued with our work day and I was sad to see it end at three o clock ! Well how did you like your first day Alice asked? I loved it ! So you'll be back tomorrow ? Oh definately I replied ! That's great news ! A lot of summer workers come the first day and then put in for a transfer to other departments ! You either love this work or you hate it she said ! I love it I replied , I'll see you tomorrow Alice . As I walked home I thought about my day , my feet hurt from being on them all day but it was a good hurt. I loved my job!

As I was approaching our house I saw the lights on inside Steven was still on night shift and would probably be still sleeping . As soon as I walked in I smelled bacon ! The smelled filled the house , it was heavenly . Then I heard

Esther's voice and realized heaven had a visitor and her name was Satan ! I walked into the kitchen and saw Steven and Esther having coffee ! There she is Steven said ! How was your first day at work ? Ok there was two ways I could play this I had to think quickly ! If I liked it to much Esther would find a way to take it away from me but If I acted like I didn't like it she would call me lazy and gloat that she knew that I was worthless and wouldn't like it when she got me alone ! I decided that I was proud of my job and I was going to let it show ! I loved it I replied ! The nurse who is training me said I'm a natural at it ! Esther glared at me ,I looked away ! Steven said that's wonderful Addie ! I made breakfast for supper since we're all working people now and won't get to eat breakfast together often . It smells great I said . I'll set the table, I thought we'd do it buffet style tonight Steven said pointing to the plates on the counter. I had no idea by what he meant by buffet style but if it meant I got to eat some of that bacon I was in ! He walked over to the counter and grabbed a plate, come on ladies grab your plates and fill them up ! Oh ok buffet style meant form a line and fill your plates from the pots , I could do that ! I waited for both he and Esther to get their food then I got mine. I made scrambled eggs with cheese, home fries with onions and bacon ! Yum, Yum and yum I said , Steven laughed dig in ! It was delicious, Steven said I think I'm going to try and get a little more sleep before work tonight. I'll do the dishes I said , thanks for cooking. You're welcome and thanks for doing the dishes , No problem.

I scraped all the dishes in the trash , filled the dishpan and got to work. Without even turning around I could feel Esther's evil stare piercing the back of my head I swung around. You think you're so smart don't you coming in here bragging about your stupid little summer job. No , he asked how I liked it I was just being honest . Well it's your first day give them a couple of days they'll find our what a useless piece of shit you really are ! Boy she was one miserable human being ! She just stood there staring at me as if she was deciding her next move . Finally she turned and walked out of the room heading for the living room ! I wouldn't let her ruin my mood ! I loved my job and I couldn't wait to go back tomorrow ! I was sad it was only Monday through Friday . I wish I could work the weekends too ! That night when Steven left for work I braced myself for Esther to storm into my room I knew she was just waiting for him to leave to rip into me. I heard her say good bye as I sat on the edge of my bed . I heard her coming up the stairs and she stopped when she go to my door. I froze, she didn't move ! Was she listening to try and tell if I was sleeping ? I know how she loved the element of surprise ! I didn't dare move ! I could hear my heart pound in my ears. Just like that she walked past my room and into the bathroom ! I know this trick oh to well , give me a false sense of security letting me think every things ok so I let my guard down then pounce ! Well I'm not falling for it ! I heard her leave the bathroom and head to her room ! What no party Something was up ! I sat there on the edge of my bed waiting for her to make her sneak attack but it didn't happen !

Just in case she was taking a nap , getting rested before she pounced I slept on the floor in front of the door so I would at least be ready. Steven had gotten me a small round alarm clock. Now that your working you need to make sure you're on time for work he said. I set the clock next to me on the floor so I would be sure to hear it if I dozed off . Exhaustion set in and I finally fell asleep. I woke to the sound of the clock I set it a half hour earlier than the time Esther always got up so I could get a shower and leave before she even woke up ! I was showered and dressed and I crept down the stairs and out the door ! I loved walking it was my me time ! I listened to the birds, smelled the fresh air. Walking cleared my head ! I arrived ten minutes early to work and my supervisor said Hey Addie good morning ! Good morning I replied with a smile . You know what the early bird gets here she asked ? I stood there , um I'm not sure . You get first pick at the donuts ! There's a pot of coffee on and some paper cups go back in the kitchen and get some. Do you want me to bring you anything I asked ? No sweetie I'm good I had a big breakfast , I might sneak a donut later. I went back to the kitchen and there was a huge pink box on the counter

. As soon as I opened the door the smell of coffee permeated the room, it was delightful ! Truth be told I never drank coffee but it was free and I was hungry so coffee it was ! Alice walked into the kitchen hey sweetie she said with her head tilted , as she came over and gently squeezed my shoulder. Oh no she knew my story , I could just tell ! My supervisor must have filled her in on my sorted details! It was always so embarrassing for me when people knew. I know my supervisor didn't tell her to gossip she like so many probably just felt sorry for me and filled her in.

Alice grabbed a cup and poured some coffee in it . She took two packets of sugar and some creamer and added it to the cup. She caught me watching her out of the corner of her eye and giggled. You ever drink coffee before Addie ? No but it smells so good I have to try it ! Well I like mine with cream and sugar like this and she fixed me a cup . I took a sip and it made a sound of pure delight as I swallowed the warm goodness! Yep your hooked she laughed ! Yes I think I am. We ate our donut and drank our coffee then went out to the nurse desk to get our assignments for the day. I shadowed Alice again until lunch and she said well Miss you're doing such a great job I think I'll give you a shot at being on your own after lunch. You go take your lunch now and I'll go when you get back . Ok I went down to the cafeteria and sat. I didn't have a lunch but was happy just to sit down and take a break. One of the other nurse from the floor came down and said can I sit with you ? Sure , she pulled out a chair and sat down. She saw that I had no lunch and said wow what was I thinking packing such a big lunch I'll never be able to eat all of this ! I knew this game , Ive played it before ! People feel the need to feed me ! I was painfully thin and here I sat the poor kid with no lunch. I just smiled , you like ham and cheese sandwiches she asked. Oh that's ok I'm good . I never waste food it's a sin please share my lunch with me she said with a smile. Ok thank you , she handed me half of her sandwich and we shared her grapes and chips. After we were done I thanked her again and we headed back up to the floor.

It was Friday morning and I was sad that I would have the weekend off from work. My co workers were all talking about their plans for the weekend and one of the ladies asked me what are you going to do this weekend? Oh I'm not sure yet I lied ! I knew my weekend would be spent in the house as usual. Well have fun whatever you do and see you back here Monday morning. When I got home Steven was in the kitchen making supper. He was day shift this week . I was helping Steven make supper before Esther came home and he asked why don't you ever go to the youth center anymore or hang out with your friends ? I wasn't sure how to answer him. What I wanted to say is because your wife it crazy and keeps me locked up in this house but I knew better ! Oh I don't know I replied . You need to socialize more Addie your young ! Yeah don't I know it I thought but what I said was yeah I will . Well tonights the night , do you have your friends phone numbers ? Yes I have them somewhere I have to go look in my book from school. Well go find the numbers and come down and call them . Oh I don't know I said nervously . Knowing Esther would beat the crap out of me ! Addie you're sixteen years old now you should be out every night ! True I was sixteen but I was so introvert and immature for my age because I never got a chance to be sixteen ! Well I'm making a executive decision right here right now he said ! You're going out tonight ! With that I heard Esther say who's going out ? I spun around , I froze in fear and said nothing ! Addie is he said ! She never leaves this house except for work it's not healthy ! Esther stared at me I turned away.

Esther walked over to Steven and in a low voice , but purposely loud enough for me to hear she said she has no friends ! Yes she does , she has their numbers. Call them Addie make planes for tonight ! Esther stood there glaring at her ! Esther's eye's were saying call and I'll kick you ass but her mouth said yes call them Addie. I ran up the stairs grabbed my notebook I hadn't touched since school and turned to the back page . Becky wrote her number down for me just in case I ever needed her. I wrote it on a scrap of paper and ran down the stairs. Steven said did you find it ? Yes I have it ,well pick up that phone and start dialing he laughed. I dialed the phone it rang once, twice on the third ring my heart sank. I looked over and Esther was smiling, oh well you tried she said with a cocky smirk. Then on the forth ring I heard the voice of my friend Becky ! Becky hi it's Addie , hey how have you been ? Good how are you ? I'm good she said. Steven said ask her what she's doing tonight. Um what are you doing tonight I asked ? Hanging out with the girls why? She wants to know why I said to Steven. He laughed really hard and said watch this is how it's done. He took the receiver from me and said Hi Becky ,um who is this Becky asked confused ? This is Steven , I'm married to Addie's mom . Ok Becky said still not knowing what was going on ! I told Addie to call you because she never leaves the house . I thought maybe you two could do something tonight . There was silence on the other end of the phone . Hello he said you there? Yes is this for real Becky asked ? Yes it's for real he laughed ! Yes definately she can come hang with us , we'd love to see her ! Ok what time is good ? She can come to my house now and we could meet up with the girls when they all get here. Steven laughed ok well were going to eat supper then I'll drive her over to your house. Where do you live ? Ok she'll be there in about an hour. Ok thanks she said as she hung up.

I stood was so excited ! There you go Addie now you have plans for tonight ! Thank you I gushed. Let's eat so I can drive you over there. Esther shot me looks everytime

Steven's back was turned . I kept looking away ! We were done with supper and I said I'll do the dishes and Esther said ok but Steven said no Addie you have plans tonight ! Let's go I'll drive you over to Becky's house ! Like a bullet I was out the door ! I jumped in the car leaving Esther standing there with her mouth hanging open ! It all happened so fast she didn't know what hit her !

Chapter 52

On the ride over to Becky's house I thanked Steven for setting this up ! No problem he said I'll be back to pick you up at ten. Ok I said as we pulled up to Becky's house . See you then ! I ran over to Becky who screamed with excitement ! We went in her house and she said how the heck have you been and tell me what's going on ! How did you get sprung from prison ? I was filling her in on all the details of what happened that night and her Mom walked in. Hey Addie so nice to see you she said hugging me ! Well I'll let you girls talk . Have fun she said as she went upstairs. Soon Ellie, Stacey and Pattie arrived ! We all hugged and caught up on what had been going on since school let out . I was the only on with job. They spent most of their days at the public pool. I told them how much I loved my job and how it didn't seem like work at all ! We talked, laughed and just hung out ! We all decided to take a walk . I had the best time ! In the back of my mind I kept thinking Esther is really going to lay into me when she gets the chance but I pushed it away ! I had time with my friends and I was going to enjoy it ! It was almost ten o'clock and Steven would be here soon. Doom set in I didn't want to go home but I knew I had no choice, Stacey said hey can I catch a ride home with you so I don't have to call my Dad ? Sure no problem , we lived in the same town . We dropped Stacey off and headed home .Thanks again I said to Steven your welcome. We pulled up in front of the house as I sat there looking at it a blanket of depression came over me then I walked in and the firs thing I saw was Esther ! Have fun was what she said but I new it meant hope it was worth it cause I'm gonna beat the crap out of you the first chance I get ! Yeah I had a lot of fun ,it was nice to see everyone again. Well it's late I'm going to go to bed . Yeah I have to get up early for work in the morning Steven said . Esther what time to you have work tomorrow ? She looked right at me and said I don't have to be there until nine so Addie and me can have breakfast together ! Well there it was , I had a beating to look forward to before she went to work !

I heard Steven leave at six thirty and braced myself for Esther to rip into me . I started pacing in my room , this needed to stop I had to make a stand ! I was sixteen years old for God's sake and still felt like that scared little girl whenever Esther was around ! I listened at my door for movement but didn't hear anything so I quietly opened my door and jumped back seeing Esther just standing there ! What the hell I thought ! She glared at me , you have fun last night ? Yes I said timidly . That's great she said in a snide tone ! She took a step toward me and I backed into my room . She kept taking steps toward me and I kept backing up until I was backed into a wall. She put her hand to support herself lurking just inches from me. So I guess you think you're all grown up now with your job and running with your friends huh ? No I said afraid to breath ! Well you're not I own your past, I own you present and I will own your future ! I didn't move ! So you got anything to say to that ? No I timidly replied ! She lurched at me and I flinched ! That's right just remember who boss here got it ! Yes was all I said looking at the ground . She just stood there in my space for a minute or so , my head was down the whole time out of fear and because I knew if I looked her in the eye she would take it as a sign of defiance punishable by a beating ! Finally she backed up ,I looked up and she lurched at me again ! This time I put my arms up covering my face . Yep I made my point she said as she walked out of the room ! I stood in that spot and didn't move ! I heard her going into the bathroom to get ready for work. I was terrified to leave my room ! I tip toed over to my door and closed it quietly. I just had to make it another fourty five minutes or so before she had to leave for work then I'd be in the clear.

She walked passed my door opened it and said I'm leaving for work when I get home this house better be spotless ! Ok I replied . By the way Esther said with a crazy look on her face I wanted to give you something to look forward to tomorrow. Steven has to work but I'm off all day and so are you , oh the fun we're gonna have ! She laughed and left for work ! I sat down on my bed and cried ! I honestly can't take this anymore ! When she's not beating me she mentally torturing me ! This had to stop , there had to be someone I could trust ! There had to be someone who would stop her! Could I tell Steven ? No although he has been very good to me he did leave me tied to a bed ! Could I ask Becky to go to the police with me ? No because I had to lie and say things were getting better when I went to her house because if not she would have confronted Steven ! Could I tell my supervisor at work ? No because I loved my job and I didn't want Esther anywhere near it ! I I laid on my be and prayed please let me make it through this ! Exhaustion must have taken over because I woke up looked around and was in a panic ! Oh my God I was supposed to clean the house ! How long was I sleeping ? I looked at my clock in horror, I slept for six hours without moving an inch ! I had two hours to clean this entire house I jumped off my bed and ran downstairs ! I tackled the kitchen and the living room then went upstairs to the bathroom. I ran the vacuum both upstairs and downstairs . I had exactly twenty minutes before Steven got home from work. I ran upstairs and took a shower. I was putting the towels away when I heard Steven come in . I came downstairs and Steven said wow the house looks great ! Thanks how was work? Good , give me a few minutes to change and you can help me with supper.

I sat on the couch , my mind wandered to tomorrow morning ! Esther was off and I just know she was at work right now plotting how she would torture me! I must have really been in deep thought because Steven walked in front of me and said Earth to Addie laughing ! What I said confused ? I said your name about five times , you were a million miles away ! You have no idea I thought ! Oh sorry I was just thinking about work on Monday . I really love my job ! That's great , there's nothing worse than going to a job you hate everyday he said ! Oh I could think of a few things that are worse I thought ! I just smiled and agreed with him. You like chicken patty's he asked? I don't know I never had them ! What you never had a chicken patty ? Nope but I'm sure I'll love them . Good cause it's what we're having tonight ! Chicken patty on a roll with mayo,lettuce and tomato with fries! Sounds great I said and I went into the kitchen to help with supper. About an hour later Esther came home and looked exhausted ! Hey how was your day Steven asked ? We were so busy , my feet are throbbing ! I'm going to run upstairs and change she said . Ok supper in about ten minutes! We ate and I

said well I'm really tired I think I'm going to go up to bed .
Addie it's Saturday night and your sixteen years old. It
eight o'clock he said laughing ! I know but I wanted to
read a little before bed and I am really tired . Ok see you
tomorrow he said . Oh Addie don't forget I'm off
tomorrow Esther said ! We have have a girls day ! My God
she was evil I thought as I walked up the stairs !

I was so thankful I slept in the afternoon because I knew I
wouldn't get any sleep tonight . I laid in my bed thinking
of all the horrible things Esther had planned for me as
soon as Steven left for work ! I drifted off for about an
hour and that was it all night ! When morning came I was
up standing in the center of my room ! I heard the front
door close and heard footsteps in the hallway . Satan was
up ! She went into the bathroom and my first thought was
I bet she's in there humming taking great pleasure in the
fact that in a few minutes she'll be wiping the floor with
me. I heard the toilet flush then listened as the bathroom
door opened. My anxiety grew to a point that my stomach
started to hurt and I could feel my heart pounding in my
ears ! I thought maybe I could fight back, defend myself ! I
was small and scrawny standing five foot two inches tall
and weighing about eigthy pounds soaking wet ! I was no
match for Esther who stood Five foot eight inches and
about one hundred seventy pounds !

She walked right passed my room and went downstairs !
Now I was really freaked out ! I knew this must be a trick !
There was no way I was leaving this room ! I stood in the
same spot and didn't move for quiet some time. I could
hear her clanking around the kitchen ! Was she planning
on poisoning me ? I put nothing past her ! I finally sat on
the floor in front of my door and waited ! Nothing
happened ! My anxiety was at a all time high ! I felt like I
was going to get sick ! Was this her new game to mentally
screw with me so much that I went insane ? Two hours
had gone by and still there I sat in front of my door ! Ok I
had to get a hold of myself ! I would sit here all day if I had
to ! Steven would be home at three thirty ! I had to pee so
bad but I didn't dare leave the safety of my room. Then all
of sudden I heard her on the steps . She was right in front
of my door I could feel my heart pounding . Why wasn't
she moving ? It was like some crazy stand off that I
wanted no part of ! Finally she went to her room and shut
the door ! This was unchartered territory , I had no idea
how to act ! I got up and started pacing because I had to
pee now and I couldn't wait any longer ! I put my ear
against the door and listened for movement ! It was eerily
silent. It was either make a dash for the bathroom or pee
my pants. I quietly opened my door and tip toed to the
bathroom . I peed then was afraid to flush the toilet ! I
washed my hands and opened the bathroom door and
holy crap there she was standing in the hallway ! I froze

were I stood terrified to move ! She just kept staring at me not saying a word ! Her eyes were so vacant !Was she on something ? It was like she was in a trance ! I was afraid movement would snap her out of it so I didn't move a muscle . All of a sudden she walked right passed me and went downstairs ! I ran to my room and shut the door ! I would stay in my room until Steven came home !

While I sat in my room I tried to make sense of what just happened ! Never in my life did I see Esther so without emotion ! It seemed like she looked right through me , like she was there physically but mentally she checked out ! I heard Steven come home and waited to see what his reaction was to the way Esther was acting ! They were talking but it was so low it was almost inaudible . I couldn't decide whether I should go downstairs or stay in my room, then I heard Steven call for me. I timidly walked down the stairs and he said your mother has a migraine, she's gonna sleep on the couch for a little bit . Want to help me make supper ? Sure I said as I peeked into the living room and saw Esther covered with a blanket fast asleep !

I guess I'll never know what happened that day and I felt a little bad that all I cared about was that I dodged a beating ! I know Esther, Steven and their friends smoked pot but maybe she tried something else ! What ever happened by the next morning she seemed to be back to her evil self.

Neither she or I ever mentioned what happened that day. It was Monday morning and I was on my way to work . My supervisor pulled me aside and said I just wanted to tell you that Alice has given you very high praise ! She said you have picked up the job quickly, you're polite and respectful of the residents and she loves working with you ! This brought tears to my eyes ! Oh Addie this is good news honey ! I know it just makes me so happy ! I love this job ! You are the sweetest thing she said rubbing my shoulder. There's donuts and coffee in the back, help yourself. Thank you I said as I walked back to the kitchen with a bounce in my step ! I was so proud that I smiled from ear to ear ! Good morning Alice said as she come into the kitchen ! Good morning Alice ! How are you today ? Well someone's very perky today ,did you already have coffee ? Nope just happy that's all ! Glad to hear it ! Are you ready for work ? Always , I threw my coffee cup in the garbage , washed my hands and was back out on the floor ! The residents were happy to see us every morning ! It made me wonder what would Esther be like at this age ? I would bet she would be combative ! I would never know for sure because as soon as I was legally allowed I was so out of that house and I would never go back ! I will sever all ties with Esther !

Chapter 53

My work day always went so fast ! I hated going home but knew I had no choice! When I got home that day Steven said I have big news! What is it I asked with excitement ? We have to wait until your mother gets home so I can tell you both at the same time ! As I helped him with supper I tried to guess what his new was ! We heard Esther open the door and he said come on I can't wait any longer ! We met Esther at the front door and he said ok you two I have great news ! Esther hated change I could see the irritation in her face although she was trying to look excited ! I'm going steady day shift as of tomorrow he said almost giddy ! This was such fantastic news ! He would be here every night ! No more would I be drug from my bed in the middle of the night and beaten ! I didn't realize I was crying until Steven said Addie are you ok ? Yes I'm just really happy for you , and me I thought ! Esther hugged Steven and with her fake voice said we have to celebrate ! She glared at me over his shoulder , I could only imagine she felt she was losing her control ! No more parties when Steven was night shift and no more sneak attack beatings in the middle of the night. Her glare was so fierce I actually took a step back ! I t sent chills down my spine ! Well suppers almost ready , give me about ten more minutes he said ! I'll help I started to say as I was yanked backwards by my hair ! Esther pulled me into the living room and hissed in my ear if you think this is your get out of jail card your fucking crazy ! Remember he works weekend and I'm off most Sunday's ! Just letting you know so you have something to look forward to she said as she headed upstairs to change out of her work clothes !

I had felt jubilation for a sweet second then the evil wrath of Esther slapped me back reality ! I got myself together and went in to help with supper. That night as I laid in bed I remembered the hissing of Esther in my ear ! God she was so filled with hate ! I thought of the day I would be free of her ! The second I could I'd be so far from here ! I had no idea where I would go but I know it to be fact ! I would stash money away from every job I had and I would get the hell out of here ! I woke up fifteen minutes earlier than usual since there would be three of us fighting for the shower in the morning now. I quickly showered and was out the door on the way to work. On the walk to work I dreamed of having my own apartment. How I would decorate it. I only needed a small space ,and I would love a dog. My apartment would be warm and inviting. It would be my space. A place that I could return to after work ,play with my dog and eat a simple meal. I would watch tv which would be a luxury . My bedroom would be my sanctuary. I would have a bed with soft ,fluffy pillows and a warm comforter. My bathroom would have pretty smelling soaps and warm ,clean towels ! I would take warm ,soaking baths in my claw foot bathtub ! Ok that would be my dream apartment but hoestly I would happy in a tiny efficiency apartment with none of the above except the dog. I would really love a dog. Before I knew it I was at work. I felt so blessed to have this job!

When I got in my supervisor said I have something for you Addie. Here you go your first pay check ! I stared the the white envelope with the clear little window which had my name in it and felt such pride. I know it's not a fortune but you can buy yourself something nice with it I'm sure she said . I carefully opened it and it said pay to the order of and then I scanned over to the right of the check and there it was three hundred and ten dollars for two weeks of work ! My mind was blown , this was like a million dollars to me ! I couldn't stop staring at it ! I walked back to the kitchen and grabbed a cup of coffee and donut and just kept running my hand over the check making sure it was real ! I held it up in the air and said yes ! Out of the corner of my eye I saw Alice and my supervisor standing in the doorway with their heads tilted and their hands on their hearts. Alice looked at me with such compassion I felt I needed to say something. Sorry this is my first check I'm just excited . No need to be sorry you earned it Alice said and we're excited for you ! We all went out on the floor and began our work day .

When I got home I showed Steven my check . Way to go Addie , your first check ! So what are you gonna buy ? I don't know yet, I have to think about it. You know your going to have to open a savings account or sign it over to your mother to get it cashed ! I'll open a savings account . Smart move ,keep adding money to your account and before you know it you might have enough to buy a used car ! Whoa, I didn't even think about a car ! I was thinking small like a bottle of perfume or school clothes .I'd worry about a car once I get established ! First things first , I would need a apartment ,furniture, rent, utilities. I would work this summer job and then I would ask if they could keep me on for after school and weekends. Esther came home and Steven said show your mom what you got today ! Crap I didn't want her to see the actual check I was going to say I made a little less than I actuall did so I could put some away ! I reluctantly took my check out and showed her ! Her eyes lit up ! Oh no way this was my check , she wasn't getting it ! It was my ticket to freedom! She stared at a little to log marking me want to go up to my room and hide it so she didn't take it. If you sign that over to me I can cash it for you she said with a glint of greed in her eye! Oh thanks but I'm going to open a savings account that way I won't be tempted to touch the money , and neither will you I thought ! She glared at me ! Suppers ready Steven said , and I tucked my check safely into my back pocket !

The whole time during supper I was trying to think of a safe hiding spot for my check but I knew there wasn't anyplace in this house it would be safe from Esther's hands after I saw the way she looked at it . I've seen her go through money like it was water ! We were on a very tight budget and I would see her blow money on booze every Friday when it was sometimes hard for us to buy groceries ! We currently were out of oil and had no hot water and winter was coming. I was hoping that would be enough incentive for her to stop partying. With Steven being on steady days I'm hoping he would tighten the reigns and we could get back on budget ! I took my check with me the next day and I asked to speak to my supervisor . Um this may sound a little strange but would it be possible for you to hold my check until Friday when I can get to the bank to open a savings account? She looked at me and without asking any questions seemed to know exactly what and why I was asking. Sure honey no problem. Thank you I said as I handed her the check. Remind me Friday to give it back to you. Why don't you leave a few minutes early on Friday so you can get to the bank on time. Thank you so much I really appreciate it.

When Esther got home that day she said hey why don't you sign that check over to me and I can run up to the bank and cash it for you ! Oh hell no I thought ! Oh I left it in my locker at work I lied ! What she screamed ! It's safe I have a lock on my locker and I'm the only one who has the combination ! I want that check home tomorrow do you hear me ? Esther, Steven said it's her check if she wants to keep it in her locker at work so she doesn't spend it than let her ! I think it shows great restraint on her part, most teens would have cashed it and spent the whole thing already . Esther was a heart breat away from reaching across the table and chocking me I could see it in her eyes ! Yeah you're right Esther said !

I went to the bank that Friday to open a savings account. I've known the bank teller who waited on me for about six years . She looked at me and said I need your birth certificate and social security card to open you a account ! I politely said Sadie you know who I am , we go to the same church ! Bank rules sweetie . I don't want to cash the check I just want to open a savings account so I don't spend the money . I'm saving for a car I lied . Sorry bring back the paperwork I need and I'll be glad to open your account ! I left the bank feeling both defeated and mad ! Esther had my birth certificate and social security card and I was trying to avoid her having anything to do with my pay checks. With no choice I reluctantly went home and asked Esther for my paperwork so I could open my savings account. Her face went pale ! I gave you your paperwork when you applied for your job and you never gave it back to me ! No I never had any paperwork for my job . I handed in my application to my principle and he gave it to my employer. So you lost your paperwork and now you're coming crying to me Ester said? I've never seen any of my paperwork in my life you know that ! She stepped toward me listen you little bitch you lost your paperwork so that's your problem ! Now sign the check over to me and I'll cash it for you and that's that ! No thanks ! I'll find another way to open a account ! Well good luck with that because you're a minor and you have to have someone co sign in order to open a account ! This was unreal , all I wanted to do was open a savings account ! She said come on we'll go to the bank right now and I'll co sign for you so you can open your account ! What choice did I have , I knew Steven would say ask your mom so we went to the bank !

When we got there Sadie said hey Esther how have you been ? Ok this boggled my mind because Sadie was a elderly religious woman and Esther was a pot smoking hippie ,but Sadie was fine with Esther co signing to open my account ! I opened the account and Sadie handed me my savings acount book and Esther turned to me and Esther asked in her fake voice do you want me to hold that for you ? No that's ok I'll keep it safe I said as I said thank you to Sadie and left the bank. Sadie raised a eyebrow to me when I said no to Esther like I was being disrespectful. Nothing could be further from the truth ! This little blue savings account book was my great escape fund ! I would save every cent and when I was legal I would use that money to start a new life ! My goal in life was never to be rich only to be happy ! I could easily do that on a modest budget ! No frills,I was a very simple person. I was walking home and I heard Esther call my name . She caught up with me and said you little son of a bitch do you realize how fucking disrespectful you were back there ? I wasn't trying to be disrespectful at all I just meant I will definitely keep this book safe. She glared at me and quickened her pace walking past me. I dropped back letting her get far ahead of me and thought about where I would hide my savings account book so it would be safe from Esther's grasp.

I got home and Steven was there so I knew it was safe to go in . Esther went directly to him and tweaked the story about what happened at the bank making me look like I did everything but curse at her ! I stood there listening to her spin her web of lies and thought wow she's been home five minutes and she came up with this elaborate lie, what could she come up with if she had more time ? Steven looked at me and said Addie this is so unlike you , apologize to your mother ! I stood there looking shocked , but felt so ganged up on that I apologized for something I never did ! I think you should go to your room and we'll call you down when supper's ready. It hurt the way he looked at me ! He had such disappointment in his eyes which was never the case because I never gave him a reason.

I went up to my room and searched for a hiding spot for my savings account book. I finally found a loose corner of carpet in my closet that I peeled back , I wrapped my book in paper and slipped it under to rug. After putting my stuff back in my closet I felt confident that I had found a great hiding spot ! Steven called me down for supper and I felt the shift immediately ! I have no idea what was said or done when I was upstairs but Steven went from someone who seemed to genuinely care about me as a step child to someone who looked at me as if I was a stranger ! When supper was done I offered to do the dishes and he said go ahead and walked out of the kitchen ! Esther followed him and gave me one of her gotcha glares ! What had I done , better question was what had Esther lied and said I did to make him have such a drastic change of opinion where I was concerned.

The days that followed were a huge adjustment for me. When I got home from work I would ask if I could help with supper and Steven seemed irritated to have me around . Finally after about four days I decided I needed to know what was going on ! I know I didn't do anything but his demeanor toward me had changed so much that I felt if I talked to him I could try and fix the situation. I came home from work and went straight to the kitchen , he saw me and gave me a look of almost disgust ! Steven did I do something to you you seem mad ? I'm not mad let's just say my eyes were opened ! Opened to what ? I don't understand ! Open tp the fact that this whole time you've been acting one way in front of me and another behind my back ! Wait what I asked ? I'm not acting anyway ! It doesn't matter he said as he was getting supper ready and turned his back to me . It matters to me I'm not sure what Esther said but , he cut me off and said drop it ! I didn't do anything I have no idea why you're mad . He spun around and yelled I said drop it ! I stepped back , I was shocked he had never so much as raised his voice to me before ! Ok I'm not sure what I did but I'm sorry I said as I turned to walk out of the room and literally almost ran directly into Esther ! I had no idea she even came in or how long she had been standing there ! She raised her eyebrows and gave me a cocky smirk ! She had succeeded in conquering and dividing Steven and I . I was now alone in hell !

The only joy I had now was work. I hadn't seen my friends since the night at Becky's house. I was more motivated than ever to save my money and get the hell out of here . Work was going great , I had gotten three more reviews all very favorable. I hated when quiting time rolled around because I went home to a house of awkward silence. Gone were the days of Steven and I being able to talk to each other. I felt like I had an ally in a house of horrors. But Esther took care of that. He honestly looked at me like he loathed me and couldn't stand to be around me. I spent most of my time in my room which was fine by me. Steven had days off during the week which meant he had to work occasional weekends. Esther always worked Saturdays but had Sundays off and she took great please in slapping me around , it was like her Sunday ritual ! She

would always say you thought you were so special . You
had Steven on your side, well how's that going for you
now ? She said it like it was something to be proud of !
She was so insanely twisted ! That's fine if he wanted to
take whatever lie she told him at face value and believe it
there was nothing I could do about it.
My summer job was almost over and I was going to miss
my co workers so much ! My supervisor sad she would put
a good word in for me because they wanted me back next
year ! I saved my money all summer ,Esther said since you
have a job now you can buy your back to school clothes.
That was fine with me I didn't need much. I bought myself
my first ever pair of name brand jeans ! They were a pair
of Lee jeans ! I walked to our local department store and
tried the jeans on in the dressing room ,they fit like a
glove. I bought three tops , underwear, bra ,socks and a
pair of sneakers. I went to the beauty isle and bought
shower to shower powder, deodorant, shampoo ,blush
foundation and eye shadow ! I felt like a princess ! On the
walk home I wondered if Esther was going to say anything
about me buying make up . As soon as I got home I
headed for my room and Esther said not so fast let me see
what you bought ! If anything is inappropriate you're
taking it right back ! She looked through my bag and saw
the make up ! Since when dd I say you could wear make
up ? I just thought that since I was going into ninth grade I
could wear a little blush . Don't let me see you wearing

tons of make up looking like a hooker ! You won't I'll only wear a little . I went up to my room and carefully hung up my new clothes.

Chapter 54

It was the weekend before school was starting and there was a knock on the front door . I was up in my room,Steven yelled for me . I came to the top of the stairs and saw Stacey ! I ran down the stairs and hugged her ! What are you doing here ? I figured this was our last weekend of freedom and I wanted to see if you wanted to go for a walk or something ? I timidly walked into the living room not realizing Stacey followed me . I instantly saw the fake smile on Esther's face and knew it couldn't be for me , I turned and saw Stacey so close it looked like we were one person ! She looked at Esther and said hi would it be possible for Addie to take a walk with me through town ? Esther's eyes shot over to me I froze. She glanced over at Steven and he shrugged his shoulders like he could care less ! Fine be back by nine ! Thank you I said as we ran out the door ! Oh my God your mother is scary Stacey said ! Oh don't I know it I replied !

I filled her in on everything that happened over the summer My job , the situation with Steven, Esther and saving my money to get out of here as soon as I could. She listened intently to every word . What the hell Addie , she said when I told her the Steven story ! I have no idea what Esther said to him but whatever it was was enough for him to basically write me off . The tension in that house is worse than ever ! Is she still hitting you Stacey asked ? Since Steven went steady days the only time she can get me alone is every other Sunday when he has to work ! It has become her Sunday ritual ! To tell you the truth I don't know if Steven would do anything if she beat me right in front of him .Stacey stopped walking , Addie enough is enough you're seventeen years old now fight back ! Don't think I haven't thought about it I said but every time I get the nerve to stand up to her she looks at me with those dead eyes ! I revert back to that once helpless little girl and I back down ! Well you're not that poor helpless little girl anymore she said , stand up to her or tell someone what the hell has been going on your whole life ! We stopped down at her house and I met her parents . They were so sweet and by the sympathetic head tilt they both gave me I sensed they knew my story . It was almost nine , I had to get home . Stacey yelled to her parents I'll be right back and since we only lived about six blocks from each other she started walking me home. Half way there I said I got it the rest of the way. See you Monday at school. I'll stop by in the morning and we can walk to the bus stop together Stacey said. See you then I waved as I headed back home.

When I got home Steven was sitting alone in the living room . He looked over at me , got up and went upstairs not saying a word. I went into my room and cried ! Thank God school was starting and I could see my friends everyday ! I woke up early Monday morning , it was my first day of high school . In a few hours I would officially be a freshman ! I laid my new clothes on my bed and went to take a shower. We still didn't have hot water which would become an issue very soon once the weather got colder. I hurried and got dressed. and attempted to put on the make up I bought . I had no idea what I was doing with the make up and it wasn't like I could ask Esther for help . I washed my face and threw the make up in my book bag . I figured the girls could help me apply it when we go to school. I grabbed my book bag and ran down the stair and stopped dead in my tracks when I saw Esther standing in the living room . Let me see your face she demanded ! I looked at her and she said , ere you to lazy to even try and put the make up on ? I tried and messed it up so I just washed it off. She looked at me and laughed you're fucking hopeless aren't you ? I ignored her nasty comment and left for school !

As soon as I got outside I saw Stacey waiting across the street. Stacey took one look at me and said you look great ! You got new clothes ! Yeah I bought them with the money I made on my summer job ! Wait to the girls see you ! We were both excited and nervous to be freshman!

We were low man on the totem pole. With that came a lot of razzing from the upperclassmen . That being said we were now in high school ! A whole new world was waiting for us ! We got to the bus stop and I was thrilled to see that it was a cool group of kids. We got on the bus and couldn't wait to get to school to see everyone ! As soon as we got off the bus we found our group of girls . Everyone made a big deal out of my new clothes which had me smiling from ear to ear . We all hoped we had classes together. The first bell rang and we went to our homeroom. The teacher handed out our schedules. I had one class with Ellie and one class with Pattie that was it ! I was so bummed ! The bright spot was we all had the same lunch so we could get together then and catch up.

It definately was a different atmosphere in high school . It was basically sink or swim atmosphere. When I brought home the paperwork last year for freshman year Esther insisted on filing everything out ! She filled in academic courses .   All my friends choose business course that's why we didn't have any classes together. After the first day I realized what a horrible mistake she made ! Those courses were so far above my head I was destine to flunk. I went to the principles office first thing the next day and asked if I could transfer to Business courses and the secretary informed me that all the classes were full and there was nothing she could do . I was in a panic I knew there was no way I was going to be able to pass these courses ! I would study like I never studied before ! As the days went by I got further and further behind. The teachers might as well have been speaking Greek ! I wrote down every words they said in class, most of the time my writing was illegible because I was writing so fast. I'd go home after school and try to decipher my notes and would be in tears ! I went back to the office this time in tears stressing to the secretary that my current courses were to difficult for me to grasp and I was going to flunk if I couldn't change to the business course. She said the only thing we can offer you is vo tech . I had no idea what that was. She explained to me that it was a trade school and you did half a day in school then you got bused to the vo tech for courses like nurses aide, nursing , ect. She said I would need a parent to sign a permission for me for tech and gave me the papers.

I went to the bathroom and cried ! Vo tech sounded interesting especially the nurses aide course but I wanted to stay in my school. I gathered myself together and went to class. When we got our first test back in two classes my fears were true ! I flunked them both. My teachers asked me to stay after class so they could discuss my grades. I told them both that I felt the course were way over my head and that I tried to transfer out but the other classes were full. Neither teacher took kindly to the fact that I wanted to give up. They both said in not so many words I needed to apply myself and work harder ! I went home that day feeling so defeated ! I was willing to work hard for what I wanted , that being said I knew my limitations! I didn't have the ability to retain material being taught in these classes . I had to go over and over it and with Algebra no matter how hard I tried I couldn't get it ! When I got home Esther was in the living room and I brought home every book in my locker! Jesus Addie why the hell do you have so many books ? I have homework I lied. Let me see what they have you studying she said as she grabbed one of the books off the pile ! Algebra ! Yeah you'll be flunking this one she said laughing ! She opened the text book and the vo tech paperwork fell onto the floor . She picked it up read it and flipped out ! No fucking way your going to tech they're a bunch of druggies ! Are you freaking kidding me I thought ! Our house looked like pot central most of my life with all her stoner friends and she wasn't worried about me then ! I went to the office because I want to transfer to business classes instead of Academic but the classes are full. You lazy fuck school just started and you want to give up already ! No I don't want to give up . I've worked so hard to get my grades up and I can't understand the material in the academic classes.

Esther stood up and slapped me across the face . Your staying in the classes your in ! You can't quit every time something is hard .If I quit every time something was hard I would have quit life long ago I thought but said nothing ! Don't be such a little bitch ! Wow there for a minute I thought she was giving me sound parental advice , that was until she added the little bitch part ! I'm pretty sure you won't find that in a how to parent your child book !If you have to study every second of everyday then that's what you'll do ! Now get out of my sight you make me sick ! I went upstairs and sat on my bed an cried ! I wasn't a quiter I was a realist ! I knew that these classes were to hard for me to grasp . I'd go into every class with the attitude ok today I'll get this but as soon as the teacher started to talk I was lost ! ! I would be brought to tears when I studied for hours and got my test back seeing F after F ! Mid way through the first marking period I received a failure notice for every major subject I had ! I came home and Esther had them open on table ! Without one word to me she slapped me across the face knocking me to the ground ! Dragging me to my feet by my hair she pressed my face against the the kitchen table screaming do you see this ? This is what I came home to today after working my ass off all day ! Five fucking failure notices ! How the fuck are you failing every major class ? Because my classes are to hard for me I tried to tell you that weeks ago ! Istudy every night , I do nothing but study and I can't retain the material ! Shut the fuck up and stop making excuses for being lazy ! With that I lost my mind and for the first time in my life I talked back ! Lazy ? I study every second I'm awake ! I have nightmare about these test ! I take notes and rewrite them over and over in hopes that

I'll remember something ! She grabbed me by the throat who the fuck do you think you're talking to ? She glared into my eyes, her face inches from mine ? You listen to me you little bitch you ever speak to me that way again and I will kill you got it ? I shook my head yes! She pushed me backwards , setting me off balance and I landed on the floor ! It was then I realized Esther filled out the paperwork choosing Academic courses because she was setting me up to fail ! She knew my limitations, she knew I would never pass those courses !

Steven came in from the store and said what the hell is going on in here I can hear you from the street ? Just like that Esther turned on the tears and said look at this ,pointing to the failure notices ! What the hell Addie he said ? I was yelling at her because of them and she screamed in my face ! You did what he said glaring at me ! Esther turned the waterworks on full blast ! If you ever raise your voice to you mother again you'll be out of here ,do I make myself clear ? Yes I said . Get the hell out of here ,go to your room he said hugging Esther ! Esther had a huge smile on her face as she glared at me over his shoulder !

Out of all my classes I hate Algebra the most ! x=? Ok x= nothing ! I don't get it ! I went to the library to look up books on algebra thinking maybe it was the teacher . Maybe he wasn't explaining it properly! That didn't explain how many of the kids in class were getting it but it made me feel better about myself so ... Well the books in the library confused me more ! No matter how I studied I still flunked all my quizes and test ! I wasn't doing any better in my other classes !I felt like such a loser ! I went back to the office one more time and pleaded my case. I'm flunking every class , I'm studying around the clock and I'm still flunking ! Like I told you before there's nothing we can do about it the classes are full the secretary said. Am I able to change my major now for next year ? Well technically if you want to go to college you should stay with Academic . I assure you I don't want to go to college ! Well I'll give you the forms take them home and have your parents sign them and bring them back and we'll switch your major from academic to business next year ! I took the paperwork but I might as well throw it away now because Esther would never sign it !

I was filling Stacey in on the walk home from the bus stop and said Esther won't let me change my major . I'm terrified I'm going to flunk my freshman year ! Why did you choose Academic in the first place ? I didn't Esther filled out my paperwork ! No way I would pass the classes your taking that's why I chose Business courses ! We got to my house and I said I have to go in I'm on lock down see you in the morning . As soon as I walked in Esther started in on me ! What did you flunk today dummy ? I stood there staring at her ! I honestly see why people snap I thought as she kept talking ! Finally I think she realized I had zoned out and she said you're to fucking stupid to fuck with get your ass upstairs ! I did as I was told !

I continued to flunk my test and I knew the second bunch of failure notices would soon be sent to my house ! At this point I was ready to give up ! I practically begged to change my major because I knew this would happen and no one helped me ! My Algebra teacher asked me to stay after class. Look your going to flunk my class if you don't get it together ! No disrespect but I guarantee I will flunk your class I've studied every night since the first day of school and I'm still getting F's ! Some people just aren't cut out for the Academic course and I'm one of them ! You're a great teacher but I'm not teachable in this course ! Is there any way you can suggest I be switched to the business major ? Last month I received five failure notices ! He looked at me shocked ! You flunked every class ? Yes this is what I'm trying to tell everyone , I have no interest in college , I never have ! I plan on getting a job as soon as I graduate . Without a degree life will be hard !Life is already hard I said before I realized it came out of my mouth ! What do you mean by that ? I just mean as far as school goes ! Oh ok well I will suggest to the office that they change your major before you get so behind you can't catch up ! Thank you thank you I said so happy I could cry ! Hey I'm not making any promises I said I'd suggest it ! You're the first person who's willing to help me with this so Thank you !

I left class and met up with the girls for lunch . I filled them in on what was going on with my courses . As soon as I hear anything I'll let you know . What's Esther going to do if the school changes your major ? She'll flip out ! Do you think she'll come to the school ? The thought of her doing that made my stomach hurt ! Oh God I hope not but knowing her thats when she'll put on the "concerned" parent act ! Three days went by and I hadn't heard anything about my Major being switched . I wanted to ask my teacher if he knew anything but I didn't want to rock the boat ! That weekend Steven had to work on Sunday which left me with an entire day of Esther ! She stormed into my room bright and early and gave me a chore list for the day ! When your done with that I'll find something else for you to do ! I was going to study this afternoon if that's ok . Sad to say but all the studying in the world won't help you ! How does it feel knowing you're going to flunk your freshman year ? I'm not going to flunk I'll make sure of that ! Yeah ok keep that dream alive she said as she laughed and walked out of my room !

I was done the chore list at two and I asked if I could go study . Bring your shit down and study at the kitchen table so your not up there screwing around ! Reluctantly I brought all my school books down to the kitchen and started studying ! I went over and over the Algebra but didn't understand it ! The answers were in the back of the book so I would do a problem then check the answer ! I did fifteen problems and every one of the was wrong ! Esther walked by the kitchen , it was more like she was patrolling the room ! Oh Algebra she said as she looked down at my textbook ! Well we both know how this is going to end don't we ? She said with a evil taunting voice ! Is it any wonder I have poor learning skills ! I mean honestly I never had a calm , non abusive home life in which to study ! I think Esther would rather be set on fire than be maternal ! I was trying my hardest but school never came easy to me I had to do four times the work of other students just to get a C . I was willing to put in the work but the Academic major was just to far above my ability ! Esther grabbed my Algerbra Book and opened to the first chapter. She started reading problems and saying what's the answer ? Immediately my stomach started to hurt ! I grabbed my paper and pencil and tried to remember the example the teacher showed us in class . I gave her the answer , she checked the back of the book and slammed me in the head with the text book wrong , next one ! This went on for about fifteen minutes , Every wrong answer earned me another slam to the back of my head ! My hands were shaking so bad I could hardly write! finally Esther threw the book down on the table and said how the fuck are you so stupid and walked out of the room !

I sat there crying , staring at the problems ! Esther came back in the kitchen and I flinched when she got near me ! She started laughing , yeah you better flinch ! Take your shit back upstairs Steven's going to be home in a few minutes and he'll need the kitchen to make supper . I grabbed my books and headed up to my room ! I threw my books on my bed and plopped down on the bed next to them ! I laid there feeling so mad and ashamed ! What was wrong with me ? Why couldn't I grasp these subjects ? As I laid these I started to imagine my life after graduating high school and free of Esther ! I wanted a simple life . One where I slept without fear, Woke up not having to to over my shoulder and just enjoyed life without threat of abuse ! I must have drifted off because when I woke up Steven was knocking on my bedroom door . I got up opened the door and he looked at me and said when you're called for supper I would appreciate you answering ! I'm sorry I must have dozed off studying ! Well suppers ready get down stairs ! I did as I was told !

After roll call in homeroom I heard my name come over the intercom. I gathered my stuff and headed to the office ! When I got there the secretary instructed me to take a seat . The guidance counselor will be with you in a minute. I sat there wringing my hands ! Was I in trouble because I was failing ? When the guidance counselor came out she introduced herself and led me to her office. Hi Addie do you know why I called you here today ? Is it because of my grades ? Yes , I see you have a failing grade in all you major classes can you tell me how that happened ! I study I swear I do , I just can't grasp the courses! I wanted to choose the Business course but my mother filled out the paperwork and insisted I took the Academic classes. You made it clear that you didn't want them to your mother she asked ? Yes but she I trailed off. She what the counselor asked ? I chose my words carefully . She just wanted me to take college appropriate course but I explained to her I have no desire to go to college. I plan on getting a job as soon as I graduate. College is great but it's just not for me. Your teachers have spoken with me as said as much. They've recommended that you be switch the Business major. With this I sat up straighter in my chair. After hearing what you just told me I'm in total agreement with them . I thought my heart was going to leap out of my chest. Thank you so much I said with tears in my eyes . Then I thought about Esther telling me there was no way she would let me change courses. My heart sank ! Do I have t take paperwork home for my mother to sign ? No this was at the request of your teachers and you so it will change as of tomorrow ! She handed me my new schedule and said now you have to play catch up so know you'll have a lot of work to do to get caught up with your classmates. I will do everything I have to I swear ! She looked at me and said I think you can do it if you work very hard . You should be all caught up by the end of the marking period ! Thank you again I said as I headed back to class !

I filled my friends in at lunch and Stacey said what's Esther going to do when she finds out ? She's going to flip out ! I'll work through it It's either switch or flunk ! When I got home that day I stood on the front porch afraid to go in . I gathered all my courage and opened the door , I was met with a slap so hard across the face that it knocked me to the floor ! Esther stood there with rage in her eyes! Get the fuck in here and close the door. I bent down to pick up my books that were blocking the door and she grabbed me by the hair and slammed the door shut ! What did I do I asked as she shook me like a rag doll ? So you got your fucking major changed she hissed ? It was at my teachers request . Don't give me that fucking shit. It was I called down to the counselors office today and she said my current teachers requested the change. Great now everyone know you're stupid ! I said nothing ! Your going to be switched to the retard class ! Boy that makes me proud ! It's the Business course it's not for slow kids I replied ! Yeah you keep telling yourself that , it a class of retards ! I'm going to that school tomorrow and I'm getting your courses change back do you hear me ? Please don't I can't pass those course, I'll flunk my freshman year

! Get your shit and get up to your room you make me sick
!

I grabbed my books and ran up the stairs. A few minutes
later I heard Steven come home and Esther filled him in
on what happened at school. Then I heard her fake
sobbing that I was going to be in the slow class ! I heard
him explain that the Business course wasn't the slow
course it was for students that didn't want to go to college
but it taught them office skills. Hey she can't do much
worse than she's been doing this year in school why don't
we just see what happens he said ! I was given my new
textbooks and a list of assignments I had to have done
before the end of the marking period along with my
current work . I got to work and was called down to
supper about a half hour later. We all ate in silence,then
Steven said Addie get the dishes ! I did as I was told. After
making sure the kitchen was clean I headed back upstairs
to get my homework done . I worked into the night ,finally
falling asleep around two in the morning. I wanted
nothing more than to continue sleeping when my alarm
clock went off nut I knew if I wanted a shower I had to get
up and get in the bathroom early ! I headed out to school
and Stacey was waiting for me across the street . How did
it go last night she asked. Esther knew before I got home
and was less than happy about it ! She said she was going
to come to school and get my courses changed back ! Do

you think she'll show up Stacey asked ? God I hope not but Esther's nuts so ...

It was so hard for me to focus with the threat of Esther coming to school looming over my head but I buckled down and got to work ! I was so thankful to have my courses changed and I didn't want to do anything to jeopardize it ! I handed in my homework and my homeroom teacher said Addie you didn't have to do so much the first night ! I know I replied but I just wanted to show you I'm thankful for my classes being switched and I'm going to work really hard to get caught up ! Well great work , I'll grade these and have them back to you tomorrow . Here's more assignments he said as he handed me a stack of papers. Thank you I said I'll get as much of this done tonight as I can. I was having lunch with the girls and all I could think about was Esther making a scene at school ! I didn't get called down to the office so that was a good sign !

When I got home that afternoon from school I pushed the front door open and jumped back just in case there was a slap waiting for me on the other side ! The coast looked clear so I went into the house . As soon as I got in I saw Esther standing in the center of the living room arms crossed in front of her chest ! I walked in and neither of us spoke . Finally she said so did you have your retard classes today ? I swear I wanted to scream at her they're business classes but being able to take the classes meant more to me than making a point so I said nothing ! You better fucking answer me when I ask you a question ? I had my business classes today was all I said . I didn't bother going to school today because you're a embarrassment ! I don't want to have any connection with you and your retard classes ! Get the fuck out of my site ! I ran up the stairs to my room brushing off her hate filled words ! All I cared about was I was able to keep my courses ! I started right in on my homework. School was a joy now that I could grasp the material !

I finished all of my make up assignments in two weeks and was able to take my first round of test. I was sent to the library under the supervision of my librarian to take my test. As I was taking them I felt i knew the material but I always doubted myself so I was a wreck waiting for the test to be graded ! The next day when I received the test back I literally cried . I got high B's on all five test ! I was so proud of myself ! I worked really hard to get all the back assignments done and studied my butt off and I did it ! When I got home I thought about showing Esther my test but then decided I'd keep it to myself. She wouldn't have anything positive to say so why bother

Chapter 55

As soon as I got home Esther said start packing your shit were moving ! I stood there staring at her ! Don't get so fucking dramatic we're only moving three blocks away ! We bought a house ! This was huge , Esther never owned a house in her life ! Go put your shit up in your room and when Steven comes home we'll walk over and go see it ! I did as I was told. We walked over and I was horrified when I realized what house it was! It looked like it should be condemned ! We have to fix it up but it's ours Esther said ! She opened the door and the inside was trashed ! It looked like it had been neglected for decades ! We're going to paint and clean it up Steven said as he beamed with pride ! We continued walking through the house and each room was worst than the one we had previously seen . I hugged my body afraid something was going to crawl out from under the debris on the floor. I turned to see Esther and Steven envisioning what it could look like and said when can we get started ? This weekend Steven replied ! we have friends coming over with pick up trucks and we're going to haul all the trash out and start painting ! In my mind I thought there's not enough paint in the world but my mouth said sounds great !

When we got back home I laid on my bed and cried ! The thought of having to move into that house , which by the way had no electricity, hot water or heat was to much ! I felt like it was a huge step backwards but what choice did I have ! I wiped my tears and started packing my room.

That weekend we started the clean out of the new house ! Esther's stoner friends lined the street with their pick up trucks and helped haul the debris away . It took a good week to get it all cleaned out but now at least we could see the floors ! Every night the stoners would hang around and drink and smoke pot by lantern light. I would go back to the house and be thankful for the quiet so I could get my homework done. This went on for weeks ! The good thing was Esther was so busy and tired from work and getting the house livable she hadn't laid a hand on me in weeks! Maybe this house had some positive points after all !

Esther and Steven had picked up some extra shifts on the weekends to cover the cost of piant and other things needed for the house. Esther told me to go over to the house and start to sweep and mop floors, wipe down baseboards and other house tasks. I did as I was told . As I scrubbed the filth away in the new house I had no way of knowing the secrets that would be unearthed and the magnitude of the events that would happen in my life when I lived there !

My life had been a roller coaster of events up to now but even I couldn't have imagined what was going to happen next !   To be continued …………..